# Praise for *Freedom at Work*

"Ideals like freedom, self-determination, and democracy are too often shelved when we show up to work, where for some reason we too willingly accept a culture of surveillance and even fear. In this powerful and engaging book, Traci Fenton lays out how we can actually bring the ideals of democracy to our workplaces—and why everyone from CEOs to workers to communities stand to benefit."

**—Daniel H. Pink, #1 *New York Times* bestselling author of**
***When*, *Drive*, and *To Sell Is Human***

"Centuries from now, when business school historians are seeking the source of truth for the undeniable renaissance in business thinking that occurred early in the 21st century, thinking that led to the flourishing of ideas, people, and profits in corporations around the world, they will find author Traci Fenton. Traci will be known as the indomitable soul and spirit fostering, over her lifetime, a movement towards freedom, democracy, and yes, even joy, in the context of work. Those historians will discover that every one of the vanguard businesses of the 21st century had well-worn copies of *Freedom at Work: The Leadership Strategy for Transforming Your Life, Your Organization, and Our World* on the shelves of their corporate libraries and the desks of their people. You, the enlightened leader, who has been searching for such inspiration and results, will have put this book there."

**—Richard Sheridan, CEO and Chief Storyteller at**
**Menlo Innovations and author of *Joy, Inc.* and *Chief Joy Officer***

"If you're not leading with freedom, you're leading with fear. That's the most striking message in *Freedom at Work*. We believe in the principles of *Freedom at Work*. Putting them into practice has helped us maintain our employee engagement of 93% and both grow our revenue and deliver value to our stakeholders."

**—Garry Ridge, CEO and chairman of WD-40 Company**
**and coauthor of *Helping People Win at Work***

"The brilliant Traci Fenton taps into a concept that is missing today—not only in workplaces, but often in our daily lives: freedom. Embracing freedom in the workplace won't just benefit your organization at every level, it will promote an important precedent that lets all individuals shine."

**—Jamie Naughton, former Chief of Staff to Tony Hsieh and**
**head of corporate Communications for Zappos**

"Freedom-Centered Leadership shouldn't be a novel concept, but it's unfortunately far from the norm. This book is a step toward changing that, one organization at a time, and it couldn't have come at a more crucial moment in our history. This book is as timely and practical as it is conceptually profound."

**—Kent Thiry, former CEO and chairman of DaVita**

"Imagine a workplace where people were trusted in their work and given the freedom to make their own decisions. In this groundbreaking book, the fabulous Traci Fenton explores organizations at the cutting edge of freedom in the workplace. It is a book that could transform your workplace."

**—Henry Stewart, Chief Happiness Officer, Happy,**
**and author of *The Happy Manifesto***

# FREEDOM
# AT WORK

# FREEDOM
# AT WORK

---

## The Leadership Strategy
## for Transforming Your Life,
## Your Organization, and Our World

---

## TRACI FENTON

BenBella Books, Inc.
Dallas, TX

*Freedom at Work* copyright © 2022 by Traci Fenton

WorldBlu, Freedom at Work, The Power Question Practice, Freedom-Centered Leadership, WorldBlu certified Freedom-Centered Organizations, and the WorldBlu 10 Principles of Organizational Democracy are trademarks of WorldBlu, LLC.

BenBella Books, Inc.
10440 N. Central Expressway
Suite 800
Dallas, TX 75231
www.benbellabooks.com
Send feedback to feedback@benbellabooks.com

*BenBella* is a federally registered trademark.

Printed in the United States of America
10 9 8 7 6 5 4 3 2 1

Library of Congress Control Number: 2021034766
ISBN 9781953295491 (print)
ISBN 9781953295835 (electronic)

Editing by Claire Schulz
Copyediting by James Fraleigh
Proofreading by Michael Fedison and Sarah Vostok
Indexing by WordCo Indexing Services, Inc.
Text design and composition by PerfecType, Nashville, TN
Illustrations by Rizky Azhari Shahrial
Author photo by Hollister Thomas
Cover design by Brigid Pearson
Printed by Lake Book Manufacturing

*For those who stand for, fight for,*
*and love freedom.*

———

*Ye shall know the Truth, and the Truth shall make you free.*
−Christ Jesus−


*Citizens of the world, accept the "glorious liberty of the children of God,"*
*and be free! This is your divine right.*
−Mary Baker Eddy−


*I prefer dangerous freedom over peaceful slavery.*
−Thomas Jefferson−


*Libertas perfundet omnia luce.*
*(Freedom will flood all things with light.)*
−Latin proverb−

# CONTENTS

*Author's Note* | *xiii*

*Introduction* | *xv*

## PART I
## FREEDOM AT WORK

Fear at Work | 3

The Promise of Freedom at Work | 11

## PART II
## FREEDOM-CENTERED MINDSET

Shifting Your Mindset from Fear to Freedom | 27

The Power Question Practice | 33

## PART III
## FREEDOM-CENTERED LEADERSHIP

The Three Attributes of Freedom-Centered Leadership | 45

Love | 49

Power | 65

Ubuntu | 73

## PART IV
# FREEDOM-CENTERED DESIGN

Organizational Democracy: The Framework for Freedom | 83

**| START |**

Principle 1: Purpose and Vision | 95

Principle 2: Integrity | 107

Principle 3: Dialogue and Listening | 121

Principle 4: Transparency | 135

**| SCALE |**

Principle 5: Accountability | 149

Principle 6: Decentralization | 159

Principle 7: Individual and Collective | 175

**| SUSTAIN |**

Principle 8: Choice | 189

Principle 9: Fairness and Dignity | 199

Principle 10: Reflection and Evaluation | 213

Seven Ways to (Accidentally) Destroy Your Successful Freedom-Centered Organization | 225

Conclusion: Why Freedom at Work Matters to Freedom in Our World | 233

Acknowledgments | 237

Resources | 239

Notes | 245

Index | 251

About the Author | 267

About WorldBlu | 269

# AUTHOR'S NOTE

This book is based on over two decades of inspiring and rewarding work my team and I have done with top CEOs, leaders, teams, and organizations worldwide. It has been a tremendous honor to work with and learn from them.

The company stories and practices described in these pages are drawn from fifty remarkable WorldBlu certified Freedom-Centered Organizations (selected from nearly two hundred worldwide). Unless otherwise noted, the stories are based on information provided directly by those organizations, as well as personal interviews I conducted with leaders, often on location. In most cases, I refer to CEOs and various leaders by their first names only, and I've avoided naming the organizations. This was intentional. These organizations deserve so much credit for the creativity they have shown in the way they have applied Freedom at Work. However, my goal is for you to read these timeless stories and transformational practices and imagine how *you* could adapt Freedom at Work within your *own* team or organization. I have provided some contextual information about these organizations so you can understand that they are substantial and successful organizations from around the world. However, I do not want you to feel limited in applying these ideas and practices simply because their industry, size, or scope may not be the same as yours. I would not want you to think, "Well, that could work for *them*, but it couldn't work for *us*," because more than likely, it can.

If you'd like to find out more, the complete list of WorldBlu certified Freedom-Centered Organizations can be found at www.worldblu.com. Welcome to Freedom at Work!

# INTRODUCTION

---

*Our unalterable resolution should be to be free.*
—SAMUEL ADAMS—

On June 15, 1215, beneath the trees of Runnymede, by the lush green banks of the River Thames, stood a council of twenty-five deeply frustrated barons who were fed up with King John's mismanagement, poor decision-making, and tyrannical leadership. On that historic day in England, they had the king sign a peace treaty known as Magna Carta, or "Great Charter," limiting his powers and creating a "year zero" in humanity's struggle for freedom and democracy.

Echoes of this pivotal document, along with inspiration gleaned from older Turkish, Greek, and Roman examples, Biblical principles, and the Native American Iroquois' model of democracy, would later influence the Declaration of Independence, the US Constitution, and the Bill of Rights, establishing the most powerful and longest-running democratic constitutional republic in the world: the United States of America.

Such movements for freedom, enshrined in these most cherished and sacred documents, would tap into a universal Truth: humankind's divine right to be free. In the words of US president Franklin Delano Roosevelt, "The democratic aspiration is no mere recent phase in human history. It *is* human history. It permeated the ancient life of early peoples. It blazed anew in the Middle Ages. It was written in the Magna Carta." And yet, despite the fact that "the democratic aspiration," as Roosevelt put it, is thousands of years old, the true promise of democracy has not penetrated where it can make the most difference in our daily lives: namely, in the way we work.

———————

Nearly eight hundred years after the barons' triumph at Runnymede, Kent was confronted with the biggest leadership challenge of his life. The Harvard MBA had just agreed to turn around a large healthcare company that was anything but healthy itself. He was about to impact thousands of customers, shareholders, and employees and their families all over the world. Little did he know then that the organization would one day become a thriving Fortune 500 company, and he and the organization would become a case study of exemplary leadership for top business schools.[1]

Yet, at that point the company's future was anything but guaranteed. They were rapidly losing cash, teetering on the edge of bankruptcy, and under investigation by the US Securities and Exchange Commission. Shareholders were suing. Morale was at an all-time low. Executives were either being fired or quitting. As Kent later shared, "If a single bank had asked for a single dollar the company might have gone under. It was a brutally negative place. People were angry and scared." He had been hired to lead everyone out of the fear and chaos—but how would he do it?

Most leaders, when faced with circumstances that must be turned around, resort to a top-down, fear-and-control style of leadership that can leave carnage and resentment in its wake. This style may be effective in the short term but hardly ever wins the long game. Faced with worry, stress, and expectations of success, many leaders can't mentally pivot out of their own fears to think from a different leadership paradigm altogether.

Despite the pressure to conform to a tyrannical, slash-and-burn leadership style typical of most turnaround CEOs, Kent had a different philosophy altogether. He envisioned an organization filled not with dejected, traumatized, and demoralized employees who were just mentally "renting space" each day, but with engaged, joyous, and purposeful citizens. To build this democratic community *first*, and a company *second*, as he later explained it, he himself would have to resist the pull toward centralized leadership. He could only realize this vision if he led in a very different way—if he led *democratically*. But would his employees follow?

When Kent announced his vision for how he wanted to turn the company around, about a third of its leaders and employees thought the idea was ridiculous and that it would take a herculean effort just to make payroll that month. Another third thought it was a "nice idea," but that a democratic leadership style would eventually buckle under the severity of the problems they faced. "I would go back to my hotel room at night in those early days and cry, wondering if I was on the right path," the CEO would later share at their annual leadership event.

————————

What exactly is this democratic leadership style Kent hoped to implement? The term *democracy* comes from the Greek words *demos*, "the people," and *kratein*, "to rule." The essence of democracy is that we the people have the unalienable right and responsibility of self-government; not the state, an oligarchy, a dictatorship, or a monarchy. A democratic leadership style, which is applicable to *every* area of life where leadership is needed, is exactly what Kent wanted to use to turn the company around. He believed that by tapping into the spirit of freedom inside each employee and leader, he could activate a remarkable turnaround from the inside out.

Kent also knew what many of us inherently understand: that top-down, fear-based leadership—whether used centuries ago or today—is highly dependent on one (or a few!) individuals' agendas, personalities, whims, moods, intellect, and shortcomings. Fear-based leadership, in all its forms, is not only an inadequate leadership style for leading in highly complex circumstances; it is also highly unpredictable and often dangerous, costing money and even lives.

There's a reason why the greatest thinkers in human history, to whom we turn for eternal guidance, weren't advocates for the monarchical, tyrannical, or dictatorial control of many by one. They had the wisdom to understand that democratic leadership was a more intelligent system of leadership. It was more just, humane, and moral. It was an act of love toward our fellow human beings. It took the long view. A democratic style of leadership has been responsible for more ingenuity, prosperity, happiness, and success in human history than any other style of leadership because a democratic style of leadership taps into the core idea that we are made to be *free*.

Now, we value democracy. We understand that nations are formed by it. We're happy to live in freedom (if we do). But the problem is, most of us don't really understand what democracy is, why it's the most effective style of leadership, and how to actually *practice* it. And if you don't understand it, then you certainly can't choose to lead with it—and ultimately, you can't reap all of the benefits it has to offer.

**A democratic style of leadership has been responsible for more ingenuity, prosperity, happiness, and success in human history than any other style of leadership because a democratic style of leadership taps into the core idea that we are made to be *free*.**

My personal journey to discovering the power of democracy began back in the fall of my senior year of college. Our college president had selected me to be the director of our prestigious, student-run public affairs conference. I asked my ambitious student team to come up with a topic for the event that would be out of the box, forward thinking, and globally aware. One fall day, after months of research, they came back to me and proposed that the theme of the conference should be . . . democracy. As I stood in the college president's boardroom, my jaw dropped in disbelief. "Democracy means voting and old men in politics in Washington, DC," I said to them, stunned. Privately, I thought, *What part of "forward thinking" do they not understand?!*

They asked me to hear them out, so I listened. They explained to me that democracy wasn't just a political concept per se, but a way of *leading and organizing* people so that they could release their full potential, promise, and purpose. And when I heard that, something clicked for me.

I had a long-held desire to help people unleash their greatness. This desire took root at a very young age, inspired by my spiritual upbringing and influenced by my family. I had a golden childhood growing up in beautiful Cedar Rapids, Iowa, a midsized family town in the US Midwest. I was blessed with two loving parents: my mother, an elementary school teacher, and my father, who taught deaf high-school students. Around our dinner table, my mother would talk about the lesson plans she was creating on character education for fellow teachers in her school district. My father, after leaving teaching when I was a young teenager, became an entrepreneur, building his own financial planning and insurance company. He was constantly listening to leadership and motivational tapes whenever he drove me to my various extracurricular activities. My inner, spiritual sense of self-worth and purpose was further reinforced by the sounds of Brian Tracy and Zig Ziglar playing each day in the car. (Perhaps inspired by their example, I have a distinct memory of counseling my fellow fourth-grade students one-on-one on the playground during recess about how to overcome their fears and live to their fullest potential while everyone else played kickball!)

I was a very joyous and trusting kid, focused on playing my flute in marching band and performing in our top-rated show choir, attending dance lessons, and participating in various athletic activities rather than anything having to do with the wider world or politics—both of which we rarely, if ever, discussed in my home. But the divine hand always has a plan for each one of us, regardless of our early beginnings, and I believe the symbols and signs can often be found around us. It was only while writing this book that I discovered some of these powerful foreshadowings.

For example, I grew up on Mason Drive. George Mason was a principal author of the Virginia Declaration of Rights, which had a major influence on the United States Bill of Rights. Historians deem him a father of that document.[2] Hiawatha, a suburb of my hometown, was named after the Native American who cofounded the Iroquois Confederacy, one of the oldest participatory democracies in the world. Elements of their Great Law of Peace inspired our Founding Fathers' writing of the US Constitution, a fact finally acknowledged by the US Congress in 1988.[3] Another suburb, Solon, was named for one of the founders of Greek democracy. The town of Fairfax, which was just a few miles down the road from my home, was named after Thomas Fairfax, 6th Lord of Fairfax of Cameron, in England. He was one of George Washington's key mentors and the individual for whom Fairfax County, Virginia (where I lived for a time while writing this book) was named. Fairfax County is also where Mount Vernon, President George Washington's estate, is located. And interestingly, Mount Vernon, Iowa, is located just twenty minutes from my childhood home.

Additionally, as I researched this book, I discovered I had several family members who fought for freedom in the American Revolution. My aunt also discovered that we were related to the distinguished Reuben Eaton Fenton. He was close friends with Abraham Lincoln and was also instrumental in founding the Republican Party, which was committed to abolishing slavery. Fenton was governor of New York as well as a congressman and later a senator of the state. He had a reputation of high integrity and a deep and passionate commitment to freedom and democracy. Upon his passing, his funeral was said to have "been attended by the greatest number of people of any funeral ever held in Jamestown."[4]

Furthermore, I discovered that on my mother's side, we were also related to King John of England—yes, the same king who signed the Magna Carta.

By the time I reached college (after graduating from the aptly named Jefferson High School!), I had been a student of leadership for years. With the possibility of a conference on democracy, however, I started to see how a democratic style of leadership created the conditions where individuals could learn self-government, develop a deeper sense of self-worth, and rise to their full leadership potential. So, I said "yes" to its theme being on democratic leadership—and how it could be applied in everything from schools to nonprofits, small to large companies.

---

**I started to see how a democratic style of leadership created the conditions where individuals could learn self-government, develop a deeper sense of self-worth, and rise to their full leadership potential.**

---

This decision changed my life. I shifted my undergraduate thesis to be about discovering the principles of democracy, and later focused my graduate studies in this area as well. I researched what democratic leadership is—and what it isn't. I studied classical democratic thought and read everything I could on democracy, from the Romans to the Greeks, the Native Americans to the Founding Fathers of the United States, religious texts as well as leading philosophers and contemporary thinkers. I studied democracy in multiple spheres of life, such as schools and businesses, urban planning, and music and the arts, and identified the core democratic principles that kept coming up. I traveled throughout democratic and undemocratic countries in North and South America, Europe, Asia, and Africa, interviewing dozens of practitioners of democracy about what they believed constituted the fundamental principles of democracy. And I attended multiple global forums and conferences devoted to exploring democracy and its various practices. (What I learned in the course of this study is beyond the scope of this book, but if you're interested in hearing more on this, please turn to the recommended reading section on pages 239–243, where you'll find a selected bibliography of works on democracy that informed my research.)

I was looking for the core *causal* principles that must be present to create a democratic system. After a decade of research, ten foundational principles of organizational democracy emerged.

# THE WORLDBLU 10 PRINCIPLES OF ORGANIZATIONAL DEMOCRACY

| STAGE | PRINCIPLE | DEFINITION |
|---|---|---|
| Start | 1. Purpose and Vision | Purpose and Vision are at work when each individual and the organization know their reason for being and have a sense of intentional direction. |
| | 2. Integrity | Integrity is at work when each individual and the organization uphold high moral and ethical principles. |
| | 3. Dialogue and Listening | Dialogue and Listening are at work when each individual listens and engages in conversation in a way that deepens meaning and connection. |
| | 4. Transparency | Transparency is at work when ideas and information are openly and responsibly shared. |
| Scale | 5. Accountability | Accountability is at work when each individual and the organization are responsible to each other for their actions. |
| | 6. Decentralization | Decentralization is at work when power is appropriately shared throughout an organization. |
| | 7. Individual and Collective | The Individual and the Collective are at work when the rights of both are valued and respected. |
| Sustain | 8. Choice | Choice is at work when each individual chooses between different possibilities. |
| | 9. Fairness and Dignity | Fairness and Dignity are at work when each individual is treated justly and impartially and is recognized for their inherent worth. |
| | 10. Reflection and Evaluation | Reflection and Evaluation are at work when each individual and the organization are committed to continuous feedback and growth. |

All ten principles must be present for a system to be distinctly democratic. (Other principles, such as ownership, trust, justice, and empowerment, came up again and again in my research, but it became clear that they are actually the *results* of democracy, not its cause. In other words, if they didn't help create a democratic leadership and organizational system but were instead *outcomes* of it, they weren't foundational principles—so that's why they didn't make the list.)

Of course, democratic leadership is not new. Many ancient and contemporary leadership thinkers whom I highly respect (please see my list of recommended reading in the resources section on page 239) have written about freedom and organizational democracy. My goal is not to repackage what has been written before; to the best of my knowledge, no one has clearly articulated the *exact* principles of democracy in this way. Rather, my express goal is to help you understand with confidence and conviction what the ten principles of democracy actually *are*, so you can use them to build more democratic organizations, and ultimately help build a more democratic world. By understanding these principles, I hope to make democratic leadership even clearer and therefore easier for you to implement in your life, team, or organization. In the following pages, we will take an exciting, in-depth look at these principles, and how, as a leader, you can use them to solve your leadership and organizational challenges in unexpected and encouraging ways.

In the spring of my last quarter of college, I was so inspired by what I was discovering about the relationship between leadership and democracy that I founded WorldBlu. We are a global leadership company teaching the mindset, leadership skills, and organizational design of Freedom at Work to members worldwide. We're called WorldBlu because blue is widely recognized as the color of freedom, and our vision is to see a world where everyone can live, lead, and work in freedom rather than fear. Our name captures our vision in a word. In the years since we were founded, my team and I have worked with thousands of CEOs and top leaders in over a hundred countries and in companies ranging from small organizations to Fortune 500s, such as The WD-40 Company, Zappos, Mindvalley, DaVita, Pandora, Hulu, GE Aviation Durham, Achievers, Menlo Innovations, Podio, RevAsia, and HCL Technologies. I have also had the privilege of speaking to leaders around the world at entities such as Harvard, Yale, the US Naval Academy, the University of Southern California, and South by Southwest. It seems that the concept of democratic leadership, while thousands of years old, is just as fresh and timely today as it was when my peers and I organized that student conference! The journey of working with these top leaders and organizations over the past two decades has been deeply educational and fulfilling, and it's why I am so excited to share their stories with you.

When I first started this work, I thought a leader could transform their team or organization's culture simply by focusing on the design of the organization's systems and processes. But after researching, observing, and working with top leaders and their organizations worldwide, I discovered there was more to it. Leading from a spirit of freedom rather than fear begins with an entirely different *mindset* and requires thoroughly different leadership skills *before* a leader is ready to focus on their team or organization's design.

This is how the Freedom at Work leadership model came to life. The model is based on three key pillars:

# THE FREEDOM AT WORK LEADERSHIP MODEL

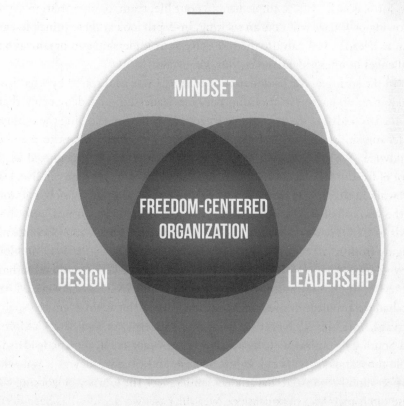

## 1: FREEDOM-CENTERED MINDSET

A Freedom-Centered Mindset lays the foundation for Freedom at Work. It is about making better decisions, being more creative, overcoming limitations, and imagining new possibilities from a mindset of freedom rather than fear. What does this mean for a leader and their team or organization? Action rather than analysis paralysis, alignment rather than distrust, and personal accountability rather than victimhood, all translating into forward progress. In Part II of this book, I'll be teaching you a five-step practice to shift your mindset instantly from fear to freedom, and then how to help others on your team do the same.

## 2: FREEDOM-CENTERED LEADERSHIP

Freedom-Centered Leadership is about leading yourself and others with skills that enhance freedom with personal accountability rather than fear and control. There are three core attributes of Freedom-Centered Leadership—Power, Love, and Ubuntu—and these develop a leader's ability to self-govern, have high self-worth, and cultivate self-knowledge. These three areas get at the root issues that cause most leadership success or failure. You'll learn about this in Part III.

## 3: FREEDOM-CENTERED DESIGN

Freedom-Centered Design is about designing your team or organization's systems and processes in accord with the WorldBlu 10 Principles of Organizational Democracy (which are the ten foundational principles I listed on page xxi). This remarkable and comprehensive system of democratic principles, when fully implemented, creates Freedom-Centered Teams or Organizations that make more money, outperform their competitors, are more sustainable during crises or recessions, use their resources more wisely and efficiently, and innovate and execute with speed. In Part IV of this book, you'll discover over one hundred transformational practices, curated from top WorldBlu certified Freedom-Centered Organizations from around the world. I chose examples that you can use both virtually and in-person, representing all different sizes of organizations and industries, public and private. My goal is to inspire you to implement a democratically-designed culture into your own team or organization more easily, effectively, and with lasting results.

## WORLDBLU CERTIFIED FREEDOM-CENTERED ORGANIZATIONS

While any company can operate using these democratic principles, some take it a step further. Companies who work with us can choose to undergo a rigorous annual assessment to analyze how the organization operates—among individual employees, leaders, and systems and processes—measured against the 10 Principles of Organizational Democracy. In this book, I share transformational practices taken *only* from organizations that are WorldBlu certified, so you can be assured that these stories aren't cherry-picked from a toxic or biased system to prove a point or because they sound catchy. Each practice comes from a healthy democratic workplace. To illustrate, let me tell you a bit more about what it means to be a WorldBlu certified Freedom-Centered Organization.

Since 2007, WorldBlu has had an open invitation for any organization (for-profit, nonprofit, schools, government, sports teams, and so on) with five or more full- or part-time employees or essential contractors to take our Freedom at Work Scorecard to determine where they fall on the continuum of organizational democracy.

The Freedom at Work Scorecard is a robust, analytical, and rigorous assessment tool that identifies how well an organization operationalizes the 10 Principles of Organizational Democracy at the levels of the individual employee, leadership, and systems and processes (read: organizational design). It must be completed by 70 percent of an organization (or, for large organizations, 100 percent of a random sample). An organization must achieve an average score of 3.5 out of 5.0 to become a WorldBlu certified Freedom-Centered Organization. They must renew the certification annually by retaking the Freedom at Work Scorecard. It is a very high standard to meet, which is why so few organizations have achieved it.

Unlike generic culture surveys, or instruments like employee engagement, satisfaction, or pulse surveys, our Freedom at Work Scorecard analyzes the *design* of an organization, pinpointing exactly where an organization is succeeding in its practice of organizational democracy . . . and where it is not.

As of this writing, hundreds of companies worldwide have taken the Freedom at Work Scorecard, but only an elite 166 organizations have earned the WorldBlu Freedom-Centered Organization certification. They come from diverse industries, including manufacturing, food, healthcare, retail, sports, education, and technology, ranging from 10 to 120,000 employees, with revenues from $1 million to $20 billion. Our work, and these top organizations, have all been researched and written about in *Fortune, Forbes, Fast Company,*

*Inc.* magazine, *The Financial Times, The Christian Science Monitor, Entrepreneur Magazine, US News and World Report, The Wall Street Journal,* and dozens of other leading publications worldwide.

These leaders and organizations do not claim to be "perfect," that they have never made mistakes, or that they have some utopian view of leadership and business. In fact, with such high standards, most are often quite unforgiving about their flaws. But they *are* actively striving for something higher each day, and that counts for a lot.

While there are undoubtedly many well-known democratic organizations that also deserve to be in this book, if they are not, it is because they did not choose to take the Freedom at Work Scorecard, so they could not be fully assessed and vetted. However, many of these world-class organizations, such as Semco, also deserve to be recognized and studied. (Please see the recommended reading list on page 239 for the books I highly recommend.)

This book is for those of you who are passionate about and committed to leading yourself, your team, or your organization with the principles of freedom and democracy rather than fear and control. That might mean you're a CEO, manager, educator, administrator, team leader, or someone who simply wants to be the best leader you can possibly be. I've written *Freedom at Work* to be your personal leadership handbook, and I hope you will refer to it over and over again. At the end of the book, I've given you next steps for how to get started in Freedom at Work, as well as many tips to support your development as a leader.

Supporting your development as a leader is my mission, but that's not the only reason I wrote this book. I believe that democracy and freedom are under constant threat worldwide due to oppressive, fear-based leadership and control-based systems in every area of our lives. There are many ways to help build and strengthen democracy in our world, but one of the most overlooked opportunities is in our workplaces. No matter the size or nature of your team or organization, the way you lead and design them to operate can weave a stronger tapestry of freedom and democracy in our communities worldwide. My hope is that the proven Freedom at Work leadership model will inspire millions of leaders to build or strengthen democracy in their countries through the way they lead their team or organization each day. I've written this book for these visionary freedom fighters who believe the spark of freedom is inherent in each one of us, and that they have a moral responsibility to create the conditions to bring it out in everyone. Through these pages, your team or organization can realize its untapped potential to help build a world more "blu."

As you keep reading, I hope you will come to love freedom and democracy as *the* most effective leadership style as much as I have . . . and as much as Kent's company came to embrace it, too.

———————

Despite two-thirds of the healthcare company being skeptical of Kent's proposed democratic leadership style, he dug in. First, he focused on creating a meaningful and fulfilling workplace for the approximately nine thousand people who still worked for the company. He hoped that as a result, they would offer their patients better care and share their gifts with the wider world.

The remaining one-third, thankfully, *did* connect with Kent's vision. Kent recalls employees sharing that they had always wanted to be part of an organization that strove to be a meaningful place to work. Over time, Kent began to convince more and more people that this dedication to creating a special place was not just going to "fade away."

One of their early democratic initiatives was developing shared core values. Leaders spent more than eight months meeting with teammates in small groups around the country, asking, "What would you like to have emphasized? What would you like to have honored?" After months of discussion, they held a democratic election and employees voted on the final set of six values—Team, Integrity, Continuous Improvement, Fulfillment, Service Excellence, and Accountability. (Their seventh core value, "Fun," was voted in later.) They also voted on a new name for the company and a new vision: "To Be the Greatest Healthcare Community the World Has Ever Seen."

"Democracy doesn't mean that we always agree, and it doesn't mean that we always get stuff right, but it does mean that we're really focused on creating citizens," explained Kent. "You can't create citizens unless they have a shared voice in what's going on, and you can't create intelligent citizens unless you share information so that each individual's voice can be well-informed. Remember, we're a community first, and a company second. We're a community that just happens to be organized in the form of a company."

Employees, or "teammates," begin their careers with an onboarding program that provides a comprehensive look at the company's mission and core values. Its internal university offers many leadership training programs as well as a two-day summit designed to teach new teammates about what their company stands for. Leaders at the local level conduct regular town hall meetings. Teammates can call into the quarterly Voice of the Village calls, and in the Q&A session at the end, anyone can ask any question or provide advice on any aspect of the company. And they don't hold back. Both the executive team and Kent—now fondly referred to as "the Mayor"—respond honestly and with transparency. The company has become a place where teammates feel like fellow citizens, where they care about each other without relaxing performance standards, and where they see themselves as stewards of the organization and its culture. They also engage with their broader community, too, through major service projects and educational initiatives.

"What do you do if you're a citizen as opposed to just a resident?" Kent asks. "You care in different ways; you vote, you participate in the democratic process. Someone who defines themselves as just a resident says, 'Well, there's a lot of stuff going on in my society, but I'm not going to bother to vote or volunteer or get engaged.' You come up with reasons to think that it's separate from you, and you don't share in a sense of ownership, you don't share in the building of the community. But citizens aren't like that and *we're* not like that."

Their now 56,000 employees manage over three thousand dialysis centers, six days a week, in a life-or-death business. With such high stakes, this company was the last place you'd expect to find a democratic leadership style. Kent had a choice: take the fear-based-leadership path of slash and burn, treating people as expendable cogs in a machine; or choose a democratic leadership style that lifted everyone up. He chose the latter for himself and his teammates, benefiting them in numerous ways. The company is now a publicly traded, $15 billion company in the rapidly growing healthcare industry and a global leader in providing dialysis services to patients in several dozen countries.

As they continued to expand globally, Kent and his team took their "Way" of democratic leadership to other parts of the world—including countries where people were living under authoritarianism or dictatorship. "We are about universal values, not anything that is just tied to America," he explained as he talked about their international growth into countries such as China and Saudi Arabia. "The experts said we couldn't take our 'Way' into other parts of the world, but we did, and it's been natural and comfortable. It's been fun to watch how our teammates globally are living our 'Way' with their heads, hearts, and hands."

By focusing on what makes a democratic community successful, the company has found its path to success through democratic leadership. Kent doesn't believe in the concept that achieving capitalistic objectives and being a force for good requires a zero-sum trade-off. It would take pages to list every way in which the company engages its employees, improves its patient care, and does good in the world, while still making money. Instead, here are a few of the results:

- They achieved the best patient outcomes, as measured by two separate programs under the Center for Medicare & Medicaid Services (CMS).

- The CMS Five-Star Quality Rating System recognized them as highest among all major dialysis providers.

- They outperformed the industry by nearly 138 percent.

- They have been on *Fortune*'s World's Most Admired Companies List since 2006.

- They have been recognized by the US Environmental Protection Agency for their efforts to reduce their footprint through measures such as building the first Leadership in Energy and Environmental Design (LEED) certified dialysis center, establishing annual environmental goals, investing in a new LEED Gold-certified headquarters, and researching methods for reducing medical waste.

Notably, they have sustained their WorldBlu certified Freedom-Centered Organization status every year since they were first certified—a testament to their ongoing commitment to democratic principles. "We embrace freedom and democracy at our company because it's fundamental to being a community first and a company second," explains Kent. "Central to that philosophy is maintaining a work environment that promotes engagement at all levels. A democratic workplace stresses collaboration and a team-based environment and ensures that everyone has a voice, thereby promoting full buy-in to a company's strategy and direction."

To mark the transformation from the old, centralized, command-and-control style of leadership that ran the company into the ground into the thriving, new, democratic community and company they built, Kent had a wooden bridge made and installed in the company headquarters. He then invited teammates to cross it when they felt ready, symbolically making the commitment to joining their democratic community and leaving behind the old ways of leading. One by one, at HQ and at conferences, teammates have crossed that bridge, at times emotional and at other times triumphant, as they made the transition within themselves from residents to citizens, committing to a cause greater than themselves. By choosing to lead with freedom over fear, they achieved breakthrough business performance, developed a culture that creates world-class leaders, and launched positive ripple effects around the world—all because one CEO, and his team, chose to lead with *freedom*.

This book invites you to do the same. Whether you lead a small team or an entire organization, virtually or in person, you can put freedom and democracy to work for you. Let's get started with a deeper dive into the promise of Freedom at Work.

# PART I

# FREEDOM AT WORK

There is a certain enthusiasm in liberty,
that makes human nature rise above itself,
in acts of bravery and heroism.
—Alexander Hamilton—

# Fear at Work

*. . . behold, a great red dragon . . .*
—REVELATION 12:3—

The Great Recession of 2008 was one of the biggest tests of Rich's democratic leadership style, and he wondered if he and his sixty-person team would survive it. When the recession hit, it created waves of fear and uncertainty at the Ann Arbor, Michigan–based custom software company. Would employees jump ship? Would they turn on their leaders? Would leadership default into a dictatorial, command-and-control mode?

Rich, their cofounder and CEO, doesn't pull any punches when he talks about their struggles at the time. "You can be resilient, but if your customers aren't, you're yelling into a very empty pipeline. All the companies that had big projects in play either stopped answering the phone or began saying, 'A month from now. A month from now.' That went on for almost three years. Fear reigned supreme. Real fear, not manufactured fear, where the main question was: 'Are we going to survive?'"

Previously in his career, Rich had been a top executive at a large company that operated with a top-down style of leadership. Rich had led this way too, without question.

That changed one annual Take Your Child to Work Day when Rich brought along his then elementary-age daughter. He set her up at a table with some crayons and paper in the corner of his office to keep her entertained while he set about his day. At five o'clock, he turned to his daughter and said, proudly, "Well, honey, what did you learn about Daddy's job today?"

With wisdom beyond her years, she replied, "I learned that you're really important, Dad, because no one could do anything without asking you first."

Rich was stunned. His daughter was observant—and right. His team could only move as fast as he did. He was the bottleneck. His team wasn't empowered, they were dependent and only as good as *his* best decision. It was a moment of lightning clarity for Rich, one that decidedly changed the way he led going forward.

Back then, Rich realized he had to find a way to decentralize decision-making on his team. He had to democratize his leadership skills and find ways to give power to his people, rather than hoarding it for himself. And he did just that at the large company, with remarkable results. He left his employer on a high note, and then went on to cofound his own custom software business and build it from the ground up with a more democratic leadership style. They'd succeeded in building a thriving WorldBlu certified Freedom-Centered Organization and had been bringing in a comfortable $5 million in annual revenue. Now, however, they were facing one of their biggest tests, and the fear was palpable. People's livelihoods depended on the company they'd all built together. Would they make it?

---

Over the two-plus decades my team and I have worked with top leaders and brands around the world, we've seen that those who make freedom and democracy central to their leadership styles and the design of their organizations see unparalleled growth, stability, and bottom-line results. We'll explore those outcomes in the next chapter, but before we get there, to fully understand why Freedom at Work *works*, we must first look at the greatest inhibitor of freedom—fear.

Is fear rampant in your leadership style, your team, or your organization? You might not think so. Fear sounds extreme, and most of us aren't ducking into a colleague's cubicle or office to say, "Hey, you know what, I'm afraid!" It's the last thing most leaders will admit, especially in the workplace. But look around and answer these questions honestly:

- How many departments or divisions are run as fiefdoms, where one individual holds all the control?
- How rampant is politicking in your workplace?

- How many layers of management and bureaucracy do you have?
- How often do people talk behind each other's backs or hide their real views?
- How high is your voluntary turnover rate?
- How quickly can you innovate and then execute on an idea?
- How much trust do you really have in the people you work with each day?

We have seen these problems and many others in most organizations. Why? Because of fear.

In most organizations, fear runs throughout every level, from the front lines to the C-suite. Most leaders feel remarkable pressure to never admit fear, even when they experience it. This lack of honesty with themselves and others can create a negative chain reaction throughout their team or organization.

In his *Harvard Business Review* article "What CEOs Are Afraid Of," Roger Jones shared his research from interviewing CEOs and other top executive leaders about their fears and their impact on both behavior and organizations. His research revealed that leaders' number-one fear is "being found to be incompetent"—what is often called the "impostor syndrome." The next biggest fears were "underachieving," "appearing vulnerable," "being politically attacked by colleagues," and "appearing foolish."

According to Jones's research, these fears led to all kinds of fear-based behavior, including a lack of honest conversations, too much political game playing, silo-based thinking, a lack of ownership and follow-through, and tolerance for bad behaviors throughout the organization. When asked about the effects of these fear-based behaviors, the CEOs and executives identified over five hundred negative consequences. In our own work with top leaders, we've found that at the core of all of these issues is the fear that they're not good enough or don't have the resources they need, and therefore are not up to the challenges facing them. Fear, in the form of stress, disengagement, lack of trust, fiefdoms, anger, bullying, discrimination, and uncertainty, hurts our teams and organizations in various ways:

**Fear kills good decision-making.** Perhaps one of the most far-reaching impacts of fear is the effect it has on decision-making. Poor decision-making came up again and again among the CEOs that Jones interviewed. Fear causes leaders to make bad, shortsighted decisions that cost them in the long term.

**Fear kills bottom-line growth.** Fear kills creativity, engagement, honest conversations, and personal motivation. Top talent leaves because it won't work in such toxicity. Opportunities are missed because of fear-induced shortsightedness. All of this adds up to a big price tag that creates a drag on the organization, hurting bottom-line revenue growth and profits.

**Fear kills productivity and engagement.** When individuals are in a state of fear, they have less motivation and desire to go the extra mile, are less likely to engage beyond the minimum required to keep their jobs, and are poor team players.

For example, the Gallup Organization annually measures the level of disengagement at work. Its most recent poll reports that 14 percent of the US workforce was "actively disengaged" at work, with only 36 percent of employees identified as "engaged."[1] Additional research found that 61 percent of employees experienced very high levels of stress on the job, which contributes to poor mental health (high anxiety, anger, and depression) and weakened physical health (aches and pains, fatigue, and weight gain).[2] This lack of engagement, which is often caused by fear in the workplace, is costing US companies up to $550 billion in lost productivity each year.[3]

**Fear kills innovation.** Elizabeth Wolf Morrison and Frances J. Milliken of the *Academy of Management Review* and Stern Business identified fear as a massive impediment to making change. In a fear-based workplace culture, employees often don't want to speak up about their ideas.[4] Fear of failure, punishment, and what your colleagues may think of you causes groupthink, stifles positive risk-taking, and is scientifically proven to induce poor decision-making and suppress creativity.

**Fear kills morale.** Fear in the workplace translates into bad leadership behavior, demotivating high performers and creating a toxic, morale-crushing workplace culture of backstabbing, politicking, and resentment.

**Fear kills agility.** When there is fear in the workplace, there is an overabundance of rules, policies, bureaucracy, silos, hierarchy, and fiefdoms that keep an organization from staying lean, agile, and competitive.

**Fear kills truth.** An environment of fear means that the truth is often not told, creating problems that could have been averted, hamstringing necessary work relationships, and fostering a culture of secrecy, distrust, and unethical behavior.

**Fear kills well-being.** As noted in the previous productivity-and-engagement point, being in a daily state of stress, anxiety, and uncertainty can take a major toll on employees' health, happiness, and well-being. This doesn't just impact their job performance; it impacts the way they engage with their friends and family. At its very worst, fear and stress can even lead an employee to take their own life. If you don't handle the fear, the fear will handle you.

**Fear kills leadership development.** Rather than creating an organization of leaders, fear cultivates a dependency or victim-based mentality, where employees look to management to tell them what to do. When people are afraid, they become order-takers rather than individuals who seize the initiative and get things done. Decisions are made at the top of the corporate pyramid, creating bottlenecks and putting impossible, unrelenting pressure on managers and CEOs. This dependency model excuses employees from being problem-solvers and adopting an ownership mentality, which can result in careless mistakes and a blame culture that costs an organization time and money. In the words of Patrick Henry, "Fear is the passion of slaves." Fear at work keeps us from developing into the leaders we're all capable of becoming.

So, what exactly is fear? I believe fear is an *imposition* on our thinking that tries to limit our ability to see the full range of possibilities. Fear, simply put, is a limited point of view.

This limited view is at the core of all dysfunctional leadership behaviors. Fear makes us reactionary when we need to be calm. It gives us tunnel vision when we need to think bigger. It provokes us to justify and make excuses when we need to take extreme ownership of our actions. It causes us to avoid difficult situations when we need to address them. And it triggers us to engage in immoral and self-centered behavior when we need to be more ethical and unselfish.

---

**Fear, simply put, is a limited point of view.**

---

Fear at work is hugely detrimental to a company's ability to achieve its goals. Can we be engaged when we are afraid? Are we innovative or creative when we are afraid? Do we make wise decisions when we're afraid? No. Unfortunately, most organizations don't even realize they are trapped in fear or see its impact on their growth. Case in point: according to a Zogby International/Workplace Democracy Poll, one out of four Americans feels like they work for a dictator. A whopping 80 percent say that if they had more freedom in their workplace, they could be more productive.[5] Unfortunately, most leaders don't realize they are trapped in a fear-based leadership style or recognize the impact it's having on those they lead.

During the Industrial Age, the largely hierarchical, command-and-control, militaristic approach worked—to a degree. Today, most organizations continue to be structured for that bygone era, and at great cost. They no longer need bodies performing simplified tasks repetitively. They don't benefit from the rubric "Do what you're told—or else." Instead, they need the competitive advantage found when human beings contribute creative ideas for products and services and the processes for delivering them. But the mindset, design, and leadership style inherent in these organizations perpetuate a disengaged, fear-based workforce unable to effectively respond to changing business conditions.

We want those we lead to be more creative, be personally accountable, and get things done, and yet each day leaders make fear-based decisions that only add more confusion and consternation to the workplace. Fear-based decisions perpetuate a fear-based mindset in employees. Eventually, these fear-based workplaces eject their best and brightest talent because they simply will not take it anymore. As leaders, all too often we address the *symptoms* of fear in our teams and organizations, without addressing the root issue of fear. This makes us feel like we're constantly playing the arcade game *Whac-A-Mole*, wondering why our problems never seem to get solved. Leaders have to get honest with themselves and ask, "Which of my actions are creating more fear in our team or organization?" and then address it.

Addressing the fear that comes from the top will help make your team more resilient in the face of uncertainty—both to a changing world and to market conditions that aren't under your control. Rich and his team are a perfect example.

———

Back in Ann Arbor, Rich and his team were facing a lot of fear and stress. It was the largest test of their democratic leadership and organizational design to date. But this time, thankfully, it wasn't all up to Rich to figure it out. He had an incredible team, and together, they had built democratic systems and processes into the way their company operated. Everyone was empowered, had a voice, and had ideas that mattered. Despite the challenges, they refused to default to a fear-induced, command-and-control style. They were in it together—and they were in it to *win* it.

So how did Freedom at Work help them survive when revenues plummeted and business dried up? A big component was their very personal approach to work reduction. "We have a 'shared pain, shared reward' pay system," Rich explains. "When our core economic engine slows down, everyone in the company begins making less money, including the founders." But this time, the leaders at the company didn't take an across-the-board approach. Instead, they asked a critical question: "Who needs work more than others?"

One team member, Dan, was close to retirement and said, "Send me home." He was financially secure, and he would use the extra time to work on personal projects, like building a small airplane. When they needed him, he would be there.

Other employees said, "I need as much work as you can give me." Maybe they had young families or spouses who had been laid off.

"We just kept gathering the team together, listening to people's stories, and paying attention," Rich explained. "Some could take one for the team and some couldn't. We empathized with them. We became a better team—more human."

It would be wonderful if I could share that all of their employees got the level of work they needed, but that's not reality. The company didn't have enough work to go around and had to shrink. Employees who needed more steady income left, but the company helped them find new jobs and told them that they were welcome to return when the economy and the business turned around. And it did.

It took about three years, but by then the Great Recession had rounded a corner, and most of those clients who had put their projects on hold were ready to start up again—immediately. The team stepped up, reformulated, and made an amazing revenue year happen. Those who were available came back on board. Employees offered to learn other parts of the process to help out where the team needed it—particularly in the intensive work that happens at the beginning of a design project. New talent was showing up at the door. For Rich and the other partners, the staff's agility was proof that their freedom-centered (rather than fear-based) mindset, leadership, and organizational design worked. "People remember how you treated them in tough times. Whether they stay or not, they tell stories about you. And that pays incredible dividends," explains Rich.

Despite the fear Rich's company felt when the recession took hold, they continued to lead with Freedom at Work. The result was the engagement, agility, and innovation that would ensure their continued growth and success would stay in place. "You have to get the people you need, but the bigger challenge is getting their minds, their hearts, their spirits," shared Rich. "If they've left those at home, you're not getting their best productivity or engagement."

But they *did* have their minds, hearts, and spirits in the work, and it pulled them through the challenge. The result? After coming out of the recession, their three-year cumulative growth rate was 69 percent, their reputation was intact, and their morale was high. And every year, even during the Great Recession, the company earned accolades, such as *Inc.*'s Most Audacious Companies award, the *Wall Street Journal*'s Top Small Workplaces award, and the Alfred P. Sloan Award for Workplace Flexibility—and they retained their certification as a WorldBlu Freedom-Centered Organization. They've even been asked to speak at the White House about their success.

"The most powerful force in our company is that every individual who walks through the door each day—employees, clients, members of the community—really wants the company to live to see another day," explains Rich. "Employees tell us they love their jobs. The community tells us what a great impact we're having. Clients appreciate our responsive approach. When you have that many people pulling for you, great things happen." Not too bad for a company that was worried about surviving just a few years earlier! Rich's company is a testament to the promise of Freedom at Work . . . which we will explore in the next pages.

# The Promise of Freedom at Work

*Everything that is really great and inspiring*
*is created by the individual*
*who can labor in freedom.*
—ALBERT EINSTEIN—

Just as Rich and his team were struggling to keep their small business alive during the Great Recession, on the other side of the globe, in a suburb of New Delhi, India, Vineet was facing the same challenge of survival . . . but on entirely different terms.

Unlike Rich, who was able to build his company with a democratic and freedom-centered style of leadership from the ground up, Vineet had inherited a publicly traded, multinational, information technology behemoth that had started decades earlier and grown to over 120,000 employees in twenty-five countries. Yet, in the highly competitive global IT market, they were struggling—losing both sales and important employees to competing companies in India and around the world.

Vineet had worked his way up inside the company. Just a few years before the Great Recession hit, he had become CEO and was determined to adopt a dramatically different leadership style—he believed in democracy in the workplace. It's one thing to grow a small, agile start-up with a freedom-centered leadership philosophy from the ground up; it was entirely different to take decades-old policies and structures and turn those—and all those employees' minds—around, too. Still, Vineet believed it was not only possible, it was the only chance they had for survival. But could they do it—and how long would it take?

———

In a farsighted 1964 *Harvard Business Review* article titled "Democracy Is Inevitable," Warren Bennis and Philip Slater argued that democracy would be the trend in both the workplace and in the world because it is the most efficient social system in times of unrelenting change.[1] Bennis, a top management expert and business school professor, and Slater, a sociologist and writer, foresaw the upheaval technological advances would bring and the need for an adaptive system that promoted freedom of thought and action.

They were right.

Today, we live in an era defined by unprecedented demands for participation, collaboration, and speed. Technological advances, generational shifts, and the global exchange of cultural, social, religious, and political ideologies are the cause, but also the modern result. Valuing each individual's potential is a current in the ocean of history that has widened and deepened with each passing century. The ideals of freedom and democracy are carrying us forward and lifting us higher. Look around and you will see the momentum of freedom and democracy in everything from education reform to our businesses, from sports teams to religious institutions. Yet that same momentum and desire for freedom is also under massive threat worldwide by repressive, undemocratic, and authoritarian leaders and systems.

So, what does that mean for us—leaders of teams, business owners, and entrepreneurs? Customers expect us to listen to their valuable feedback as we develop the next version of our products or services. Employees are desperate to contribute their best ideas and greatest talents. Communities want us to be part of the conversation about their development and growth. If we ignore their demands, we'll suffer the consequences. To succeed, leaders must be engaging, responsive, efficient, moral, and adaptive. It can feel exhilarating for some, but it's overwhelming for those who are unclear about how to lead using this strategy. Outdated management practices only make meeting these challenges even harder. Instead, organizations, leaders, and employees need to recognize the limitations of the past and evolve into a new, freedom-centered style of leadership that meets the demands of the times.

## WHAT IS FREEDOM AT WORK?

When I began exploring the concepts of leading with freedom and democracy in the business world, only a small number of organizations were even interested in the topic. I had to literally travel the world to identify those few that were trying to prove the economic and social value of freedom and democracy in the workplace by practicing it. It took me, and WorldBlu, ten years of observation, study, and analysis to develop a clear leadership model for a world that is complex, interconnected, and desperately in search of more humanity in the way we lead and work. The result was the Freedom at Work leadership model, and its three pillars (Freedom-Centered Mindset, Leadership, and Design), which codify how leaders and leading organizations are creating optimal environments for success.

What exactly do I mean by freedom? Freedom is when we live our fullest promise, potential, and purpose *without* fear. I believe freedom is our divine right. Freedom requires personal accountability, discipline, and integrity. Democracy, then, is the framework for freedom, and guides us in structuring our teams and our organizations for maximum success.

---

**Freedom is when we live our fullest promise, potential, and purpose *without* fear . . . Democracy, then, is the framework for freedom, and guides us in structuring our teams and our organizations for maximum success.**

---

Freedom at Work does not mean anarchy or a laissez-faire, free-for-all approach to building an organization. It is a well-researched, structured, and proven leadership strategy for capturing every ounce of potential for greatness and leveraging it into an environment that creates better leaders, smarter decisions, increased revenues, and a workplace culture people love.

Simon, formerly the CEO of a California-based web provider, explained their commitment to Freedom at Work like this: "We understand that the future of business is less about pomp and more about participation, less about titles and more about meaning. Working in a democratic environment makes employees feel more connected to the work that they do because they feel like they can take ownership of their individual tasks. They know if they have a better way to do something, they can do it—instead of mindlessly doing something the way someone thinks it should be done. The result is empowered employees who are prepared to tackle all sorts of challenges." The promise of Freedom at Work shows in the company's accomplishments: with 230 employees, the company serves millions of clients and brings in over $50 million in annual revenue.

| FEAR AT WORK | FREEDOM AT WORK |
|---|---|
| Authoritarian, centralized command and control | Democratic leadership |
| Personality-driven | Principle-based |
| Favoritism | Meritocracy |
| Slow, unsustainable growth | Fast, sustainable growth |
| Secretive | Transparent |
| Perks and incentives | Living your purpose |
| Survival of the fittest | Ubuntu |
| Division | Unity |
| Disengagement | Engagement |
| Moral relativism | Moral |
| Rules and policies | Common sense |
| Unfair and disrespectful | Fair and respectful |
| Order-takers | Critical thinkers |
| Controlling | Stewarding |
| Censorship | Free expression |
| Destroying self-worth | Building high self-worth |
| Conformity | Individuality |
| Narrative | Truth |
| Head-driven | Head-, heart-, and hands-driven |
| Power to the top | Power to the people |

Freedom at Work delivers on five bold promises that make it a highly effective leadership strategy for you, your team, or your organization:

**Freedom at Work addresses the *root* cause of your problems.** Unlike other leadership methods that just address the symptoms of most team and organizational problems (such as distrust, poor communication, micromanagement, toxic behavior, lack of innovation, and poor growth), Freedom at Work addresses the *root* fears causing these roadblocks and how to effectively overcome them once and for all.

**Freedom at Work cultivates a high-performance mindset throughout your team or organization.** High performance starts with your mindset, yet most leadership models out there completely overlook it, trying to create leaders by teaching skills and tactics that, while necessary, aren't the right starting point. Freedom at Work starts from the inside out.

**Freedom at Work develops world-class leaders.** Freedom at Work shows every leader how to develop high self-worth and self-knowledge, and how to self-govern effectively. The result is leaders who are confident in their leadership abilities with the understanding, and the moral courage, to resist the pull of fear-based leadership tactics.

**Freedom at Work outlines a proven framework for democratic organizational design.** Most CEOs and top leaders do not intentionally design their organization. Instead, they default into the traditional, hierarchical pyramid structure that doesn't work in a postindustrial age. What *does* work is a democratically designed organization based on the proven 10 Principles of Organizational Democracy. A *principle-based* versus practice-based approach is more adaptable, scalable, and flexible to your organizational needs. Additionally, democracy gives power to your people, unleashing top ideas faster, developing team spirit, and massively impacting your bottom line.

**Freedom at Work builds a more democratic world.** Democracy and freedom are continuously under threat in our world from numerous sources, ranging from subtle to overt forms of authoritarian leadership and economic, technological, biological, and mental slavery. We cannot rely on government officials to be the guardians of democracy in our world. Instead, as leaders, we can design our organizations, from businesses to nonprofits, schools to churches, to function *democratically*, by teaching people how to be engaged democratic citizens in the workplace each day. By doing so, we weave democracy into the social fabric of our lives, which ultimately has an unstoppable ripple effect, building more robust and democratic communities and societies, and bringing more stability and economic prosperity to our world.

Freedom at Work is the leadership strategy to transform and ultimately save our organizations and our world. Save us from what, you may ask? From the fear, which clouds our mindset, distorts leadership skills, builds toxic workplace cultures, and destroys vibrant societies. Instead, as leaders, we must consciously and intentionally choose to lead with freedom.

———

As CEO, Vineet began to completely redesign their immense, bureaucratic, and hierarchical IT company. Couldn't he choose to just reign supreme, bark orders, cash in, and fulfill his ego? Of course, he could have. However, it wasn't the leadership approach Vineet believed in—and frankly, he saw it wasn't working.

"To grow and prosper, companies must create value for their customers," he explained. "To do so, the organization must support those employees who work in the *value zone*, the interface between the company and customers where value is genuinely created. But traditional organization structures, with many layers of management and top-down decision-making, often make it more difficult for frontline employees to do their jobs. So, we have worked very hard to turn the organizational pyramid upside down, by giving employees in the value zone much greater access to information and more power to resolve problems, and, in every way possible, increasing the transparency with which we do business. Such efforts redefine how employees think of themselves and how they go about their work. They come to view themselves as the fundamental source of the company's value. They generate ideas and new sources of business and most importantly, they take on the responsibility for change and transformation."

Vineet had spent the three years leading up to what would become the Great Recession democratizing every area of the company: decentralizing decision-making, dismantling fiefdoms and secret communication channels, and disincentivizing corrupt or ineffective practices. However, the recession was the first real system-wide test of how well organizational democracy would work during challenging, even panicked, times. While Freedom-Centered Organizations aren't immune to economic crises, could their democratic design help them to at least weather them better?

Unlike fear-based organizations, Vineet's company was able to take a radically different approach to problem-solving. While he watched his competitors retreat and lay off employees as their profits tanked, Vineet decided to be unconventionally transparent with his employees. Taking to his company-wide blog, Vineet let them know that they needed to find a way to save $100 million fast or they would have to let hundreds of people go. He asked for their ideas and their help. He didn't know if his openness would scare his employees even more or if they would rally together. He would soon find out.

Hundreds of ideas came pouring in from every department and every office around the world with ideas for how they could cut costs and save jobs. Vineet and his core executive team reviewed every idea, discerning which ones they could act on quickly and which ones would have to wait.

Leveraging their employees' creativity, they identified seventy-six ideas that could hold down costs and increase revenues. Doing so also allowed them to cultivate an ownership mentality among employees, strengthen their morale, and turn the recession into an opportunity to prove the robustness of their democratic structure.

The result? Instead of just saving the company the $100 million needed to keep everyone employed, their employees' ideas saved it $260 million—and no one was laid off. In fact, Vineet's company grew 21 percent and stayed profitable during the Great Recession, even while their competitors were suffering losses and reducing head count. This only created more anxiety and distrust throughout the competitors' organizations, the consequences of which continued their agony long after the recession ended.

---

**Instead of just saving the company the $100 million needed to keep everyone employed, their employees' ideas saved it $260 million—and no one was laid off.**

---

Just six years after Vineet had transitioned the company to organizational democracy and endured the Great Recession, their bottom-line numbers spoke to the powerful relationship between organizational democracy and growth. They became one of the world's fastest-growing IT companies, doubling their market cap to more than $20 billion, tripling their revenue and income, quadrupling their number of customers, and becoming #1 in "Employee Satisfaction" according to Hewitt Associates. They also earned our certification as a WorldBlu Freedom-Centered Organization and won several other awards, including being named in *Fortune* as having the "World's Most Modern Management."

## THE BOTTOM-LINE IMPACT OF FREEDOM AT WORK

I've just shared the stories of Rich and Vineet, two CEOs whose companies—although very different—both saw great bottom-line results due to democratic leadership and organizational design. But were their bottom-line results simply exceptional, or do they prove that democratically designed organizations really can outperform traditionally designed and led organizations, particularly in severe economic circumstances? We at WorldBlu wanted to find out.

To measure the bottom-line impact of Freedom at Work on an organization, you first have to figure out how to measure the level of democracy in a workplace. However, no assessment existed to test for the presence of democratic principles in an organization. So, in 2006, we built our own rigorous assessment tool called the WorldBlu Freedom at Work Scorecard, which grades companies on the presence of the 10 democratic principles, such as Choice, Transparency, Decentralization, Accountability, Fairness, and Integrity. Next, we developed a deep database. Dale Matheny, an expert in business analytics and sustainable business practices and a professor at Principia College, helped us analyze the revenue data voluntarily supplied by participating WorldBlu certified Freedom-Centered Organizations from around the world. The oldest of the companies was founded in 1953; the youngest in 2010. They represented a wide range of industries including biotechnology, education, financial services, food and beverage, healthcare, household products, professional services/consulting, software and application, design and development technology, and warehousing and distribution. Some had a few employees; others had thousands. Some were private, some were public, some were nonprofits, and some were employee owned.

Now, with our assessment, we could move beyond anecdotal evidence by comparing WorldBlu certified Freedom-Centered Organizations' outcomes against national averages and the S&P 500. We could leverage our data to prove that freedom and organizational democracy delivers powerful, tangible financial results—that it really is the best path to sustained growth and the most effective way to weather global changes.

Here's what we found.

## Freedom Creates the Conditions for Revenue Growth

Revenue growth is one of the greatest measures of a company's health and sustainability. Consider the companies that have never earned a profit yet still went public—all because of the strength of their revenue growth. Now, for most companies, eventually profit matters—a lot. But top-line growth is proof that the company is doing some essential things right, such as product innovation and customer engagement.

To judge the strength of the WorldBlu organizational results, we compared the revenue growth of companies we certified to that of S&P 500 companies. We decided to make it even more "real" by looking at cumulative revenue growth just as companies were emerging from the Great Recession. We examined this growth over a three-year period, from 2010 to 2013, the earliest period of time for which we had data. What were the results?

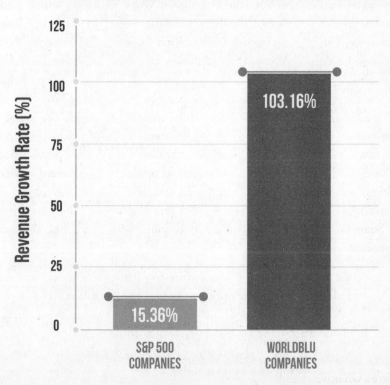

**Average Cumulative 3-Year Revenue Growth Rate**

The S&P 500 companies achieved a 15.38 percent average cumulative growth rate. The WorldBlu companies in our study achieved a staggering growth rate of 103.16 percent. In other words, WorldBlu certified Freedom-Centered Organizations saw an average cumulative revenue growth rate over a three-year period that was nearly *seven times* that of the S&P 500 companies.

Revenue growth is only one piece of the organizational health puzzle. Profit matters, margins matter, turnover matters, and cost control matters. But such strong revenue growth rates, particularly during a period when the economy hadn't fully recovered from the recession, helped cement our trust in freedom as a driver of success.

## Freedom Increases Resilience

We also wondered about the impact of Freedom at Work on a company's ability to survive and thrive during times of change. Challenges large and small in the economic and business environments will keep appearing, and in recent decades they have been greater than at any time since the Great Depression. Because we began assessing companies in 2007, we were able to examine how democratically designed companies fared throughout the Great Recession of 2008.

WorldBlu certified sixty-five companies as Freedom-Centered Organizations in 2007, 2008, and 2009—before or during the official span of the Great Recession. According to the National Bureau of Economic Research, the recession began in December 2007 and ended in June 2009. The negative effects of the recession certainly extended through 2011, though. So, we tracked each organization to determine if it still existed at the end of 2011. What did we find?

More than 95 percent of WorldBlu-certified companies survived the Great Recession.

On its own, that seems like a promising number. When compared to national averages for 2008 through 2011, it is even more impressive. Only 4.6 percent of WorldBlu certified Freedom-Centered Organizations ended operations during a time when the average national establishment exit rate—or rate of failure—was 10.33 percent.[2]

The Great Recession was a bleak time for many businesses, and even those who made it through were not unscathed. Leaders of WorldBlu certified Freedom-Centered Organizations, just like others, had to make sacrifices to keep the lights on during the toughest years. But strong democratic leadership and organizational design produced smart long-term decisions that helped the companies survive—even when others didn't.

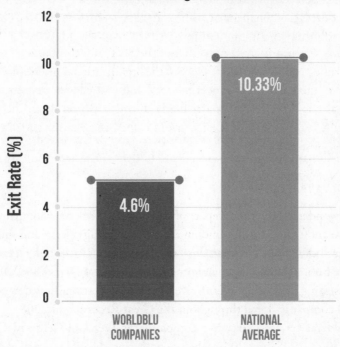

**Exit Rate During the Great Recession**

So, is Freedom at Work for every leader, industry, and organization? Based on our experience, yes—but with a caveat. To reap the rewards, you must work through the three pillars in the following order:

**First, Freedom-Centered Mindset:** Kent, Rich, and Vineet all had a mindset of freedom rather than fear, and that clear mindset was something they were able to develop in their organizations as well. When challenging times arrived, they were able to take a broader, unconventional view, which steered them to new ideas and ways of problem-solving.

**Second, Freedom-Centered Leadership:** All three CEOs had high self-worth, self-knowledge, and the ability to self-govern—and teach others how to do the same. They had the strategic leadership skills needed to confidently guide their organizations through the maze of fear into new realms of possibility and success.

**Last, Freedom-Centered Design:** Because they built robust democratic systems and processes throughout their organizations, they were able to quickly pivot to address their challenges, without defaulting into centralized command-and-control behavior and undermining all the trust they'd built.

These three pillars will also shift you and your team into new levels of personal and organizational growth, with substantial results.

A note up front: making lasting change can take time. In working with client companies, we've observed five stages of transformation that an organization often moves through as it transitions from a fear-based to a Freedom-Centered Organization. It's important to understand where your organization is on the transformational journey.

**Stage 1—Fear-Based Organizations:** Employees are miserable, governed by fear, control, secrecy, greed, and manipulation.

**Stage 2—Benevolent Dictatorship:** Employees are governed by a leader who is kind but doesn't trust them enough to give them real power and influence.

**Stage 3—The Rich Dad or Mom:** Management is "Dad or Mom" and the organization is financially well-off enough to provide nice perks for employees, such as free beer, foosball, Bring Your Dog to Work Day, and gym memberships, temporarily masking the fact that they still have almost no influence or decision-making power.

**Stage 4—Forward-Thinking Models:** At this point, there has been a positive shift in the design of the organization, giving more power to employees through more forward-thinking practices such as employee stock ownership plans (ESOPs), co-ops, servant leadership, self-management, and other methods; these include sociocracy,[3] ROWEs (Results-Only Workplace Environments), Best Places to Work, or Agile. However, mindset and leadership training may still be missing, and the organizational design may not yet be *fully* democratized.

**Stage 5—Freedom-Centered Organizations:** Here, leaders, as well as the overall organizational mindset, leadership style, and design, have fully shifted from fear and control to the Freedom at Work model, producing a freedom-centered culture. The WorldBlu 10 Principles of Organizational Democracy are *all* in operation throughout the organization. With these thriving democratic systems and processes established, CEOs, leaders, and employees can now fully engage for scalable growth and success.

These are the common stages that an organization may move through or leapfrog into as they become more freedom-centered in their mindset, leadership approach, and design. If you are a CEO, you have the power right now to make changes across your company that will move you ever closer to Stage 5. As a manager or employee, you can begin applying these ideas to yourself or your team. No matter your title or the scope of your duties, I encourage you to do the inner work and implement as much of Freedom at Work as you can within yourself and your own team. I've observed that there's a ripple effect—once others catch on to the amazing results you've achieved, you will inspire them to follow your lead.

---

**The Freedom at Work model is a timely and timeless leadership strategy because it is based on democratic principles adaptable to any organization, in any industry, of any size, anywhere in the world.**

---

The Freedom at Work model is a timely and timeless leadership strategy because it is based on democratic principles adaptable to any organization, in any industry, of any size, anywhere in the world. Through a freedom-centered mindset, leadership, and organizational design, Freedom at Work impacts every core element of a team or organization. And the effects are therefore far-reaching—and inspiring. In Part II, we'll take a deeper dive into the first pillar, upon which any Freedom-Centered Team or workplace rests: Mindset.

# PART II

# FREEDOM-CENTERED MINDSET

---

For God hath not given us the spirit of fear;
but of power, and of love,
and of a sound mind.
—2 Timothy 1:7—

# Shifting Your Mindset from Fear to Freedom

*Nothing can stop the man with the right*
*mental attitude from achieving his goal;*
*nothing on earth can help the man*
*with the wrong mental attitude.*
—Thomas Jefferson—

One of the great myths of leadership is that your mindset does not matter; what matters is that you have the right skills, get results, and make money. But in truth, *everything* starts with your mindset. It drives your behavior and decisions. And your team or organization inevitably follows your mindset trajectory.

I believe it is our sacred right to lead from a mindset of freedom, rather than fear. Mental freedom is our surest path to human progress. When we overcome fear in our own thinking, decisions, and behavior, we can more effectively self-govern and help others do the same. As leaders, however, there is often a lot of fear in our thinking that we aren't even aware of (or are too proud to admit). Don't believe me? According to research by the Cleveland Clinic and the National Science Foundation, the average individual thinks around sixty thousand thoughts a day. A staggering 95 percent of those thoughts are the *exact* same thoughts they had the day before, and 80 percent of *those* thoughts are negative and fear based.

Some leaders like to think that fear is a good motivator. They have whispered to me that they *want* their employees to be a little bit afraid of them "so they get things done." But fear is not a motivator or a friend; rather, it has been proven to make us less intelligent and more reactionary. Research shows that when we are in a mindset of fear, the peripheries of our brain shut down. We become myopic and get tunnel vision, unable to see the diversity of options available to us. Who hasn't felt the fog of fear overshadowing our thinking when we are dealing with an overwhelming problem, stealing our energy and ability to think clearly? A downward-focused mindset of fear causes a leader to make shortsighted, reactionary decisions that can cost you time, money, and relationships.

Have you ever heard the phrase "Feel the fear and do it anyway"? It may *sound* brave, and it's usually meant to inspire. But not addressing the fear in our thinking means that we either ignore it, get angry, withdraw from others, or try to cover it up with unhealthy, escapist behaviors. While these methods might temporarily mask the fear we feel as leaders, they are Band-Aids, not a cure. They keep us trapped in a negative cycle of ignoring the fear and soldiering on.

What if there were a way to recognize and handle the fear so that we could get unstuck, make better long-term decisions, and achieve breakthrough results—and help the people we lead do the same? A Freedom-Centered Mindset creates the optimal conditions to do just that, empowering us to lead ourselves and others with real courage, clarity, and conviction. But to shift your mindset, you must have the humility to recognize when there is fear in your thinking, be accountable for it, and then understand how to overcome it.

---

**To shift your mindset, you must have the humility to recognize when there is fear in your thinking, be accountable for it, and then understand how to overcome it.**

---

I learned how to recognize and shift my own mindset in an unexpected way. When I was in my mid-twenties, living in Washington, DC, I hit a crisis point. I was a full-time graduate student, juggling a part-time job for the Nasdaq Stock Market Educational Foundation, building WorldBlu, and traveling and speaking around the world.

Even though I was doing what I loved, I had reached a point where it was all just too much, and I felt completely overwhelmed, exhausted, and stressed out. I worried that I was about to hit a breaking point, but I didn't want to give up anything—it all felt too important. So, I called one of my mentors.

After listening to my long list of problems, she said to me, "I have just one question for you."

"What is it?"

She paused. "What would you do if you *weren't* afraid?"

With that one question, I saw how fear was completely controlling my mindset, decisions, and behavior—and what I needed to do to be set free.

## THE POWER QUESTION

While the question "What would you do if you weren't afraid?" is not new, it was new to me. I started to call it the "Power Question" because when we are in a fear-based mindset, we are out of our power, having given it away to fear. But when we think and act from a mindset of freedom and possibility, we are back in our *true* power. I have now had the privilege of teaching the Power Question to leaders all over the world—with remarkable results.

Take Nathan, the CEO of a thirty-person software development company based in Wellington, New Zealand. One day, Nathan realized he was heading into a major crisis: looking at their financial projections going into their new fiscal year, he could see that in about five months they were going to be $300,000 short. He knew he didn't have the cash, and he could feel himself rapidly deteriorating into a fear-based mindset and starting to panic.

"My first thoughts were, 'What am *I* going to do about this? How am *I* going to control the situation to get the outcome *I* want? How am *I* going to fix it?'" Nathan knew clearly *what* his fear was—that the business wouldn't stay in operation and thirty people would be out of a job. He knew *why* he was afraid—they simply didn't have the money to keep operating, and he couldn't see how they could come up with it in time.

"My initial gut reaction was to go into the office and start telling people what to do, get really intense, and start some hustle," he shared. Fortunately, Nathan lives in a different city from where his business is based, so on the plane ride back to Wellington, he had some time to stop and reflect.

At that point, Nathan asked himself the Power Question, "What would I do if I *weren't* afraid?" and realized that his answer wasn't to go into a fear-based command-and-control mode and scare everyone into taking action. As the leader of a WorldBlu certified Freedom-Centered Organization, he knew what effect fear could have, and he didn't want to create a panicked atmosphere that would crush morale and stifle creative thought. "I realized I needed to take a step back and support the team in solving the problem themselves, because I knew they would be able to get a better result than I could on my own.

"I went to our leadership team, which we call the 'Navigators,' and I laid out our situation to them and where it looked like we would be on April 1, and they agreed that we needed to do something about it. I suggested they all take a week and have a think about what we could do to overcome the situation." The team came back with a plan to lower costs over the next four to five months, drum up more business with current clients, and attract new ones. They then put their plan into operation.

As Nathan explained to me in a podcast interview, "Where we ended up on April 1 wasn't with a loss of $300,000, it was with an extra $200,000 in the bank. We also achieved this at what was normally our slowest time of year. It was an outstanding result."

By shifting from a fear-based mindset to a Freedom-Centered Mindset with the Power Question, Nathan and his leadership team came up with breakthrough solutions that saved the company, strengthened their democratic culture, and deepened their confidence in their ability to solve their problems together.

"If I had gone in there and tried to take control, I would have made the whole thing about me. But there was a whole team there whose livelihoods were tied up in this as well. It wasn't about just me; it was about all of us."

The bottom line for Nathan and his team? "As an organization, we were consciously in a place of fear, but when we took a step back and embraced a Freedom-Centered Mindset, we saw amazing results . . . When we got to the first of April, the feeling of satisfaction, of feeling empowered, and of actually being able to make a difference was huge."

Over the years, in conversations with leaders, when I started to ask them the Power Question, they would pause and reflect. Some leaders, with just that one question, would have a breakthrough. Their eyes would light up, their voice would sound happier, and you could see the stress leave their face. Then, they would give me their answer. I began to see how months and even years of fear-based thinking would leave their minds in just a few minutes because of the Power Question. It was incredible.

But other leaders struggled to identify their fear or even admit to it. They needed a bit more help uncovering their fear before they could come up with a real solution to what they would do if they weren't afraid. That's when I developed the Power Question Practice, a five-step exercise that helps leaders identify the real fear in their thinking more quickly, get unstuck, and take action.

That's what happened for Garry, the CEO of a publicly traded, multimillion-dollar manufacturing company based outside of San Diego, California.

While at a recent retreat, the executive team was discussing some strategic decisions and had reached an impasse. As the CEO of a WorldBlu certified Freedom-Centered Organization, Garry had been trained in the five steps of the Power Question Practice. At that point, Garry took his team through it and they had a collective breakthrough. "I love the Power Question," he told me. "And now I use it almost every day." In the next chapter, I'll take you through it, too.

# The Power Question Practice

*Fear has two meanings: "Forget Everything and Run"
or "Face Everything and Rise."
The choice is yours.*
—Zig Ziglar—

The Power Question Practice is a proven approach to help you shift your thinking in an instant. As a leader, you can use the Power Question Practice any time you are making a decision, feeling stuck or stressed, or want to think more creatively. You can use it individually or collectively to pivot your thinking and find meaningful answers that lift everyone up. As Amy Edmondson points out in her book *The Fearless Organization*, it is every leader's responsibility to create a psychologically safe environment for people to express and work through their fears. The Power Question Practice gives you the ability to do just that.

The Power Question Practice has five key questions:

1. What am I afraid of?
2. Why I am afraid?
3. The Power Question: What would I do if I weren't afraid?
4. How would I feel without the fear?
5. Why is it okay to let the fear go?

To get started, I invite you to think of a personal or workplace challenge you are currently facing. Perhaps it's an issue with a friend or colleague, a strategic question, or a financial challenge. As we go through the five steps of the Power Question Practice, put your challenge through each question and see what happens as you uncover your fears and shift your mindset from fear to possibility.

## QUESTION 1: WHAT AM I AFRAID OF?

The first question, "What am I afraid of?" helps us *awaken* to the fear in our thinking. It's all about awareness. You simply cannot shift your thinking if you aren't even aware of exactly what is causing the fear. Often, what we *think* we are afraid of is not *really* what we are afraid of. We have to go deeper.

---

**You simply cannot shift your thinking if you aren't even aware of exactly what is causing the fear.**

---

So, when you think of your challenge, what is it you are *really* afraid of? Failure, looking bad, or making the wrong decision? Other people's opinions, impostor syndrome, or damaging your reputation? Sometimes I find it helpful to ask leaders a worst-case-scenario question: Are they afraid of losing their home, their marriage, their job, their savings?

When I put it that way, most leaders start to chuckle and say, "Well, I don't think it would ever be *that* bad. I could always move in with my mom or dad, a friend, or my aunt. If I had to, I could borrow money. I think my spouse would actually understand." While there *are* times when the worst-case scenario may seem possible, most people realize that it is highly unlikely, which helps to dispel their fear.

Sometimes, though, when we ask a leader this first question in the practice, their response is, "I'm not afraid of anything." Maybe that was your first thought, too.

Actually, that's understandable. In many countries, cultures, and individual households, admitting any level of fear is considered weak or totally inadmissible—even dangerous. In various workplace cultures, to say you are afraid of something might lead to someone being teased, ostracized, or even fired. Connecting with the emotion of fear and owning it can be difficult and painful, so we have to be patient and kind with individuals in this process. Often, as a survival mechanism, people have buried the fear so deeply that they might need extra time to identify it.

For others, this response is driven by pride and ego, or the fear of feeling vulnerable. It can also be the characteristic of a leader who is out of touch with themselves.

The thing about fear is that if we are not alert to its tactics and aware of how it is trying to use us, it wins. You know you are in fear if you find yourself not reflecting on a situation but instead obsessively ruminating about it over and over again. That is one of fear's main ploys, to get us myopically focused on something so it can slowly take over our thinking, our relationships, our day, and our life. It exhausts us as it works us into a frenzy, usually with a story about another individual or circumstance that probably isn't entirely true.

That is why unpacking what it is we are *actually* afraid of is vitally important to this process. It takes the fear out of the shadows and into the light. Just that action alone can help destroy the fear. We are empowered and even liberated simply because we become aware of the unconscious fear in our thinking. In my own life and years of using the Power Question Practice, when I find I am ruminating about something, this first question gets me out of the worry and into possibility.

Once you feel at peace with your answer to this first question, it's time for the next step.

## QUESTION 2: WHY AM I AFRAID?

Am I afraid because of something that happened in the past, or something I saw happen to someone else; a fear of getting hurt; or of something I am projecting into the future? The second question is about taking *accountability* for the fear in our thinking. You can't have freedom without personal accountability.

In our courses, we ask leaders to complete a worksheet listing all of their fears. We call it a "Fear Purge" because you get out all of your fears by writing down every worry you have, from small to large, in every area of your life—work, money, career, children, marriage, retirement, traveling, health, and so on. It's a deeply eye-opening and humbling experience as leaders realize how much fear is actually hiding in their thinking. Many leaders have come up to me and said, "I was sitting here resisting everything you were saying, feeling pretty good about myself for not having a lot of fear. But then when you asked us to do the Fear Purge and write down every fear I could think of, I realized how much fear I really *did* have in my thinking."

After they've completed the Fear Purge, I ask leaders to identify if each item they wrote down is a past fear, a future fear, or a present-day fear, and tell me where the majority of their fears lie. Most people say all their concerns are in the present. So, I challenge them: "At this *exact* moment, is this really a fear that is troubling you?" They usually realize this prompt was a bit of a trick question. Almost all our fears are future fears. We are afraid of what *might* happen. We are anxious about the unknown.

Various studies have found that 85 to 90 percent of our fears and worries about the future never, *ever* come true, usually because they are based on feelings, not facts.[1] As French Renaissance philosopher Michel de Montaigne once said, "My life has been filled with terrible misfortune; most of which never happened."

---

**Most of our fears are nothing more than exaggerations, misperceptions, and stories that simply are not real or true.**

---

When we aren't thinking in the now and are too focused on the fear-based "what-ifs" of the future, a "Fear Gap" is created. This is the gap between the present and the future where all the uncertainty can rush in. The solution to the Fear Gap is to stay in the now. As a friend remarked to me recently, the word *now* spelled backwards is actually the word *won*. When you're in the now, you've won out over the Fear Gap.

But what about the 10 to 15 percent of our fears that *do* come true? Research shows that 79 percent of people found that even when their fears came true, they were able to handle the challenges better than they thought they could. Additionally, they realized that the challenge had a silver lining: teaching them something worth learning.[2] This means that most of our fears are nothing more than exaggerations, misperceptions, and stories that simply are not real or true.

# QUESTION 3—THE POWER QUESTION:
# WHAT WOULD I DO IF I WEREN'T AFRAID?

You have now become more aware of the fear in your thinking and you have taken accountability for it, so now it is time to move to *action*. We do this with the third question, which is the Power Question I introduced in the last chapter.

What I love about the Power Question is that it invites us to dream big, abandon smallness, and see all of the possibilities available to us. This is the point at which we get to put aside our ego, pride, and stories and get unstuck, break through limitations, and fulfill our goals.

When I ask leaders the Power Question, often they say to me, "That's like the question 'What would you do if you knew you couldn't fail?'" However, it is not quite the same thing. "What would you do if you weren't afraid?" asks more of us and has a greater healing impact. It invites us to acknowledge that we do have fear in our thinking, to take accountability for the fear, and then overcome it. We never compromise with fear because if we do, it will slowly sabotage us.

A leader named Turner, who lived on the coast of England, came to our Power Question workshop in London. He was a top leader at a multinational chemical company but was feeling trapped in his current job. Despite performing successfully, his self-worth and self-confidence were flagging, and he was looking for a way out.

When Turner was introduced to the Power Question Practice, he was shocked by what he uncovered. For the first time, he recognized the impact fear was having on him: the anxiety that he would never be good enough to shift from sales to leading the company's people agenda, which made him feel insignificant; his distress that the new global human resources director would never see him as capable of growing the company's People Department; and his dread that he would be trapped in a sales role for the rest of his life. His breakthrough moment came when he realized that his alarms were all self-imposed.

Asking himself the Power Question gave Turner the clarity and courage to proactively contact the new human resources director. He made it clear that he had a passion and desire to support group projects related to personal and organizational development. To his surprise, this resulted in multiple meetings culminating in an agreement that he would get to do just that.

Turner told me, "Without being introduced to the Power Question Practice, understanding my fears, and building confidence about who I am and the value of what I have to offer the world, I would still feel trapped and without choices. Today, however, I know who I am, and I am confident that I will continue to move myself towards a future where every living second of my life is spent being in service to others."

In finding his Power Answer to the Power Question, Turner rediscovered his purpose, found a sense of renewal for his job, and regained a spirit of meaning and fulfillment in his life. He was able to build up his self-confidence and belief in himself and what he had to offer to the world.

The Power Question, however, only works if you *really* want to let go of the fear to find your answer. I've seen some people cling to their anxieties because they give them a feeling of identity. After all, who are they without their fears?! For many people, fears are what define them, and to ask them what they would do without them feels like you're asking them to give up a part of themselves.

I have been deeply moved by listening to leaders' answers to the Power Question over the years. Sometimes, leaders have small breakthroughs; other times, they are quite significant. And while the Power Question Practice itself is highly transformational for leaders and teams building Freedom-Centered Organizations, it can be just as transformational for a leader's personal life as well.

## QUESTION 4: HOW WOULD I FEEL WITHOUT THE FEAR?

When leaders hit the fourth question, they usually sit back in their chairs, relax, and say, "I would feel great!" Often, we don't even realize how much the fear is fatiguing us, weighing us down, and demotivating us, keeping us from fully engaging in life. Without all the stress, we would feel liberated, inspired, and a lot happier. I have seen leaders suddenly realize how much concern they've been carrying in their body because of their fears, and how, by letting it go, they feel profoundly emotionally, spiritually, and even physically healthier. This question makes us more *aware* of how the fear is impacting us and how we might feel and behave without it. So, how would we feel without the fear? We would feel *free*.

## QUESTION 5: WHY IS IT OKAY TO LET THE FEAR GO?

The final question in the Power Question Practice helps leaders move completely out of fear and into *accomplishment*.

I am always fascinated to hear leaders' answers to the last question because *how* we get to our answer to that question says a lot about our core beliefs. If we don't know *why* we can let go of our fears, then we will never be able to let the fear go completely.

The reason why most people can let go of their concerns and anxieties is because they have finally realized the fear isn't as insurmountable as they thought, and it is logical to let it go. Another reason why individuals feel that it's okay to let go of their fears is that they feel, as I do, that there is a higher power that is good and in control, operating on their behalf. It's okay to let go of the fear because of this control that divine Love has over all.

What I've found is that ultimately, fear is *not real*. Danger may be real, but fear is not. Fear is an emotional choice, and you have a right to choose to live, lead, and work with a mindset of freedom instead.

Fear is also *not true*. When you see what looks like water on the highway on a hot summer day, do you pull over, stop driving, or try to go around it? None of the above, because you know that what looks like water on the road is an illusion. To overcome fear, you have to know what *is* true. The opposite of fear isn't love, it's *understanding*, and when we understand what is and is not true, the fear dissipates.

Last, fear is *not you*. Fear tries to mesmerize you into thinking it's your thought, but it's not; it is just another form of the "gremlins"—what I call those inner voices that try to sabotage our thinking and our sense of self-worth. A gremlin stops knocking on your mental door when you stop answering it. Understanding that your true identity is to be fearless and free, you reclaim your power as a leader. You can let go of the fear because it's *not* real, it's *not* true, and it's *not* you.

| THE POWER QUESTION PRACTICE | THE RESULTS |
| --- | --- |
| 1: **What am I afraid of?** | Helps us *awaken* to the fear in our thinking. |
| 2: **Why I am afraid?** | Helps us take *accountability* for the fear. |
| 3: **What would I do if I weren't afraid?** | Helps us break the mental chains of fear to take *action*. |
| 4: **How would I feel without the fear?** | Helps us become more self-*aware* of how we feel. |
| 5: **Why is it okay to let the fear go?** | Helps us move out of fear into *accomplishment*. |

Here are a few tips to help you in your Power Question Practice:

**Tip 1: Don't use the Power Question to override your intuition.** Once you put your challenge through the Power Question Practice, you will know that you've arrived at the right answer if you feel peace in your heart about it. If you do not, you are off track and need to go back and really listen to your intuition about what you would do if you weren't afraid. Don't let other people's opinions persuade you, either. If you feel at peace about your answer, then it's most likely the right one.

**Tip 2: Don't distort the Power Question Practice to justify reckless answers.** Please do not use the Power Question Practice to justify abandoning your family to run off with the pool boy, cashing in your retirement for a 24-karat diamond ring, or telling a board member exactly what you think of him. That is not courageous fearlessness, that is reckless fearlessness, and that is *not* what this practice is about.

**Tip 3: Don't stay on the surface. Go deep—and then go deeper.** You know when you are lifting weights at the gym and you start to feel that burn in your arms or legs? I always want to quit at that point because I don't like that feeling, and yet that feeling is *exactly* what you want to get to—the burn is the "results zone." So, as you do the Power Question Practice, make sure with each of the five questions you are really going deep into the results zone, because that is where you are going to get the most transformational impact.

**Tip 4: Don't become judgmental of yourself or others.** The purpose of the Power Question Practice isn't to feel bad about yourself once you start to notice all of the fear that is in most of our thinking. This happened to one of my clients. Once she got exposed to the Power Question Practice, she realized how most of her life decisions—from her current career even to whom she married—were all made out of fear. She started to get down on herself until she realized that she could use the practice to reframe her thinking about her life instead. And that's what she did.

The Power Question Practice will also make us more compassionately aware of how much fear drives others. Again, you don't need to become judgmental. Rather, if you are given the opportunity, respectfully ask that individual if you can help them address their fears with the Power Question Practice. If they say yes, guide them through the five questions. If they aren't ready for it, then just let it go.

**Tip 5: Put it into practice.** Make sure you take all of your Power Answers and put them into practice. You can't just *think* about how you would overcome fear, you have to actually *do* it. This is how you transform the way you live, lead, and work. Have that difficult conversation you've been putting off, take the next step to advance your career, or address that problem you've been running away from for months. You can do it, so *do* it!

---

Leading a Freedom-Centered Team or Organization begins with the right mindset, and the Power Question Practice is a proven tool to help get you there. When we learn how to cultivate a mindset of freedom rather than fear and control, we have taken the first step to successfully practicing Freedom at Work.

## REFLECTION QUESTIONS: DEVELOPING A FREEDOM-CENTERED MINDSET

Identify a challenge you are facing and then put it through the five-step Power Question Practice:

1. What am I afraid of?
2. Why I am afraid?
3. The Power Question: What would I do if I weren't afraid?
4. How would I feel without the fear?
5. Why is it okay to let the fear go?

# PART III

# FREEDOM-CENTERED LEADERSHIP

---

Let your light so shine . . .

—Christ Jesus—

# The Three Attributes of Freedom-Centered Leadership

*Be sure you put your feet in the right place,*
*then stand firm.*
–ABRAHAM LINCOLN–

John was a top marketing executive at a publicly traded Fortune 500 company. He had a cushy job, nice salary, and colleagues he enjoyed. Everything was great except for one thing—the company's CEO was a fear-based leader. During weekly meetings, John and his colleagues would watch in horror as the CEO would tear people down, belittle them, laugh as they struggled to answer his questions, and even throw objects at them in the conference room. Everyone was walking on eggshells wondering when they would be his next victim.

John and his coworkers developed a code to warn each other when their fear-based CEO was going to blow. They would watch him get angrier and angrier. When someone noticed they had reached the first critical moment, they would text the others the word "vein"—meaning the vein in his temple was starting to bulge out.

The next level up was "red," which meant his face was turning red. And the third and final stage was "ACP," short for "Assume the Crash Position"—as chairs were literally about to fly.

John described his experience as "sickening." He watched his own self-worth, and his colleagues', slowly erode. He would spend hours counseling his crying coworkers after the drama-fest meetings. It would take him days to regain his composure and dignity before he could start to feel productive again.

This went on for years, and the cumulative effects eventually took a major toll. John realized he couldn't take it anymore. He left the organization to start his own company. After a time, the fear-based CEO was also fired—but not before violating the souls of many people in his path.

---

Unfortunately, John's story isn't unusual. Many leaders—from Main Street to Wall Street and around the world—constantly use fear-based tactics to coerce, manipulate, bully, and control others under the guise of "leadership." Have you ever experienced (or even practiced!) this style of leadership before? I know most of us have experienced it at work, in our community organizations, in school growing up, and even in our homes.

These leaders use fear-and-control tactics, bulldoze and harass, micromanage and intimidate. Fear-based leaders usually have a chip on their shoulder or something to prove. Controlled by their egos and their insecurities, they fail to see the leadership capacity in others. That's why fear-based leaders love hierarchy (as long as they're at the top!), derive their power by withholding information from others, and generally feel threatened by people who are more secure in themselves than they are.

The result of fear-based leadership is that it creates a team or organization filled with adults who learn to keep their heads down and just do what they are told out of self-preservation. Even if your leader doesn't resort to actual verbal and physical abuse the way John's CEO did, over time, being in this kind of environment steals an individual's sense of self-worth and self-respect. No individual can realize their full potential in a place like that.

---

**Freedom-Centered Leaders have high self-worth, own their power within, and are living their purpose for their life.**

---

Freedom-Centered Leaders, in contrast, are committed to leading themselves and others from a place of freedom with personal accountability. Freedom-Centered Leaders have high self-worth, own their power within, and are living their purpose for their life. They don't create fear and drama—they mitigate it. They are selfless and self-governed, and act with integrity. They are the kind of leaders who attract and keep star players on their team.

## WHAT IS FREEDOM-CENTERED LEADERSHIP?

The second pillar of the Freedom at Work model is Freedom-Centered Leadership. Once you understand and practice the *mindset* skills of freedom rather than fear, you're ready to learn the *leadership* skills for how to lead yourself and others with freedom rather than control.

Freedom-Centered Leadership is about practicing three core attributes: Love (self-worth), Power (self-government), and Ubuntu (self-knowledge).

The first attribute of Freedom-Centered Leadership is Love. It is impossible to embrace freedom for yourself and others if you do not believe in your *own* self-worth *and* that of others. Your level of self-worth proportionally impacts your level of effectiveness as a leader.

---

**Your level of self-worth proportionally impacts
your level of effectiveness as a leader.**

---

The second attribute of Freedom-Centered Leadership is Power. Power relates to our power *within* and our ability to practice effective self-government. Freedom-Centered Leaders have a keen awareness of what takes away their power and ability to successfully self-govern.

The third attribute of a Freedom-Centered Leader is Ubuntu, which is a term used throughout South Africa. It means, "I can only be at my best when you are at your best, and you can only be at your best when I am at my best, because we are one." Ubuntu is about the self-knowledge each leader must possess to help their team perform at their peak.

When a leader intentionally practices all three attributes of Freedom-Centered Leadership—Love, Power, and Ubuntu—it equips them with the skills they need to develop themselves while bringing out the highest potential in their team or organization. Freedom, rather than fear and control, creates the optimal conditions for success for *everyone*. Over the next three chapters, we'll explore each of these attributes, beginning with Love.

# Love

*Every human longs for peace and love.*
—HIAWATHA—

A few years ago, I spoke at a leadership conference in the US. About one hundred CEOs were seated in a sunny hotel ballroom, ready to hear about Freedom-Centered Leadership. I asked them, "On a scale of one to ten, with ten being the highest, how would you rate your level of self-worth, and why?"

After giving the CEOs a few minutes to think about their answers, I asked them to close their eyes to keep things anonymous and raise a hand. Then I told them, "Leave your hand up if you gave yourself a five or higher." A few hands went down.

"Leave your hand up if you gave yourself a six or higher . . ." More hands down.

"A seven or higher . . ." Even more hands went down.

"And leave your hand up, please, if you gave yourself an eight or higher." Only three hands were still raised.

"How would you rate your level of self-worth?" has become the single most important thing I can ask a leader or someone who wants to be one. I've found that self-worth is the number-one determinant of a leader's success over the long term. You simply cannot be a successful Freedom-Centered Leader without having high self-worth. I consider anyone who gives themselves an eight or higher to be in the "high self-worth zone." It's not scientific; it's based on experience. People who give themselves at least an eight in self-worth are usually trending in the right direction.

That day, in a room of around one hundred CEOs, just three gave themselves an eight or higher. Unfortunately, while it was striking, it wasn't surprising. I've consistently found that most leaders struggle with self-worth, and it massively impacts the way they lead.

When I speak about Freedom-Centered Leadership, many leaders are often surprised by this conversation. "Love" and "self-worth" can sound soft or touchy-feely to business-minded people who are trained to focus on hard skills and bottom-line results. Yet, Love—specifically in the form of *self-worth*—is the first key attribute of a Freedom-Centered Leader. Your self-worth is your sense of your inherent value. It is how much you love yourself and feel secure in who you are.

---

**Your self-worth is your sense of your inherent value. It is how much you love yourself and feel secure in who you are.**

---

Having *high* self-worth means having an innate understanding that you don't have to do anything to "earn" love and significance. You derive that validation from within, regardless of external conditions, other people's opinions, how you were raised, where you live, how many degrees you have (or don't have), what your job title is, the mistakes of your past, or any other circumstances. It means being a friend to yourself. It doesn't mean you think you're perfect or have nothing to improve upon; high self-worth individuals are constantly growing and improving. But your value, your worth, is independent of what you are still working on.

On the other hand, individuals with low self-worth feel that they are never good enough, need to be externally validated through constant achieving, and are hot and cold with their attitude toward others. They are often negative, indifferent, moody, and self-absorbed; they can be closed off and unnecessarily private and may lack self-control.

It's important to understand that self-worth is *not* the same thing as self-confidence or self-esteem. The word *worth* comes from the Old English word *weorþ*, meaning "value," whereas *esteem* comes from the same root as the word *estimate*. High self-worth leaders *know* their inherent value—they don't have to estimate it! The word "confidence" is also Old English and means *trusting in oneself.*

I have met many people who act very self-confidently but who do not truly feel secure in their innate value. Self-confidence can sometimes be a mask for deep-seated insecurity. For example, a fear-based leader can appear confident but have low self-worth. Arrogance, hubris, and narcissism are often clear giveaways that an individual has low self-worth. (Think about John's CEO from the last chapter, laughing at his colleagues and acting as though he were superior to them.)

Self-confidence is more situational. You might trust yourself to bake a great cake if you're good at baking, but not trust yourself to fly a plane if you've never done it before. Self-worth, however, is understanding your constant, inherent value, and is *not* situational.

## WHY DOES SELF-WORTH MATTER TO LEADERSHIP?

Your sense of self-worth determines the way in which you will lead yourself, your team, and the style of organizational design that you will most readily embrace. Your degree of self-worth impacts the way you structure your day, your boundaries, how you interact with others, your level of joy and happiness, the decisions you make, and so much more. It determines your level of effectiveness at leading yourself and others. When you love yourself, you want to create a workplace environment that is loving to others. Conversely, when you *don't* love yourself, you create a workplace environment that isn't loving to others.

High self-worth leaders know they are good enough even when they make a mistake. They are consistently positive and upbeat; they commit to always learning; they do not judge others; they have a clear purpose and are courageously living it; and they exhibit a high level of self-control and self-discipline. They are focused on serving others over serving themselves, and they act with integrity. A high self-worth leader is willing to be personally accountable and takes feedback as an opportunity to grow. They are humble, open to new ideas, and deeply loving and kind toward their colleagues. As leaders, they tend to be solution oriented (rather than ruminating on the problem), and they love to create environments where everyone can realize their full potential.

On the other hand, many leaders have low self-worth, and this dramatically impacts the way they lead. They are much less inclined to be open to building teams or organizations where everyone can take the initiative and flourish; that feels threatening to them. Instead, they prefer to micromanage. They might not be able to bring out the best in others because they are too focused on what others are thinking about them. Low self-worth leaders hear feedback as a personal attack. They aren't willing to take personal responsibility when they make a mistake, and instead they self-justify and make excuses. They are problem-focused and controlling of others.

In short, high self-worth leaders operate in freedom, while low self-worth leaders operate in fear. And while it may seem blunt, the bottom line is that your team, division, or organization is only as strong and as freedom-centered as *your* level of self-worth as a leader.

I discovered this the hard way. After about fifteen years of working with client companies at WorldBlu, my team and I had observed that some leaders immediately "get" it and put the principles of Freedom at Work into operation right away, while others struggle to build a Freedom-Centered Team or Organization, even if intellectually they love the idea. We wondered why; we'd been working hard with these companies, and their lack of progress felt like we were failing them somehow. After we took a closer look, a clear pattern emerged. The CEOs and leaders who'd built and grown thriving, Freedom-Centered Teams or Organizations all had one thing in common: they all had *high* self-worth. The CEOs and leaders who were struggling to grasp Freedom at Work all had *low* self-worth and, most importantly, were *unwilling to acknowledge it and work on it.*

Case in point: we had worked with a client over a period of several years before we'd figured out this connection. They were a multimillion-dollar manufacturer and their leadership team loved the idea of building a Freedom-Centered Organization. They came to our live trainings and conferences and always left on fire. They would go back to their offices and try to implement the ideas we taught them, but they kept hitting roadblocks with their CEO. His leadership team was growing increasingly frustrated with the subtle and often unconscious things he was doing to undermine the Freedom-Centered Organization they were working so hard to build. Eventually, the leadership team convinced their CEO to come to one of our immersive trainings in the Freedom at Work leadership model.

At the training, we talked about self-worth. The CEO had a moment of insight and clarity about his low self-worth behavior and how it affected the company. He had inherited the company from his father and was still trying to prove to himself that he was "good enough" to be the CEO, which led to all

| CHARACTERISTICS OF LOW SELF-WORTH | CHARACTERISTICS OF HIGH SELF-WORTH |
| --- | --- |
| Never feels good enough | Knows they are inherently good enough |
| Derives validation externally | Derives validation internally |
| Emotionally hot or cold; goes to extremes | Consistently joyous |
| Is overly self-critical | Recognizes they are always learning |
| Manipulative | Honest and direct |
| Critical and judgmental | Judges righteously |
| Has a negative outlook | Has a positive outlook |
| Is indifferent or neutral | Takes a stand |
| Lacks self-control | Has high self-control |
| Is self-absorbed | Serves others |
| Self-justifies and acts defensive | Acts with integrity |
| Refuses to take personal responsibility | Takes personal responsibility |
| Feedback feels like a personal attack | Feedback is an opportunity to grow |
| Rarely compliments others | Enjoys complimenting others |
| Lacks compassion and empathy | Is highly compassionate and empathetic |
| Tears others down | Builds others up |
| Doesn't forgive | Forgives |
| Arrogant or egocentric | Humble |
| Closes their mind to new ideas | Opens their mind to new ideas |
| Secretive | Appropriately open |
| Problem-focused | Solution-oriented |

kinds of dysfunctional leadership behavior. He recognized that he was unconsciously sabotaging his employees' efforts to build a high-performing Freedom-Centered Organization because of it. By the end of our training, he voluntarily stood up in front of everyone and committed to working on improving his level of self-worth.

After our training, his leadership team went back and started doing even more inner work through our courses. The CEO, despite his public commitment, did not. He continued to wrestle with self-doubt. His team grew more and more discontented. They knew what the problem was, but the CEO had too much pride to do the work necessary to really change. It became increasingly clear to the leadership team that they would never be able to truly move the company forward, because he would keep sabotaging their efforts. Eventually, his high self-worth leadership team and other top employees resigned, feeling deeply disappointed. The CEO ended up selling the company to a competitor. It was incredibly difficult for us to observe.

The degree to which CEOs and top leaders love themselves ultimately impacts the culture they create in their organization, no matter its size, public or private status, or service orientation. Research by Gallup shows that 75 percent of people who voluntarily leave their job do so because of a bad boss or manager.[1] You can read every leadership book out there to try to improve your leadership skills, but if at your very core you don't have high self-worth, it will be difficult to build a high-performing team and healthy organizational culture. You will be the bad boss people leave.

---

**You can read every leadership book out there to try to improve your leadership skills, but if at your very core you don't have high self-worth, it will be difficult to build a high-performing team and healthy organizational culture.**

---

Garry, the CEO I introduced in Part II, puts it like this: "Leadership is not a game for the weak. As leaders we navigate across both calm and rough seas. As with a master mariner, if we have clear sight to the desired destination and we've been thoughtful and deliberate about what assets and resources we need to get to the destination, we have confidence we can get there. But then unexpected rough weather interrupts our journey. *This is when we need to dig deep into our favorable opinion of ourselves.* This is not arrogance or hubris. It is taking the time to reflect and refresh, to find a place of solace that reminds us that we can sail those rough seas and get our vessel and those that serve on it safely to our destination." Because of their belief in themselves *and* in others, Freedom-Centered Leaders naturally inspire confidence, loyalty, and a sense of certainty during the inevitable challenging times.

The entire premise of freedom and organizational democracy is built on the idea that each one of us has inherent worth and therefore *deserves* to have a voice, to have decision-making power, and to be free rather than ruled over by another. As a leader, you simply cannot believe in Freedom at Work if you don't believe in each individual's inherent worth—your own and others'. Freedom and low self-worth are completely incompatible. That's why you never see a high self-worth dictator.

In fact, at WorldBlu, we won't work with low self-worth CEOs or leaders who are *unwilling* to acknowledge that they struggle with low self-worth, are unwilling to grow, and who are not coachable. (If they *are* willing to grow and are coachable, we are happy to work with them!) Why? Because building a Freedom-Centered Organization is all about giving power to your people. If you don't have high self-worth, this will feel very threatening to you. When we have high self-worth, we *want* to see others succeed. As Freedom-Centered Leaders, we want to create environments that help release others' potential. We are not threatened by other people's success but instead take joy in it. A Freedom-Centered Leader must wholeheartedly embrace the characteristics of high self-worth and must consciously and intentionally choose to leave the characteristics of low self-worth behind.

## DO YOU KNOW YOUR WORTH?

So, where is your level of self-worth on a scale of one to ten? Most people give themselves a six or seven, thinking that's not as "bad" as anything below a five, but not as "good" as an eight, nine, or ten because, as they believe, "they are still improving." Among my clients, I've had some leaders tell me they are a one and some leaders tell me their level of self-worth is "one hundred"! But most leaders I've met sincerely believe that they don't have a lot of value, or, sadly, that they haven't "earned" enough worth yet.

Now, why do you give yourself the score that you do? Most individuals derive their self-worth from external factors—their title, the quality of their things, the car they drive, where they live, what their parents thought of them when they were kids, their body shape, how attractive their spouse is, how much money they make, and so on. I remember one CEO telling me that he was a six in self-worth because he hadn't hired a new COO yet!

The problem with all of these reasons is that self-worth is based on *external* circumstance, things, or other people's opinions of us. But your worth—your inherent *value*—has nothing, absolutely *nothing* to do with anything external. As I mentioned, self-worth is all *internal*.

Often, people don't feel good about themselves because they have made mistakes in the past, they don't feel like they've achieved their dreams, or they have regrets. Their sense of self-worth is low because they are basing their worth on their *performance* in life, usually in comparison to others. But this isn't where your worth comes from. The mistakes and bad choices may be *what* you did—but they are not *who* you are. You can buy a bigger house, drive a better car, get that promotion, make more money, and still not know and believe in your worth.

External things are superficial and might increase your *net* worth, but they don't impact your *self*-worth. As the saying goes, your self-worth is not your net worth. Your true worth must be found *within*. When it comes from within, it is grounded, not on the sands of doubt that constantly shift and change, but on the rock of knowing who you are.

Still other leaders tell me that their national or religious culture tells them they are not worthy. To admit that they have worth would be frowned upon because it is viewed as not being humble. But this act of faux humility obscures an important point: Letting go of self-centered, low self-worth thinking in order to embrace our true worth is one of the most humble things we can do!

I often have leaders tell me that their sense of self-worth changes depending on the day. Some days it's high, and some days it's low. Again, that is deriving self-worth from external things or accomplishments, or from what the gremlins are telling them. Ultimately, high self-worth individuals love themselves *consistently* and *unconditionally*.

## THE TRUTH ABOUT YOUR WORTH

One day when I was living in Washington, DC, I happened to glance up from my desk and look out the window at the exact moment a city bus passed by, emblazoned with an ad on the side. It had an all-white background with a Citibank logo in the upper right corner. In giant black letters it said "You were born *pre-approved*." Now, this may have been just advertising, but the message made an indelible impact on me.

The truth about our worth is that we were *all* born "pre-approved." I firmly believe that we are all tens in worth. You are *already* a perfect ten, whether you are willing to accept it or not!

Each individual must find their inherent sense of worth in the way that makes sense for them. I understand it through a spiritual path, as many leaders do. Mine comes from knowing I am the very *expression* of divine Love, or God, and therefore inherently and unchangingly worthy. As one of our client CEOs, Matthew, says, he knows he is a ten because "to not believe I am would be an insult to the Maker." Everyone has equal worth in the eyes of God. For other leaders, it's different, and it can be hard to articulate. Another client CEO, Nathan, doesn't believe in a higher power but he still knows that he has worth. "I just know it," he told me.

When we understand that we all are inherently tens in worth, this can truly change the way we lead in *every* area of our lives.

## IMPROVE YOUR WORTH TO LEAD OTHERS MORE SUCCESSFULLY

How do you develop self-worth so you can lead from a place of self-completeness and freedom?

First, ask yourself if you *really* want to improve your sense of self-worth. While it might seem like an obvious "yes" to some, sometimes pride, ego, and fear block us from doing the inner work needed.

If you truly want to lead yourself and others with freedom rather than fear and control, you must do this inner work. That's what Ann had to learn.

Ann was the new CEO of a retail business that was a part of a national chain. When she bought it, she inherited fifteen employees and anticipated that sales would continue as they had before. However, a few months later, there was a steady decline in sales and high employee turnover, forcing Ann to realize that she needed to change her leadership style.

Previously, Ann was a self-professed, hands-on, centralized, command-and-control leader, thinking it was the most effective way to lead her team. But through our coaching work together, she realized that this was a result of low self-worth on her part, which led to fear-based decision-making.

Ann started to embrace her inner sense of worth and became a more transparent and trusting employer. "Instead of me leading every discussion and decision, each team member was given a legitimate voice to express new ideas as well as concerns," Ann explained. "Together we created our mission statement, goals, and desires for the business based on what we value and how we think a healthy environment should look for both customers and employees. Team members now feel more valued and a part of the organization.

"Shifting my mindset to become a more fearless, open, and democratic leader allowed me to let go of numerous responsibilities by handing them off to team members who were eager to take on additional tasks, giving them the opportunity to grow and learn beyond their basic job requirements. This gave team members a heightened sense of ownership and accomplishment; plus, it freed me up to focus on higher priorities. The added bonus of this mindset shift was that it helped establish a more transparent and supportive environment, which resulted in a stronger culture built not just by me, but by everyone on the team. Now, two years later, long-term team members say things like, 'This isn't just my job, it's my family.'"

Today, team members recommend their friends apply for job openings at Ann's business, proving that its culture is positive. On top of that, Ann's realization didn't just yield a happier and healthier workplace environment; it also impacted the bottom line. Sales increased 10 percent in year one and, when I spoke with Ann, they were on track to realize another 10 percent increase in year two.

Ann was able to develop a higher sense of self-worth, and as a result, build a better team and a higher-performing business.

Improving your sense of self-worth is really about three key things:

1. Recognizing your *current* level of self-worth.
2. Making the *choice* to develop high self-worth.
3. Practicing and *living* it.

First, you have to be honest with yourself about where your sense of self-worth is, and—if you don't yet *know* you're a ten—examine what is holding you back from considering yourself a ten. You have to become much more aware of how the gremlins are trying to mess with you in order to put up a clear boundary in your thinking so they stop bullying you. Second, having high self-worth is a *choice*. You have to consciously and intentionally choose to love yourself and be the ten that you are. There are no conditions on your worth. You don't have to earn it. Mary Baker Eddy sums up this point perfectly: "Conscious worth satisfies the hungry heart, and nothing else can." Last, you need to *practice* high self-worth behaviors each day at work and at home.

Here are ten things I've done with our clients that, when practiced together, are proven to help develop a higher sense of self-worth.

1. **Get clear on your real identity.** Stop listening to the gremlin voices that constantly tell you that you're not good enough, giving you a negative sense of your identity. Instead, make a list of twenty-five things you love about yourself. Write them down and focus on the *truth* of your real identity, which is always good enough, worthy, and deeply

valuable to our world. Post the list at work and at home in places where you'll see it, reinforcing the ten that you inherently are.

2. **Notice the patterns of the gremlins.** For one week, write down all of your negative self-talk and notice the patterns. Gremlins aren't creative and usually like to say the same things over and over again, which boils down to the same fear—that you're not good enough. Then take a sheet of paper and draw two columns. In the left column, list the lies the gremlins are telling you. Then, in the right column, counter each lie by writing out what is *really* true about you. Waking up to the patterns helps you take control of your thinking. Once you identify the fear, you can overcome it. In the words of Ralph Waldo Emerson, "You become what you think about all day long."

3. **Develop a butt-kicking mantra.** Once you spot a gremlin trying to take away your sense of self-worth, you need a mantra that breaks its mesmeric hold on you, tells it to go away, and puts you back in your power. On the rare occasions that I hear a gremlin knocking on my mental door, I say, "Shut the fuck up, you stupid-ass lie!" Yeah, that's my (very blunt!) mantra. You can make one, too. It can be pointed like mine, or more gentle, yet firm. Use your mantra when the gremlins try to shout at you, and it will help you reclaim your worth—and get them to leave fast!

4. **Shut your mental door.** When you hear a gremlin voice knocking for admission into your headspace, slam the door in its face. Too often, we *compromise* and invite the bullying thought to come in, sit down, and put its feet up rather than locking the dead bolt. When you stop letting the gremlin voices in as mental houseguests, they stop showing up.

5. **Forgive yourself.** So, you messed something up? We all do! Instead of harshly judging yourself, truly forgive yourself. And then do #6.

6. **Reframe failure into Learning Moments.** Low self-worth thinking says, "*I* am my mistake." But that is not true. Reframe so-called mistakes as "Learning Moments" and see them as stepping-stones to inner growth and wisdom. (We'll revisit the concept of Learning Moments in Part IV.)

7. **Develop mental discipline through denials and affirmations.** Every time a gremlin tries to tell you that you're not good enough, *deny* its power with your mantra. Next, *affirm* the truth about who you are. Stop letting low self-worth thinking impose on you. Develop mental discipline and dominion through this daily practice.

8. **Focus on gratitude and serving others.** I'm not the first or last one to say it, but focusing on what you are grateful for throughout your day and living in service to others is a wonderful way to deepen your sense of worth. Low self-worth thinking is ingratitude and an intense focus on yourself. Instead, focus on what you're grateful for and live your purpose in service to others.

9. **Defeat fear with the Power Question Practice.** Fear drives low self-worth thinking. Identify and then overcome your fears with the Power Question Practice so you can break through and reclaim your sense of self-worth.

10. **Practice being a ten.** How would you *talk*, *behave*, and *lead* if you already knew you were truly a perfect ten? Start practicing being this way and you will become it!

Increasing your sense of self-worth is like developing a new muscle, and you must practice it regularly until it sticks. Enroll in a highly transformational leadership course, such as one of the ones we offer at WorldBlu, and work regularly with a coach who will teach you the skills of a high self-worth leader, such as how to handle conflict well, how to set healthy boundaries, how to live your purpose, and how to lead from a place of love, not fear.

These ten practices will get you on the path to developing a deeper sense of self-worth so that you can lead yourself and others from a place of freedom rather than fear.

## LEADING DIFFERENT LEVELS OF SELF-WORTH IN YOUR TEAM OR ORGANIZATION

Now that we've explored how to develop your own sense of self-worth, we need to talk about leading and working with people who have different levels of self-worth.

Freedom-Centered Leaders need to be aware of their colleagues' levels of self-worth so they can successfully navigate challenges that may arise while providing them with the opportunity to grow. Your colleagues' level of self-worth will dramatically impact your team's level of performance, engagement, trust, and morale.

Working with high self-worth people is deeply fulfilling, fun, and quite frankly, very easy. You can focus more on achieving goals than dealing with drama. Therefore, as a leader, you must think through who you have on your team.

How do you know someone else's level of self-worth? The characteristics of low and high self-worth that I outlined in the chart on page 53 will give you a surprisingly accurate grasp. Ask yourself, "On a scale of one to ten, how would I rate their level of self-worth and why?" to get a general benchmark. Go with your gut. Understanding where a colleague is with their level of self-worth will guide you in how to best interact with them and support their growth.

Self-worth can be taught to those who are struggling yet sincerely want to grow and are coachable. But for those who do *not* want to acknowledge their low self-worth issues and who are *not* coachable, you will want to think deeply about whether having them on the team helps move you forward or holds you back. Then, you will need to take the appropriate actions necessary to either invest in those who are willing to grow or, if they're not, to let them go. This is not a decision to be taken lightly, and you should thoroughly analyze their past performance, how low self-worth may be impacting their behavior, and if they are coachable or not before taking action.

Now, let me give you a few tips for working with people who have different levels of self-worth within the workplace.

## High Self-Worth Leaders Leading Low Self-Worth Employees

If you are a high self-worth leader (meaning you can honestly give yourself an eight or higher in self-worth) working with a low self-worth employee (anyone you'd rate as a seven or lower), here are a few things to be aware of as you work with them:

**It may be difficult for them to receive feedback.** Those struggling with low self-worth will hear feedback as a personal attack and shut down, retaliate, get angry, or beat themselves up. Check in with them soon after giving the feedback to reinforce that it is not a value judgment on them as a *person* but is specific to a task, situation, or project. As you see them improve, give them a fair amount of sincere recognition to further reinforce their growth.

**They will need a lot of ongoing praise.** Low self-worth employees who engage in mean, bullying, or manipulative behavior are the kinds of people that you might not want to compliment at all. Find a sincere and honest way to regularly applaud them and they may blossom and grow over time.

**They still need to be held accountable.** Low self-worth behavior can be slippery at times. Often such employees will scapegoat and manipulate others, doing everything they can to avoid taking personal responsibility for their actions. It may be difficult, but as a leader you must lovingly and firmly hold them accountable for any negative actions while helping them engage in healthier, high self-worth behaviors.

**See their inherent ten-ness—but don't get duped.** As a high self-worth leader, you must see the inherent ten-ness in colleagues who struggle with lower self-worth—but remember that change will not happen overnight. One leadership course or a good conversation will not totally end bad behavior related to low self-worth, so stay wise to the best way to interact with and support them. Schedule routine check-ins to reinforce their ten-ness.

**Don't take their negative behavior personally.** Do you remember the Aesop fable of the scorpion and the frog? The scorpion asks the frog if he will give him a ride across the river on his back. The frog initially says no because he knows the scorpion will sting him. The scorpion promises he won't, climbs on the frog's back, and, halfway across the river, stings him. As they both are drowning, the frog asks the scorpion why he stung him. "I couldn't help myself, it's my nature," replies the scorpion, and they both sink to the bottom of the river. The lesson: don't take low self-worth behavior personally. Hurting people hurt people.

**If they're not improving, don't be slow to let the employee go.** Nathan, the CEO of a then-struggling New Zealand tech company, had a difficult choice to make. Despite investing thousands of dollars in his chief operating officer's leadership development over the course of several years, nothing changed; she was continually challenged by the unhealthy leadership behaviors associated with low self-worth. Finally, he made the choice to let her go. You must have the courage to take this step if needed because such employees will poison the Freedom-Centered Team or Organization you are building.

## High Self-Worth Leaders Leading High Self-Worth Employees

By contrast, how should high self-worth leaders manage high self-worth employees (those who give themselves an eight or higher)?

**Give them clear and direct feedback.** They take feedback as a learning opportunity and will rise to the task.

**Give them recognition and praise, but don't assume they need it.** Such employees get their sense of significance from internal rather than external factors. While they don't need recognition, they will appreciate it.

**Give them a challenge that is aligned with their personal purpose.** Assign them significant, demanding, well-aligned work to keep them highly engaged and fulfilled.

**Treat them with respect.** Because such people truly respect themselves, they can shut down if they don't feel respected by others. Even if you disagree with them, make sure that you always treat them with respect, and they will stay open to what you have to share with them.

**Create a Freedom-Centered Team or Organization where they can thrive.** High self-worth employees flourish in environments where they are not micromanaged or told what to do. Build a Freedom-Centered Team or Organization for them and they will be loyal and excel.

## HIRING FOR HIGH SELF-WORTH

As you build a Freedom-Centered Team or Organization, you must think carefully about who you hire. Most hiring managers focus on a candidate's skill set, experience, values alignment, résumé, or performance on various exams. Some even run algorithms to see how a candidate matches up. But that's not where you should *start*.

The first thing you must look for in hiring if you want to build a Freedom-Centered Team or Organization is *a candidate's level of self-worth*. Remember, a lot of dysfunctional workplace behavior comes from low self-worth people, so you must hire for self-worth *first* above everything else if you want to build a high-performing team.

Even one low self-worth employee, no matter how impressive their résumé or CV, can drag down an entire high self-worth team. A low self-worth team is negative; doesn't work well together; engages in backstabbing and gossip; and is mentally, emotionally, and spiritually draining. This kind of team will exhaust you and waste hours of your time on endless drama while crushing your bottom line. Under such circumstances, high self-worth employees will leave.

By contrast, with a high self-worth team, you can *truly succeed together*. Everyone has each other's backs and works well together. Trust levels are high, people are engaged, and they love going the extra mile. Best of all, they are consistently joyful and thrive on helping everyone they work with look good and be set up for success.

One WorldBlu certified Freedom-Centered Organization in Madison, Wisconsin, has taken this approach to their hiring process. Its CEO, Matthew, explained: "In the application process, we have a question asking about their level of self-worth on a one-to-ten scale, and then when we get to the interview process, we ask them to first define what self-worth means to them, then tell us their score, and then reflect on the score they gave themselves."

Matthew detailed how they put it into operation using a sample set of data for a recent position: "We had 315 applicants and three-fourths of those applicants gave themselves an eight, nine, or ten. Two percent gave themselves an eleven! The lowest score was a three, and 11 percent of applicants chose not to answer the question. A total of 25 percent of the applicants gave themselves a ten. Of those 315, we hired seven, five of which gave themselves a ten and two of which gave themselves a nine. I have to say, they are absolutely rock stars in the organization."

Matthew's experience proves the value of high self-worth at every level within an organization. Remember, self-worth is all about loving yourself, and when you do, you can create an environment that is loving to those around you, too. Once a leader has embedded Love into their leadership style—or at least committed to improving their self-worth—they can move on to the second component of Freedom-Centered Leadership: Power. In fact, Matthew learned a key lesson about Power that I'll share with you in the next chapter.

## REFLECTION QUESTIONS: LOVE

1. On a scale of one to ten (with ten being the highest), how would you rate your level of self-worth and why?
2. Is your level of self-worth internally or externally derived?
3. What would have to change in your thinking to move just one number up in your level of self-worth (if you didn't already give yourself a ten)?
4. What would have to change in your thinking for you to give yourself a ten in self-worth?
5. Think of five to seven close coworkers or team members in your organization. How would you rate their level of self-worth and why? What do you think is the best way to lead or work with them?

# Power

*Power proves the man.*
—SOLON—

"**T**oxic Executives Create a Culture of Fear and Intimidation." This was the scathing headline that one of Matthew's employees had used to post anonymously about his leadership on a company-rating website. "It felt like a punch to the gut," he said. "It felt like the whole organization must be silently burning around me, in mutiny."[1]

This was not a normal review for one of our certified Freedom-Centered Organizations, and it felt personal to Matthew, a chief executive who was deeply conscientious about leading from a place of freedom rather than fear while developing his colleagues to lead in the same way. How could he not take it personally? Even worse, what was he, the CEO with the "power," supposed to do about it?

Power is one of the three core attributes of a Freedom-Centered Leader. After all, democracy literally means *power* to the people. So, to be free, we must understand our Power. Yet when some people hear the word *power* it conjures up negative, domineering images. The famous quote by British historian Lord Acton sums up this sentiment: "Absolute power corrupts absolutely."

However, Freedom-Centered Power is not about absolute power *over* others. It is not about power *to* or power *with* others. And it's not about *empowering* others either. It is, quite simply, about accepting and owning your power *within*—and helping those you lead do the same. Your power within is partly an expression of claiming your self-worth. Knowing that you are a ten in self-worth can help you tap further into your infinite power within.

The word *power* originates from the Latin word for "potent." And the word *potent* comes from the Sanskrit for "master." When we are embracing our power within, we are in *mastery*. This level of mastery is what allows us to fully unlock our potential in every area of life.

So how would Matthew own his inner power to deal with this situation? Would he default into a "power-over" approach out of fear of what others thought of him, or would he find a higher way? And how would he navigate staying in his power as a leader when being attacked—and while not even sure who was attacking him? Adversity can be one of the best tests to determine if we are in our true power as leaders.

Matthew's approach was to turn to a few different books, as well as his faith, for inspiration. He realized that he needed to identify the sense of injustice (he felt their style of communication had been venomous), truly forgive (he was ready), and then empathize with the reviewer's point of view (his turning point).

Once he did all of this, he realized a few ways the company culture had failed and how they could improve. One was that their internal grievance process was new and more people needed to be aware of it. While people were encouraged to talk with their managers if there was a problem, not everyone was comfortable doing so.

He also recognized that their promotions and career advancement process was not as clear as it could be and that they were lacking in racial and ethnic diversity. Last, he identified that the company needed to improve their managerial training and communications processes so employees didn't feel that there was favoritism, fear, or intimidation happening at any level of leadership.[2]

By working through this process and trying to understand rather than taking offense or reacting to the situation, he stayed in his power rather than giving it away to anger or a feeling of injustice. By taking accountability—and ultimately taking action—Matthew was able to feel grateful for the situation overall. Matthew demonstrated the difference between Freedom-Centered Power versus fear-based power.

To own our inner power as leaders, we have to understand what real power is and how to use it. As a leader, you are in Freedom-Centered Power when you know what is true and are being moral, fearless, and humble; living your purpose, embracing your inner worth, and being personally accountable—in short, leading with Love. This is what true power looks like, and it is what enables us to successfully practice self-government.

| CHARACTERISTICS OF FEAR-BASED POWER | CHARACTERISTICS OF FREEDOM-CENTERED POWER |
|---|---|
| Silence or violence | Constructive and healthy interactions |
| Passive-aggressive | Frank, open, and honest communication |
| Confusing | Clear and direct |
| Victim mentality | Personally accountable |
| Promotes personal agenda at the expense of others | Supports both individual and group needs |
| Territory over relationship | Relationship over territory |
| Takes from others aggressively | Holds clear boundaries |
| Serves ego | Serves others |
| Creates fear and drama | Mitigates fear and drama |
| Competitive | Cooperative |
| Fearful | Calm |
| Extreme | Even-handed |
| Abusive | Caring |
| Provokes change through intimidation | Inspires change through leadership |
| Prideful | Humble |
| Reactionary | Responsive |
| Merciless | Graceful |
| Undisciplined | Disciplined |
| Lacks self-government | High level of self-government |

So what does it take to own our inner power as leaders? Let's take a deeper look at the core elements of Freedom-Centered Power.

## FREEDOM-CENTERED POWER KNOWS THE TRUTH

As a Freedom-Centered Leader, first and foremost, you are not in your power unless you know what is true and you are standing for it. We only have a feeling of dominion if we know the truth about a person or situation. So, what is the truth and why does it matter? Understanding what is *really* true (not just what is *your* truth) is the pathway to accepting and owning our power; it gives us a solid foundation to rest upon amid challenges and shifting circumstances. Otherwise you will be manipulated and deceived by lies.

So, how do we get to the truth? We have to be able to constantly discern between opinions and facts, personalities and principles, stories and reality. In Matthew's case, he knew the truth was that they were an excellent company committed to Freedom at Work, with plenty of evidence for this fact. That core truth kept him on track as he figured out how to handle the criticism.

I believe the path to truth can also often involve a spiritual journey. But you simply cannot be in your power as a leader if you don't deeply know what is true as you navigate complex leadership situations.

## FREEDOM-CENTERED POWER IS MORAL

As Freedom-Centered Leaders, we own our power within when we are ethical and make decisions from a place of moral courage. Why? Because when we are in alignment with a higher moral standard, it guides us, keeps us safe, gives us courage during difficult times, and keeps us centered in our power.

Unfortunately, we all know fear-based leaders who make unethical and immoral decisions because they lack a conscience and character, which ultimately undermines their team or organization. Even worse, during challenging times, fear-based leaders have no moral capital built up with their colleagues to call upon because they are morally bankrupt.

For leaders to own their inner power, they *must* have a moral compass—and use it. They must also understand that there are universal moral principles; they cannot be a moral relativist. Matthew could have defaulted into fear-based power and never even acknowledged the negative review, sidestepping accountability and dismissing an employee's point of view. Yet because of his inner standards, he faced the situation and used it to improve as a leader while improving company culture, too.

---

**For leaders to own their inner power, they *must* have a moral compass—and use it.**

---

Freedom-Centered Leaders live moral lives and do their best to make decisions aligned with high ethical standards—even when it's difficult. This requires a deeper level of maturity and taking the longer view. Freedom-Centered Leaders also strive to help their colleagues adhere to ethical principles, which provides the stability and trust that builds a solid foundation for their teams or organizations. But being moral must also be coupled with humility, or else we can become self-righteous, willful, and unyielding.

## FREEDOM-CENTERED POWER IS COMPASSIONATE

When we are acting from a place of compassion rather than fear and control, we are in our power as leaders. And acting from this place of caring for and considering others keeps us in our power.

Fear-based leaders do not think of others' feelings and instead try to gain power through trying to abuse or control them. This abuse of power looks like discriminatory practices, unfairness, censorship, and other forms of uncaring behavior. These tactics take a leader out of owning their power within and erodes any social capital they may have developed with their colleagues or customer base.

Being compassionate and empathetic is not about being a pushover or wishy-washy. On the contrary, awareness of another's feelings takes backbone. Matthew's reaction toward the negative review illustrates what I mean. He cared deeply about his employees' points of view and honored them by listening to their perspective and looking for ways to improve as a leader. Compassion also looks like knowing when to make the tough, unpopular calls and hard choices to maintain a standard of freedom rather than fear. It is about communicating clearly with your colleagues, defining expectations, and knowing how and when to express genuine care, grace, and kindness.

## FREEDOM-CENTERED POWER IS FEARLESS

As we explored in the Freedom-Centered Mindset chapter, when we are in fear, we are not owning our inner power. Fear can be obvious, but most of the time, it is subtle. That is why, as Freedom-Centered Leaders, we have to use tools such as the Power Question Practice to guide us away from making decisions based on fear, which gives our power away.

Yet too often we give our power over to fear-based thinking and therefore make bad decisions, especially in times of stress, upheaval, and change. Matthew admitted that he worried everyone was against him in the organization because of that one anonymous comment. This would make any leader want to run and hide! But when fear is at the helm, it breeds resentment, anger, apathy, and indifference within us—and with those we lead.

As fearless leaders, when we endeavor to keep learning with each barb thrown at us, don't react, stay the course, and overcome the common fears of failure and others' opinions of us, we stay in our inner power and can make more insightful and strategic decisions that benefit everyone over the long term.

## FREEDOM-CENTERED POWER IS PURPOSEFUL

Freedom-Centered Leaders have a clear sense of their purpose and vision for their lives. They are in their power because they know what they stand for. Ideally, leaders should have a one-sentence Purpose and Vision statement to help guide their decisions and behavior (and at WorldBlu, we teach a course on how to find it). Your purpose is your reason for being, and your vision is what you want to see as a result of living your purpose. Knowing your purpose and vision for your life helps you to inspire others with your clarity, focus, and certainty. When we do not know our purpose and vision for our life, we do not know what we stand for, why we are here, or the true north toward which we are headed. This can result in countless missteps; wasted time, money, and relationships; and a lack of meaning and fulfillment in our lives.

Matthew's Purpose statement is to "celebrate life and promote human flourishing." He was able to use his clear sense of purpose to guide how he handled the anonymous review and still stay in his inner power. (We will return to the idea of Purpose and Vision—and how it matters on an even larger scale—in a later chapter.)

## FREEDOM-CENTERED POWER MEANS HAVING HEALTHY BOUNDARIES

Have you ever said "yes" to doing something that you didn't want to do? Most of us have, but every time we do, we are not setting or honoring healthy boundaries. Part of having healthy boundaries is holding the boundary on fear consuming you and your life. It allows us as leaders to think clearly and resist emotionalism and drama. Freedom-Centered Leaders hold the boundary in challenging times, stay calm, and do their best not to act in a reactionary way. Without healthy boundaries around our time, resources, emotions, bodies, spirits, and purpose, we inadvertently give our power away.

A fear-based leader, in Matthew's situation, could have given his power away to fear, demanding his employees tell him who wrote the negative review, shaming and embarrassing that individual, and even firing them.

As a Freedom-Centered Leader, however, Matthew did the opposite by listening to the feedback and improving as a leader. Healthy boundaries give Freedom-Centered Leaders a sense of peace that helps ensure they can live their purpose and achieve their goals.

## FREEDOM-CENTERED POWER IS ABOUT OWNING YOUR INHERENT WORTH

As we explored in the chapter about Love, Freedom-Centered Leaders know and claim their inherent sense of self-worth. By contrast, fear-based leaders do not own their worth, and therefore engage in behaviors that take them out of their power. The higher an individual's sense of self-worth is, the less they succumb to fear-based power. The lower their sense of self-worth, the more they use fear-based power to control and manipulate others.

As a high self-worth leader, Matthew not only addressed the review and improved; he also ended up writing an article about his learning journey from the experience for a major business magazine.

Self-worth and power are inextricably linked. When we know our true worth, we are loving ourselves and honoring the worth and dignity inherent in each individual, while tapping into our inherent power.

---

**Self-worth and power are inextricably linked.**

---

## FREEDOM-CENTERED POWER IS ACCOUNTABLE

When we own our power as leaders, we take accountability for our thoughts, actions, and the impact our behavior has on others—positive or negative. Freedom-Centered Leaders like Matthew do not make excuses and are willing to do the difficult work to address the challenges life inevitably brings each one of us.

Fear-based leaders, however, always see themselves as the victim of another individual's actions or an untoward circumstance and refuse to ever be accountable for *anything*. If only they knew how much power they cede through this lack of personal accountability.

## OWNING OUR POWER RESULTS IN SELF-GOVERNMENT

Owning our inner power as leaders means we know what is true; we are ethical and moral, loving and fearless; we embrace our inherent worth; know and live our purpose; and take personal accountability for our lives and our impact on others. All of this results in effective self-government. Freedom-Centered Leaders do not take away an individual's autonomy, trading their independence for dependence. Instead, they strive to help those they lead embrace their power within. Self-government creates a high-performing team managed not through unnecessary bureaucracy, policy manuals, and rules but through Freedom-Centered Power.

Let's now turn to the third component of Freedom-Centered Leadership: Ubuntu.

---

## REFLECTION QUESTIONS: POWER

1. On a scale of one to ten, how much are you in fear-based power and why?
2. On a scale of one to ten, how much are you in Freedom-Centered Power and why?
3. When are you most in your power within? When are you *not* in your power within?
4. How would you change your behavior if you consciously led yourself and others with Freedom-Centered Power?
5. What are three things you can start doing differently right now to start leading with more Freedom-Centered Power rather than fear-based power?

# Ubuntu

*Freedom is knowing who you really are.*
—Bill Vaughan—

In 2004, I traveled to South Africa for the first time, attending the World Movement for Democracy's global assembly and meeting with world leaders and business leaders who were working to advance democracy in South Africa and beyond.

While I was there, an unexpected yet life-changing opportunity opened up. I got to meet Wendy, then CEO of the retail division of South Africa's largest bank, high up in her offices overlooking Johannesburg. Wendy had been charged with finding a way to unify the employees of the bank in the post-apartheid era. As we sat in a beautiful conference room, Wendy, a soft-spoken yet confident leader, explained to me how, under her leadership, they transitioned from a fear-based organization to one centered in freedom. When I asked her how, she said, "One word: Ubuntu."

I had never heard of it before, so Wendy further explained. "Ubuntu means, 'I can be my best only if you are at your best, and you can only be your best if I am at my best, because we are one.'"

As a result of practicing the spirit of Ubuntu, they made a significant shift from being a fear-based division to a Freedom-Centered Team, became a role model for the rest of the company, and massively improved their bottom line.

Within five years, they grew by 100 percent, raised employee satisfaction to the ninetieth percentile, and lowered overall turnover.

But the benefits didn't just stop with their financial success; they also rippled out to impact the community. Over ten thousand of their twenty-two thousand employees, many of whom had never volunteered before, began volunteering in their communities in the spirit of Ubuntu. As a result, Wendy was recognized for their remarkable turnaround; she proudly shared with me that she (with the help of her team!) had been voted South Africa's "Top Woman in Business."

It is commonly agreed that the exact meaning of the word *Ubuntu*, a Nguni Bantu word from South Africa, can be a bit difficult to pin down. Nelson Mandela, former president of South Africa, explained it like this: "In Africa, there is a concept known as 'Ubuntu'—the profound sense that we are human only through the humanity of others; that if we are to accomplish anything in this world it will in equal measure be due to the work and achievement of others."

In his article "Practising Ubuntu and Leadership for Good Governance," T. I. Nzimakwe of the School of Management and Governance at the University of KwaZulu-Natal in South Africa explains, "Ubuntu is an old African term for 'humanness'—for caring and for sharing. It is a way of life and stresses the importance of community, solidarity, sharing and caring. As an ideal, Ubuntu means the opposite of being selfish and self-centered. It promotes cooperation between individuals, cultures and nations. Ubuntu thus empowers all to be valued to reach their full potential in accord with all around them."

Ubuntu is the third attribute of Freedom-Centered Leadership. It captures, in a word, the values of self-knowledge, interconnectedness, teamwork, and mutual accountability we have to one another. When we live the Ubuntu spirit, it allows us to build very high-performing teams.

---

**Ubuntu captures, in a word, the values of self-knowledge, interconnectedness, teamwork, and mutual accountability we have to one another.**

---

One notable example comes from the world of sports. Back in 2007, the Boston Celtics basketball team was massively struggling after coming in last in the NBA Eastern Conference season standings. Their new coach, Doc

Rivers, was searching for a philosophy that would bring his team together and get them on a path of success. While at his alma mater, Marquette University, in a chance encounter, he met Kita Matungulu, an expert in Ubuntu who is also the head of Hoops for Hope in South Africa. Kita asked Doc if he had ever heard of Ubuntu and told him he needed to get his team to practice it.[1]

"The definition of Ubuntu is I am who I am because of you. My shine is your shine. My success is your success," Kita explained to Doc, who loved the concept and took it to his team.[2]

Doc explained to the players that Ubuntu would be their new philosophy, and ultimately it unified and guided their previously fractured and failing team. Everything they did was about Ubuntu. If there was a problem, they solved it with Ubuntu. If egos flared up, they calmed down with Ubuntu. Before their games, their cheer was, "1-2-3, Ubuntu!" The Boston Celtics' embrace of Ubuntu led to a remarkable one-year turnaround that propelled them to win the 2008 NBA championship—their first title since 1986.

Ubuntu delivers several benefits that help Freedom-Centered Leaders further develop themselves and their teams. Let's explore each one.

## UBUNTU IS SELF-KNOWLEDGE

If Ubuntu is about showing up at our best so that everyone else can be at their best, then what exactly is our "best"? To answer this requires self-knowledge.

Why does self-knowledge matter so much? Well, as a leader, if you don't know yourself, how can you show up at your best for your team? When you know who you are and you know your strengths, then you know how to use them in service to your goals.

Ubuntu also helps us when, as leaders, we are dealing with burnout, mental exhaustion, decision fatigue, and stress. When we get realigned with what we need to do to be at our best, we draw a mental boundary in the sand around anything that is draining us, finding refreshment and renewal.

As I mentioned, I believe self-knowledge begins with knowing your purpose and vision for your life, then consciously and intentionally living it each day. Everyone on the WorldBlu team knows their purpose and vision for their life. This allows us to ensure that every member of our team is engaged in purpose-aligned work, which ultimately gives them a feeling of meaning and fulfillment.

And while self-knowledge may start with having a clear purpose and vision, a Freedom-Centered Leader must also know what it takes to be at their best mentally, physically, spiritually, athletically, socially, and financially so they are set up for success in *every* area of life. Take some time to reflect on this question: What does being at your best actually look like in each of those areas? Having a clear picture helps you set priorities. You can also revisit and refresh this vision as you move through the seasons of your life; what your best looks like today may be very different one, five, or ten years from now.

I recall at one point I felt like I was doing a million things that weren't in alignment with my Ubuntu. Not only was it making me miserable, it also meant I couldn't show up at my best as a leader for my team. So, I sat down and wrote out what I truly needed to be doing to be at my best— my Ubuntu—in every major area of my life. Then, I shifted, delegated, or stopped doing the things that were not Ubuntu-aligned for me, and started doing more of what *did* enable me to show up on purpose. This liberated me to be more freedom-centered and less fear-based in my personal and professional lives. This simple activity was deeply rejuvenating and got me back on track.

As leaders live their Ubuntu each day, they are modeling, creating, and supporting the conditions for those on their team to identify and live their Ubuntu as well. I've noticed that whenever someone at WorldBlu is underperforming in the necessary tasks of their position, it's best to check first and make sure that—in addition to having the skills and training they need to succeed— their position is aligned with their Ubuntu. If not, we work with them to shift them to a new role or new work that better aligns with their best.

## UBUNTU IS INTERCONNECTEDNESS AND TEAMWORK

The spirit of Ubuntu perfectly sums up the fact that all of us are interconnected and therefore interdependent. This spirit of inherent interconnectedness also helps counter feelings of isolation and division. Ubuntu heightens the awareness of our mutual responsibility to each other to think and act as one team.

In the case of the 2007 Boston Celtics, the team comprised many individual superstar players—and that was the problem. They were on the court playing to make *themselves* look good rather than thinking about how their actions could help the entire team succeed.

Once they figured this out through the spirit of Ubuntu, the players stopped being so self-centered and instead thought about how they could make each other perform at an even higher level. The improvement was not just marginal—after all, they went on to win the NBA championship!

This recognition of our interconnectedness invites us to consciously look for opportunities to help someone else rise up so that our entire team stays strong. For example, we have a practice at WorldBlu where we invite anyone to share an example of when they saw someone on our team living the spirit of Ubuntu—helping another be at their best so we all could be at our best.

When a team is leading with Ubuntu, it shifts us from thinking of just ourselves to recognizing our interconnectedness and how our actions impact the greater team for failure or success. It is about being in service to each other.

## UBUNTU IS HONORING OUR HUMANITY

Fear-based leaders treat the people in their organizations as cogs in a machine, whereas Freedom-Centered Leaders, through the practice of Ubuntu, recognize the humanity in each individual and build an environment that honors our humanity.

Archbishop Desmond Tutu, a Nobel Peace Prize winner and South African Anglican theologian known for his human rights and anti-apartheid work, anchors Ubuntu in the ideals of forgiveness and reconciliation. He explains it like this:

> One of the sayings in our country is Ubuntu—the essence of being human.
>
> Ubuntu speaks particularly about the fact that you can't exist as a human being in isolation. It speaks about our interconnectedness. You can't be human all by yourself, and when you have this quality—Ubuntu—you are known for your generosity. We think of ourselves far too frequently as just individuals, separated from one another, whereas you are connected and what you do affects the whole world. When you do well, it spreads out; it is for the whole of humanity.[3]

Ubuntu is about *humanity*, about being humane to one another, about recognizing that we are not cogs in a machine. Rather, we are in constant relationship with one another, and we become more human and caring through recognizing this vibrant interconnectedness.

## UBUNTU IS CHARACTER

Last, Ubuntu is about being an individual of character. It is about treating everyone with dignity and respect, building universal brotherhood and sisterhood, making a positive contribution, sharing with others, and being a contributing member of your community. Ubuntu requires ethical and moral behavior, because it is impossible for anyone on a team to show up at their best if someone on that team lacks a dependable character.

The spirit of Ubuntu is about building high-performing teams where, through self-knowledge, each individual feels a shared responsibility to show up at their best so that everyone on their team can be at their best and achieve breakthrough results. When we realize that your success is my success, and vice versa, potential jealousy is removed. We don't have to dim our light; we can shine so *everyone* can shine.

---

We have explored the first two dimensions of the Freedom at Work model—how to develop a Freedom-Centered Mindset and how to be a Freedom-Centered Leader. Now it is time to explore the third pillar of Freedom at Work: Freedom-Centered Design and how to design your team's or organization's culture using the principles of organizational democracy.

## REFLECTION QUESTIONS: UBUNTU

1.  What do you need to do to live your Ubuntu in the following areas each day?
    * Physically
    * Mentally
    * Athletically
    * Spiritually
    * Financially
    * Career
    * Friends
    * Family

2. On a scale from one to ten (with ten being the highest), how much are you living your Ubuntu at *work* and why?
3. On a scale from one to ten, how much are you living your Ubuntu in your *personal* life and why?
4. What healthy boundaries do you need to set so that you have the time and resources to live your Ubuntu each day personally and professionally?
5. What needs to change in your team or organization so that people can more fully live their Ubuntu in your workplace?

# PART IV

# FREEDOM-CENTERED DESIGN

Democracy is based upon the conviction that there
are extraordinary possibilities in ordinary people.
—Harry Emerson Fosdick—

# Organizational Democracy:
# The Framework for Freedom

*Always stand on principle . . . even if you stand alone.*
–John Adams–

**W**hen you look at most people riding the bus or train, sitting in bumper-to-bumper traffic on their way to work, or staring back at you through their computer screen, you can usually see it: the light in their eyes is gone. Few of us are truly excited to clock in, because most people are still spending their days working at traditionally bureaucratic organizations. With unnecessarily hierarchical structures, policy manuals a foot thick, and endless drama from bosses and colleagues, fear-based companies steal the light in people and slowly, painfully, extinguish it.

In their book *The End of Management and the Rise of Organizational Democracy*, Kenneth Cloke and Joan Goldsmith write about the results of command-and-control work environments on employees:

> Through years of experience, employees learn that it is safer to suppress their innate capacity to solve problems and wait instead for commands from above. They lose their initiative and ability to see how things can be improved. They learn not to care and to accept things the way they are. They justify making mistakes and are allowed to be irresponsible and pass

the blame to others for their mistakes. They become mindlessly obedient, fatalistic, intransigent, and hostile. Yet in spite of the obvious limitations created by these responses, managers continue giving orders rather than helping employees learn for themselves what needs to be done and how and when to do it best.

In my view, this is nothing short of immoral and unethical.

So how did the entire pyramid structure of organizational design come to be the dominant model for companies around the world? Before the eighteenth century, people in Europe and the United States were mostly gathered in agrarian societies and didn't have much need to figure out how to organize and lead large groups of people. Then, from approximately 1760 to 1840, new machines like the steam engine and the power loom replaced farmers' old hand tools, and industries were concentrated into big establishments. With the birth of these Industrial Age factories came the need to organize larger workforces to get things done. Men of industry at the time had two types of organizational models to choose from: the military model and the newly formed democratic model of the United States of America. They overwhelmingly chose the military model, and, as I briefly mentioned in the chapter "Fear at Work," a mostly centralized command-and-control structure became the dominant paradigm for structuring an organization. As big industry took root around the world, the model followed.

The innovations of the first Industrial Age led to several more, followed by the digital revolution and the Information Age that began in the mid-twentieth century. I believe the Information Age has given birth to an entirely new age—an era of power to the people unlike anything we've ever seen. Despite the major forces trying to slow or stop it, I believe we are rising into a Democratic Age.

In this new Democratic Age of decentralized power to the people, the rigid and pervasive command-and-control model of organizational design will be completely inadequate. It is a linear, inflexible, and cumbersome structure that can't adjust fast enough or attract and retain top talent long enough to stay competitive.

What all types of organizations today need is a model that is nonlinear, highly adaptive, agile, ethical, and systems-based. What is this optimal model?

Russell Ackoff, professor emeritus at the Wharton School, University of Pennsylvania, and author of *The Democratic Corporation*, explains democracy as a system that "can respond to the unpredictable changes inherent in turbulent environments and can deal effectively with increasing complexity" through "active adaptation." The optimal model for organizational design—one that can rapidly adapt to market changes, global crises, and economic booms and busts while still inspiring loyalty and bringing out the best in human potential—is *organizational democracy.* If more freedom—which translates to revenue growth, a high-performing team, and a great culture—is our goal, then organizational democracy is the optimal framework for bringing freedom with personal accountability into our workplaces. Organizational democracy, simply stated, is a way of leading and organizing people in order to release their full potential rather than limiting it.

> **Organizational democracy is a way of leading
> and organizing people in order to release their
> full potential rather than limiting it.**

But what, exactly, is organizational democracy? Well, before we get to that, let's back up even farther. It's important to understand what *democracy* itself means—and it might not be what you think.

## WHAT IS DEMOCRACY?

Most of us think democracy means voting, politics, or government. While it may challenge your paradigm a bit, these features are not *synonymous* with democracy or *guarantees* of its presence. For example, too often democracy is defined by the capacity to vote in elections or the existence of a free press. But these actions alone don't prove that a country is democratic. (Iraqi citizens voted under Saddam Hussein, but they had only one choice—him! Did that make their nation democratic? Of course not.) Voting is a way of making a decision but does not itself make a system democratic (especially if the voting process lacks integrity or is fraudulent). And a system that only defines democracy as a simple majority vote can easily deteriorate into the "mob rule" that thinkers throughout history have warned of. And some countries have a "free" press that is sensational and inaccurate.

Additionally, there are also many forms of government, such as republics, monarchies, or constitutional polities, that may or may not be democratic in their structure, leadership style, or operations. *Democracy* is not politics per se or a governmental system, but a distinct style of *leadership* applicable in various settings such as government, education, and business.

In truth, democracy is not a collection of one-size-fits-all *practices*. Democracy is a leadership *system* that empowers people to determine their individual and collective paths to freedom and prosperity. The essence of democracy is that every individual should have the power and ability to shape their lives and futures as they choose. While I will not dive into a deep historical explanation of democracy in this book, its origins are commonly recognized as beginning with the Greeks around 507 BC—although there is evidence that democracy is even older than that.[1] Today, it has branched beyond being used in government or politics into all areas of life, from business to education, media to religion.

Democracy serves three functions in one: as a leadership style, a system of organizational design, and a system of governance. It gives power to the people in a way that releases human potential so we all may flourish. For this reason, it is applicable to *every* area of life that needs to be designed to work well. And by understanding the *principles* of democracy, you can choose how to apply them in the unique way that makes sense for your team or organization, just as the same principles of architecture apply whether you are building a tiny home or a skyscraper. My goal is to equip you with these principles so you can adapt them in the way that makes sense for your context.

## THE 10 PRINCIPLES OF ORGANIZATIONAL DEMOCRACY

After a decade of research, I identified the exact principles needed for a truly democratic system. All ten principles must be in operation to create a robust, scalable, and distinctly democratic organizational design. While I will talk about *organizational* democracy, I believe these principles are really the universal principles of democracy. I and other top leadership thinkers use the term *organizational democracy* to denote it as a method for bringing democracy to *any* type of organization. (It's also important to note that there are other styles of democracy in the business space, such as workplace democracy or industrial democracy, which touch on and align in some but not all ways with what I'm exploring here.)

Statistical analysis by Dr. Lisa Kensler of Auburn University found the ten principles to be all highly interrelated and interdependent without clustering, which suggested they were equally valuable, distinct, and not duplicative.[2] If all ten of the principles are in operation, you have organizational democracy. If even one is missing, like a wheel with a broken spoke or a human body missing a core organ, you do not.

# THE WORLDBLU 10 PRINCIPLES OF ORGANIZATIONAL DEMOCRACY

| STAGE | PRINCIPLE | DEFINITION |
| --- | --- | --- |
| Start | 1. Purpose and Vision | Purpose and Vision are at work when each individual and the organization know their reason for being and have a sense of intentional direction. |
| | 2. Integrity | Integrity is at work when each individual and the organization uphold high moral and ethical principles. |
| | 3. Dialogue and Listening | Dialogue and Listening are at work when each individual listens and engages in conversation in a way that deepens meaning and connection. |
| | 4. Transparency | Transparency is at work when ideas and information are openly and responsibly shared. |
| Scale | 5. Accountability | Accountability is at work when each individual and the organization are responsible to each other for their actions. |
| | 6. Decentralization | Decentralization is at work when power is appropriately shared throughout an organization. |
| | 7. Individual and Collective | The Individual and the Collective are at work when the rights of both are valued and respected. |
| Sustain | 8. Choice | Choice is at work when each individual chooses between different possibilities. |
| | 9. Fairness and Dignity | Fairness and Dignity are at work when each individual is treated justly and impartially and is recognized for their inherent worth. |
| | 10. Reflection and Evaluation | Reflection and Evaluation are at work when each individual and the organization are committed to continuous feedback and growth. |

**If all ten of the principles are in operation, you have organizational democracy. If even one is missing, like a wheel with a broken spoke or a human body missing a core organ, you do not.**

I have grouped the principles into three categories: Start, Scale, and Sustain. The phases provide a road map for implementing the principles. That said, bringing organizational democracy into your team isn't always linear. Another starting point may also make more sense for your particular team.

While all ten principles are vital to making a democratic system, we found through independent research that *four* of the ten principles are the biggest drivers of the democratic system: Transparency, Accountability, Decentralization, and Choice. If these four principles fail to be implemented successfully within an organization, then most likely the six other democratic principles in the system will fail as well.

It is also important to understand that I am very intentionally using the word *principles* rather than *values*. A principle is inviolate, universal, and unchanging, and points to a true north. Principles give *structure*, such as the principles of mathematics or aerodynamics. Values, however, guide *behavior*, and they can change based on the environment or the circumstance. These are the principles of organizational democracy—they do not change.

As you will discover in the following pages, what makes organizational democracy superior to other organizational design models is that it is a complete system that values the human spirit. Whereas other structural systems are overly engineered and static, leaving out the humanity, a sense of real community, or vital principles that keep the system in balance, the 10 Principles of Organizational Democracy deliver a perfectly balanced system that meets our *human* needs for community, connection, and voice while also meeting our *organizational* needs for flexibility, adaptability, and growth. Organizational democracy is also timely, timeless, and universally applicable across small to very large organizations, as well as different industries and geographies.

And what role does culture play in all of this? According to independent research completed on our WorldBlu certified Freedom-Centered Organizations, *a staggering 75 percent of an organization's culture is determined by the*

---

**The 10 Principles of Organizational Democracy deliver a perfectly balanced system that meets our human needs for community, connection, and voice while also meeting our organizational needs for flexibility, adaptability, and growth.**

---

*design of its systems and processes.*[3] This makes it critical to understand how to design those systems and processes, also known as *transformational practices*, by knowing the right design principles, which I will discuss in the chapters that follow. Culture is the outcome of having the right mindset, leadership, and design in place—and that design is organizational democracy. The result is a world-class workplace.

## THE TOP 10 REASONS TO USE ORGANIZATIONAL DEMOCRACY

1. **Organizational democracy is more profitable.**
   Companies that practice all ten democratic principles are proven to have a healthier bottom line, even during economic booms and busts.

2. **Organizational democracy is more adaptable, responsive, and robust.**
   Unlike rigid command-and-control structures, organizational democracy is, by definition, designed to easily handle and adapt to perpetual change.

3. **Organizational democracy inspires full engagement and a sense of ownership.**
   By creating a principle-based system where individuals can have a voice, be accountable, and take action, employees feel an enhanced sense of ownership and can reap the rewards of their full engagement.

4. **Organizational democracy minimizes waste.**
   Because democratically-designed organizations operate on trust, timely access to accurate information, and integrity, there is less need for layers of hierarchy, bureaucracy, and inefficient interactions, all of which waste time and money.

5. **Organizational democracy is faster in the execution and implementation stage.**
   Democratic decision-making generates substantial buy-in from employees in the developmental stages, which translates to the alignment needed to execute quickly in the implementation stage.

6. **Organizational democracy achieves bottom-line goals without killing employees' souls in the process.**
   With clear accountability, open access to relevant financial information, minimal hierarchy, and streamlined execution, a democratic design allows teams to achieve bottom-line goals without trampling on employees' hearts, minds, and desire for work–life balance.

7. **Organizational democracy is more humane.**
   Democratic design means seeing employees as people rather than a means to an end. It gives employees a healthy and constructive framework to guide their interactions and relationships, resolve conflicts, and achieve their personal and professional goals. Democracy is as much of a lifestyle choice as it is a way of working together.

8. **Organizational democracy is more fun and meaningful.**
   Most people find it much more enjoyable and fulfilling to work in an environment where their voice matters, their work aligns with their purpose, they have the information they need to make intelligent decisions, and they like the people on their team.

9. **Organizational democracy is stabilizing.**
   Because democratic organizations cultivate leaders at every point throughout the organization, they are less susceptible to instability and volatility when there are changes in senior leadership or the marketplace.

10. **Organizational democracy helps build a more democratic world.**
    Gretchen Spreitzer, a professor of management and organizations and a researcher at the University of Michigan Ross School of Business, quantitatively found that organizations that operate on the principles of freedom and democracy increase the level of economic prosperity, civic engagement, and peace in their communities.[4] Democratically designed organizations also create a bulwark to the advances of authoritarian leadership in society because they teach employees the critical thinking and leadership skills of engaged democratic citizens. Freedom at work literally advances freedom in our world.

## DESIGNING A TEAM OR ORGANIZATION WITH THE 10 PRINCIPLES OF ORGANIZATIONAL DEMOCRACY

In the chapters that follow, I will be introducing you to each democratic principle and over one hundred of the top transformational practices in organizational democracy. They have been curated from thousands of practices at fifty of the world's top WorldBlu certified Freedom-Centered Organizations. Each practice, and the accompanying stories, comes from the companies themselves. I didn't pluck any of these out of a toxic system to prove a point; each practice comes from a healthy, certified, democratic system. I selected these practices out of the thousands in our library because they are inspiring, highly adaptable to a range of organizations, and distinctly democratic. Plus, most are applicable for both in-person and virtual teams.

Before we move on, however, I want to make a few things clear. First, please don't get overwhelmed by thinking that you have to implement all one hundred practices in your organization in order to exercise Freedom at Work. In fact, I am *not* recommending that you try and implement them directly into your team or organization, or that all of the practices will make sense in your unique situation. Why? Because while principles are universally applicable and scalable, practices are not. Practices are specific activities that may work in one context but not in another. Instead, you could consider *adapting* some of your favorite practices in a way that makes sense for your context (or create your own!) and then implement them democratically.

The one-size-fits-all, plug-and-play approach to implementing other organizations' best practices is a shortcoming of other organizational design systems, which put forth a series of practices that may not be universally adaptable or scalable. As Ralph Waldo Emerson once said, "A man who grasps principles can successfully select his own methods. The man who tries methods, ignoring principles, is sure to have trouble."

For example, the democratic principle of Transparency might look one way in a team of five people and entirely different in a division with one thousand people, but the principle is still the same. Too many other quasi-democratic systems out there are missing key principles or are too formulaic and practice-rather than principle-based, which is why they ultimately fail to scale.

Second, you will see some transformational practices that will resonate with you and others that will not—and that's okay! Be sure to highlight the practices that excite you, might help you get unstuck or solve a problem, or that you could most easily adapt for your team or organization.

I've organized the transformational practices into beginner, intermediate, and advanced categories. These are not fixed, but they will guide you generally as you think about your team's or organization's culture and where you may be in the process of intelligently shifting from fear to more freedom.

Last, if you're a CEO or top leader responsible to employees, shareholders, a board of directors, or the bottom line, you might feel hesitant about organizational democracy because you think it means you'll lose control. Or perhaps you're unclear about how accountability works within a more decentralized system. I've worked with hundreds of CEOs (and I, myself, am one!), so please know I understand that the buck still stops with you. There are still things for which you will be accountable. I am also not advocating for an entirely flat organization, not having a CEO (or equivalent person or team of leaders), or no decisions being made (how would an organization even work if that were the case?). Even healthy democratic organizations still have some hierarchy, and, as you will learn, there are several highly effective ways to design democratic systems that ensure clear accountability and decision-making.

I hope you will discover that the shift you are making is away from centralized, toxic, command-and-control-based systems and processes into more healthy, scalable, and high-functioning democratic practices. I am not asking you to give up control per se: instead, I am inviting you to skillfully design democratic systems and processes that will do more of the heavy lifting for you. Your job is to be a *steward*, accountable to the democratic systems and processes that will make your organization more profitable, innovative, joyous, and of greater benefit to our world.

I hope you will be inspired by the examples presented in each of the principle chapters, and come to deeply value the role each principle plays in building a highly adaptive, robust, and healthy democratic team or organization.

# START

---

Begin with the end in mind.
—Stephen Covey—

# PRINCIPLE 1

## Purpose and Vision

*Decide upon your major definite purpose in life
and then organize all your activities around it.*
−Brian Tracy−

It's Tuesday at 2:00 PM, which means it's time for the weekly Awesomeness
Report at a $42 million personal growth publisher. When 250 employees
come into their bright and colorful "Hall of Awesomeness," there is a palpable
sense of joy and enthusiasm. The day before, their CEO, Vishen, had emailed
everyone to send him their "moments of awesomeness," which he'd share at this
regular meeting.

But awesomeness wasn't always happening at this thriving company. Several years earlier, they had had a sudden influx of new recruits, practically
doubling the company overnight. Things started getting messy, trouble was
brewing, and people weren't happy with each other. All of this started to impact
the company's performance. To align their employees, the company decided

to rewrite their Purpose and Vision statements together and then give them meaning and context. Their goal was to unify everyone around their Purpose and Vision statements in order to make better decisions together.

The agreed-upon Purpose statement, describing *why* the organization existed, was: "To bring enlightenment and personal growth to the world in a scalable way using a hybrid of marketing and technology." Their Vision, or what they hoped to *achieve* as a result of living their Purpose, was: "To spread enlightened ideas to 500 million lives by 2050."

Now, when Tuesday comes around, the hour-long Awesomeness Report starts with thirty minutes of stand-up comedy, fun, music, and games, along with hearing everyone's moments of success and joy. (One week, replies included tweaks to a website that increased a conversion rate, a new client, a big sale that someone closed, an amazing weekend, a holiday trip, someone who found a girlfriend, a new baby, and a team delivering beyond their quota.) Anyone who has set a new record for the week gets to ring the "Bell of Awesomeness," which can only be rung in "moments of sheer and total awesomeness." The top five performers that week win the Community Award, where a higher percentage of the profit-sharing pie is allocated to them. The company also welcomes any new hires with a strange little ritual involving them sitting on a giant plastic puppy and taking an Oath of Awesomeness.

The second part of the Awesomeness Report focuses on setting new visions and goals for quality standards, marketing campaigns, revenue goals, or a new strategy they want to achieve together. Then, seated on yellow, green, and orange beanbag chairs, employees are invited to pick a date and visualize achieving a meaningful goal they're working toward. It's fun, but it's also serious business!

The Awesomeness Report contributes something vital to the company's success by keeping everyone aligned around their shared Purpose and Vision statements. It's also a time to celebrate, appreciate, and give gratitude to people for achieving goals while setting new goals for the week going forward. As a result, in the challenging industry of publishing, they grew their revenues to over $42 million in just ten years since the company's inception. And, for many employees, it's their favorite hour of the whole week.

Their chief operating officer, Ezekiel, says, "The democratic environment at our company literally awakens the inner you. No idea is too small or too crazy. If you believe in the difference your idea can make, you can literally come up to anyone, and put the idea forward. If people like it and believe that it will be successful, you get to spearhead the movement. If that's not a sign of being able to say what you want, do what you want, and learn from it at the same time, then I don't know what is."

## WHAT ARE PURPOSE AND VISION?

Purpose and Vision are at work when each individual and the organization know their reason for being and have a sense of intentional direction. It is the first step in the Start phase toward building a Freedom-Centered Team or Organization because it provides a clear direction for the entire organizational system. Without a clear Purpose and Vision, there will be confusion and a lack of meaning and alignment on decision-making and strategy. So, ideally, just as a leader should have one-sentence purpose and vision statements to help guide their decisions, behavior, and life, companies should develop similar statements to steer the whole organization. Boiling it down to one succinct sentence makes it easier for everyone to remember and use regularly.

---

**Purpose and Vision are at work when each individual and the organization know their reason for being and have a sense of intentional direction.**

---

A Purpose statement is an organization's reason for being; it's *why* it exists in the first place. A Vision statement is the "big finish" that a Freedom-Centered Organization strives to achieve by living its Purpose. You don't always have to know exactly *how* you will achieve your vision, but you do have to have a true north to lead your team toward. The Purpose and Vision principle acts like riverbanks, keeping an entire organization flowing in the right direction.

Many leaders, however, confuse a Purpose statement with a mission statement. A mission is what your organization *does*, not its reason for *being*, and it can change as your organization evolves. However, your Purpose and Vision—why your organization exists and what you want to achieve as a result—usually stays the same. It's fine to have a mission statement, but it won't deliver the same long-term strategic and inspirational benefits as clear Purpose and Vision statements will.

Ask an employee in a fear-based organization what their employer's Purpose and Vision is, and I can guarantee you that they don't know. It's not their fault; their employer doesn't know either! Fear-based organizations often lack a clearly defined Purpose and Vision (beyond making money) that everyone can rally behind. As a result, a clear sense of direction and meaning—and the passion and innovation that can come with it—is missing. It's hard to know how to make smart decisions when you don't know what the boundaries are or what you're aiming for. These kinds of lackluster workplaces are often less efficient, highly bureaucratic, and have a harder time attracting and retaining bright and motivated talent.

Purpose and Vision statements diminish the fear of not having a clear direction for the organization. They make an individual's work more meaningful, unify employees on a shared path, and set the organization's rhythm. They help everyone make faster and smarter decisions that are in closer alignment with the entire team or organization. Purpose and Vision statements make it easier to hold people accountable to goals and healthy behavior while eliminating unnecessary layers of hierarchy or bureaucracy. They also create greater trust, cohesion, and team spirit. Furthermore, they are a smart way to attract top customers who support what your organization stands for.

Garry, the CEO of a WorldBlu certified San Diego–based company, explains the value of a Purpose and Vision like this: "As the world economy fumbled through the aftereffects of the Great Recession, our Purpose and Vision coupled with our strong values ensured we stayed focused and united in building an enduring organization we will be proud to pass on to others." A clear Purpose and Vision makes an organization more resilient during times of uncertainty and challenge. It will empower employees to make faster and more strategic decisions, inspire and appeal to top talent, and bring meaningful direction to your team.

## PURPOSE AND VISION AT EVERY LEVEL

Not only should leaders and organizations have clear Purpose and Vision statements; the individuals who comprise the team or organization should as well. If team members don't know their Purpose and Vision, Freedom-Centered Leaders should offer them access to a course to help them develop one, such as the ones we offer at WorldBlu. When an individual knows their Purpose and Vision, they can navigate life more effectively, confidently making choices that are both personally and professionally beneficial and meaningful.

Freedom-Centered Leaders can also cut turnover rates and boost motivation by ensuring that they have the right people in the right seats on the proverbial bus by hiring people for positions that are purpose-aligned. Leaders can also drop expensive perk programs that "motivate" employees in favor of leaders placing employees in positions that are aligned with their greater purpose.

## THE PROMISE OF PURPOSE AND VISION

The democratic principle of Purpose and Vision delivers the following results to help create a Freedom-Centered Team or Organization rather than a fear-based one.

**Purpose and Vision produce smarter and strategically aligned decision-making.** With well-defined Purpose and Vision statements, every employee understands why the organization exists and the direction in which it is aiming, which keeps decisions and individuals strategically aligned.

**Purpose and Vision attract top talent—and help you keep it.** A clear Purpose and Vision statement will help your organization engage the right talent, reduce voluntary turnover, and breathe a deeper sense of meaning and belonging into your organization.

**Purpose and Vision mean fewer rules, managers, and layers of bureaucracy.** With a clear Purpose and Vision at the helm, an organization can be led on the basis of these guiding statements, rather than piles of policies and rules, costly layers of bureaucracy, and unnecessary hierarchy.

**Purpose and Vision enhance efficiency.** With everyone pulling in the same direction within your core organizational riverbanks, everyone knows where they are going and why, making your team much more efficient.

**Purpose and Vision increase innovation**. Clarity of Purpose and Vision gives everyone a greater understanding of what your team is trying to achieve, inspiring creativity and innovation.

## FINDING YOUR ORGANIZATION'S PURPOSE AND VISION

The first step in practicing Purpose and Vision is to create these statements for your organization. How do you do it? Follow these three guidelines:

1. **Develop your Purpose and Vision statements democratically.**
   Get the input of all the individuals within your organization and consider inviting the contributions of key outside stakeholders, such as board members, investors, vendors, and even customers you respect. Create your Purpose and Vision statements from everyone's voices, not just the

CEO's or the executive team's. After getting input from everyone, narrow it down to key themes and then to one sentence. Take a vote for the final Purpose and Vision statements, then celebrate this milestone.

2. **Continually implement your Purpose and Vision statements.**
   It's critical that leaders go beyond just putting their Purpose and Vision statements on a wall in the reception area or on their website. These statements should be talked about daily, brought into your decision-making process, and lived and celebrated by everyone—like how the Awesomeness Report helps the publishing company's employees keep their Purpose and Vision top of mind. I will show you how to do this in the transformational practices that follow.

3. **Refresh your Purpose and Vision—but only if absolutely needed.**
   While Purpose and Vision statements should remain largely unchanged (whereas a mission can change more regularly), you may need to refresh them if there is a large, strategic change within your organization. That's fine when done sparingly, but when you do change them, make sure you do so democratically.

Some examples of strong Purpose and Vision statements might help you get started. Here are a few Purpose statements from WorldBlu certified Freedom-Centered Organizations:

- **"To end human suffering as it relates to technology."** (From an Ann Arbor, Michigan–based software development firm with about sixty employees and $5 million in annual revenue.)

- **"To help make positive lasting memories for people."** (From a publicly traded manufacturing company based in San Diego with a market cap of $2 billion and more than 530 employees worldwide.)

- **"To create a vibrant, mutually cooperative community of two million committed participants trading fairly one billion dollars a year in a way that transforms the world."** (From a fair-trade, worker-owned cooperative with $70 million in revenue and about 150 employees based in West Bridgewater, Massachusetts.)

- **"To transform the way leaders lead with Freedom at Work."** (You may recognize this last one—it's our purpose statement at WorldBlu! And our Vision statement is, "To see a world where every individual can live, lead, and work in freedom.")

## TOOLBOX ─────────────────────────────

# TRANSFORMATIONAL PRACTICES IN PURPOSE AND VISION

Before you can implement any of the following practices, you must have clear, one-sentence Purpose and Vision statements. As you read, I invite you to highlight one or two practices that you could see adapting into your organization.

### The Recall Game | Beginner Level

Each week, employees at a small North Carolina–based firm read the company's Purpose and Vision statements. Then, they play "The Recall Game." Leaders ask if anyone would like to recite the statements from memory. When someone recites both statements perfectly, they get a round of applause and some fun recognition. The goal is to quickly get both statements integrated into employees' thinking while keeping it top of mind to help with strategy, decision-making, and team cohesion.

### Help Your Employees Discover Their Purpose and Vision for Their Lives | Beginner Level

What if each one of your employees knew their individual Purpose and Vision for their life and was doing work that was aligned with it? How might this alignment impact turnover, motivation, engagement, trust, and productivity? At a Wisconsin-based digital asset management company with 150 employees, the CEO understands how vital the alignment of an individual's and the organization's Purpose and Vision can be. He and his leadership team thus decided to give all of their employees the option of taking the WorldBlu course on how to find their personal Purpose and Vision. As a result, many have found a deeper meaning in their work, some have transitioned to new roles within the company that are more purpose-aligned, and two have left the company after realizing their work wasn't entirely aligned with their Purpose and Vision. The result has been a more energized and Purpose-driven workforce committed to personal and organizational growth.

### The 3 Most Important Questions | Beginner Level

One of the most important things that Freedom-Centered Organizations do when hiring is make sure there is alignment between an individual's Purpose and Vision and the work they do at the company, helping to ensure people are put in the right position, are naturally motivated, and feel supported and fulfilled.

To achieve this, employees and job candidates at an Estonian publishing company complete an exercise called "The 3 Most Important Questions," which asks:

1. What are the things I want to experience out of life?
2. How do I want to grow?
3. What do I want to contribute to the planet?

They then share their answers publicly so that fellow teammates can support and help them in their careers—even if that means moving to another part of the organization or seeking opportunities outside the company to truly fulfill their dreams. Their leadership team understands that when people are in a workplace that aligns their personal Purpose and Vision with their work, the entire organization is happier and more freedom-centered.

### The "Are We Living It?"
### Pulse Test | Intermediate Level

It's one thing to come up with a clear Purpose and Vision; it's another thing to make sure you are living it. How can you do this? Over 52,000 teammates at a global healthcare company headquartererd in Denver, Colorado, regularly receive a survey that asks, on a scale of one to ten (with ten being the highest), "How well are we living our Purpose and Vision and why?" It's a great way to quickly check and see if you're staying on track—or not.

## A "Can You Imagine?" Wall | Intermediate Level

Fear-based organizations don't do anything to generate enthusiasm for their Purpose and Vision statements (if they even have them!), and they certainly don't care about how their employees' Purpose and Vision for their life might align with the organization's. But one junk-removal company with over 250 franchises based in Vancouver, Canada, has a "Can You Imagine?" wall that gives employees the opportunity to post a specific dream for the company's future as a result of achieving their Purpose and Vision. In addition to the wall, employees are also invited to share their *own* Purpose and Vision for their life and how they get to fulfill it at work, further supporting a meaningful work environment.

## Change the World | Intermediate Level

An international customer support company in San Diego encourages their employees to do something each week that helps advance the company's Vision of changing their community, nation, and our world for the better. Employees have done everything from small to "above and beyond" acts, including having a customer tell them that the actions an employee took helped save the lives of fifty police officers during a crisis situation.

Employees then share how they are living the company's Vision during their Friday financial meetings. During this time, they pass a microphone around, and anyone who wants to share something they did that week to advance the company's Vision to change the world can do so. To date, they have shared over one thousand examples of things they have done to help change the world, with *an average of twenty examples shared each week!*

This "Change the World" practice demonstrates to all the role they have in working toward the organization's Vision and how even the smallest action can have a significant and meaningful impact on their clients, vendors, and even their employees' families.

### A "Directions" Retreat | Advanced Level

One of the critical elements of living your Purpose and Vision in an organization is ensuring leaders align their strategy with it. At an IT company based in Noida, India, with 150,000 employees, their company-wide off-site retreat day called "Directions" focuses on doing just that. They bring together representative leaders, managers, the board of directors, and employees from all parts of the organization from around the world to take part in strategic discussions that other organizations often reserve for closed-door board meetings. At the Directions retreat, they talk about the company's Purpose and Vision and how their goals and strategies are aligned with them. The retreat actively engages everyone, inspiring them to get aligned in order to understand how their individual contributions fit into the larger organizational Purpose and Vision.

### Align with Your Clients | Advanced Level

It's one thing to have a clear Purpose and Vision statement for your organization, but what if your client's Purpose and Vision aligned with yours as well? At an entirely virtual corporate training company with 150 employees based in 14 countries, they clearly communicate their Purpose and Vision both internally and externally to achieve this goal. They then actively seek clients with similar or complementary Purposes and Visions to ensure values alignment, which they believe helps strengthen their client relationships. They also discuss the intersection of their Purposes and Visions in their external project kick-off calls and throughout their work together.

### The Awesomeness Report | Advanced Level

As described at the beginning of this chapter, every Tuesday the whole staff at a Tallinn, Estonia–based publishing company gathers for a one-hour meeting called the "Awesomeness Report" that allows them to bring their Purpose and Vision to life. It starts with thirty minutes of games and entertainment, all designed to celebrate the past week's individual and team accomplishments. The week's new record-setters ring the "Bell of Awesomeness." New hires are officially welcomed. And the CEO presents company strategies, directions, and innovations. This celebration includes applause for individuals and teams, an update on company targets, and recommitment to their Purpose and Vision.

### Link to Strategic Anchors | Advanced Level

The value of having clear Purpose and Vision statements lies in using them to make better decisions. One digital advertising and web design company based in Watsontown, Pennsylvania, implemented a planning process that identifies "people, problems, and philosophies" as the "Strategic Anchors" around which all decisions are made. Clearly identifying the organization's strategic anchors allows programs, initiatives, and decisions to be made that align with them. Each anchor addresses their Purpose and Vision in results-driven goals for clients, and they continuously evaluate each strategic anchor for success.

START

# PRINCIPLE 2

## Integrity

*The foundation . . . will be laid in the pure and
immutable principles of private morality.*
–GEORGE WASHINGTON–

Mike, the CEO of a national franchise company based in Dillon, Montana, had an extremely challenging situation on his hands. He and his leadership team had recently made a decision that, while guided by democratic principles and communicated openly and transparently, their 250 "freedom-franchise" owners nationwide did not agree with—at all. He had just gotten word that they all planned to gather in Chicago in a few weeks to plot a rebellion.

"What do I do?" he asked me. "Do I pull rank and say that it's my way because I'm the CEO, or do I take a different approach and genuinely support their need to gather and be heard?" Even the strongest Freedom-Centered Leaders can be tempted to slip back into a fear-based mindset and violate their democratic principles. Despite doing an exceptional job creating a WorldBlu certified Freedom-Centered Organziation, and maintaining certification for years, Mike suddenly and unexpectedly found himself in just that spot.

Mike understood that a moment of leadership integrity was upon him. One undermining move where he pulled rank, putting himself above the principles of democracy and freedom that they'd all agreed to, would erode the democratic system they had worked so hard to build and betray the standards to which he and the franchise owners all adhered. So, would he momentarily become a dictator out of fear and shut it all down, or would he choose to lead with Integrity?

## WHAT IS INTEGRITY?

Integrity is at work when each individual and the organization uphold high moral and ethical principles. It is doing what is morally and ethically right, even when it is not convenient to you or your agenda. The *Merriam-Webster Dictionary* defines *integrity* as "firm adherence to a code of especially moral values; an unimpaired condition, the quality or state of being complete and undivided." Integrity comes from the Latin word that means "integer" or "entire," so when we are operating in Integrity, we are leading from a powerful place of wholeness. As the author C. S. Lewis put it, "Integrity is doing the right thing even when no one is watching."

---

**Integrity is at work when each individual and the organization uphold high moral and ethical principles.**

---

Integrity is the linchpin principle of the entire democratic system, for without adherence to virtuous and ethical behavior, no matter how successful a team or organization, or how strong its systems and processes may be, it will eventually fail. The Purpose and Vision principle establishes *why* an organization exists and where it is headed. Integrity is the next democratic principle in the Start phase because it helps instill a solid *foundation* of world-class leadership behavior on which a high-performing team can be built. Interestingly, I have found that it is by being disciplined and having high ethical and moral standards that we gain the *most* freedom. Why? Because true freedom is only gained by doing what is morally right. A lack of Integrity keeps us enslaved to a toxic and dysfunctional way of operating.

In fear-based organizations, there is little commitment to acting with Integrity. Feelings of inadequacy and insecurity often trigger unethical and immoral behavior in fear-based leaders who work to advance themselves at the expense of employees, investors, customers, and shareholders. A lack of Integrity is a drag on an organization's morale, creating instability and uncertainty, which makes it difficult to grow. Fear-based leaders operate by their own set of "rules" and think they are above the law in order to justify their greed, unethical behavior, and a me-first attitude. In the long run, this kind of manipulative behavior usually results in higher monetary and emotional costs to everyone. Some of the well-known failures of organizational Integrity include companies such as Enron, Tyco, WorldCom, and others.

The principle of Integrity *removes* fear from an organization. Integrity prevents lying, hiding, pretending, or trying to cover up its absence. Fear manipulates and plays by its own rules. Integrity doesn't manipulate—it's out in the open, transparent, and demands that everyone abides by the same standards. Integrity brings stability and consistency to organizations, allowing them to truly flourish.

That's the path Mike chose to take with the frustrated franchise owners. As he explained, "I decided that instead of shutting the meeting down, causing irrevocable damage to that trust we had and undermining our decades of commitment to being a freedom-franchise, not only would I support the gathering in Chicago, we would pay for everyone to go."

And that's exactly what he did. The support instantly removed the resentment and self-righteousness that had been building in everyone. The franchise owners met in Chicago—on the CEO's dime but without him there—and discussed what they wanted to see changed. They came back and presented their ideas to Mike and the leadership team. With a shared commitment to organizational democracy, they were able to reach a compromise that made everyone happy. Mike and his team modeled that no one—not the CEO, the board of directors, a customer, or the owner—is above the "law" of democracy. The situation could have triggered disengagement, created resentment that may have taken years to repair, hurt their reputation, and caused economic fallout. However, it was quickly resolved because Mike and his leadership team put principle above ego and modeled real Integrity.

| FEAR-BASED ORGANIZATIONS WITHOUT INTEGRITY BELIEVE: | FREEDOM-CENTERED ORGANIZATIONS WITH INTEGRITY BELIEVE: |
|---|---|
| Select people are above the law | No one is above the law |
| Do whatever it takes to make more money and advance your agenda | Never violate ethical or moral standards in order to make more money or advance your agenda |
| Corruption is fine | No corrupt dealings |
| Violating core values is fine | Core values must be followed |
| Unethical and immoral behavior should be overlooked, tolerated, and even promoted | Ethical and moral behavior is the linchpin of the entire organization |

In Freedom-Centered Organizations, one of the most effective ways to operationalize Integrity is through succinct core values that teach employees the behavior expected within a Freedom-Centered Culture.

For example, at a publicly traded, multinational manufacturing company based in San Diego, California, they have six core values that guide behavior. I've made several visits to this company, and when you walk around, you see their core values up everywhere, constantly reinforced by everyone in their "tribe," as they call employees. Their core values are clear, easy to remember, and guide the actions of everyone, even top leaders. No one is above the "law" of their core values. As their CEO, Garry, shares, "Values set our people free. They know where they can go, how to make decisions, and how to operate." As they have written them, their six core values are that they believe in:

1. Doing the right thing.
2. Creating positive lasting memories in all our relationships.
3. Making it better than it is today.
4. Succeeding as a tribe while excelling as individuals.
5. Owning it and passionately acting on it.
6. Sustaining our company's economy.[1]

But core values must go beyond nice phrases posted on a wall. So how does this Freedom-Centered Organization bring their core values to life? By teaching them in their Leadership Lab curriculum and making them a routine part of leadership's discussions on any business decision. The values are also embedded in their professional code of conduct and used to inform decisions about engaging in or terminating third-party relationships. Tribe members share how they are living their core values in their performance and coaching discussions. They also use their internal media to communicate their core values each day. Further, these values are also embedded in their employee-led peer recognition award categories, called the People's Choice Awards, and are used to determine promotions. Candidates for internal promotions are evaluated more heavily on their history of being able to live their values than on their experience or current knowledge.[2]

Core values also guide the company's hiring process. All candidates for employment must respond to values-centered questions when they first apply for a position or to be included in the company's pipeline of interested potential candidates. Their behavioral-interviewing and candidate-evaluation methods include specific questions and assessments designed to reveal whether or not the candidate is truly aligned with their values. They hire first for a match to their core values and then for culture. They believe that knowledge and skills can be taught, but values and character are less likely to be learned successfully by the time an individual reaches adulthood.

If an employee breaches the company's core values, according to Stan, their vice president of global organizational development, "values violations can result in counseling, disciplinary action, and the possible separation of employment, even if other performance metrics were achieved. We have several examples of terminating someone's employment due to values violations, even when they 'hit their numbers.'"

Core values teach those in your organization how to be distinctly *democratic* citizens. This is why having core values is so important to reinforcing Integrity-based behaviors within your Freedom-Centered Organization. And this is why your core values should be memorable, short, and specific to the kind of cultural norms you want reinforced. I strongly encourage you to limit your number of core values to seven, so they can easily be remembered.

At WorldBlu, our core values are Humility, Excellence, Accountability, and Love. They also form an acronym—H.E.A.L.—capturing what we do in part and also making them more memorable.

What if your organization does not yet have core values? How can you figure out what they are and decide on them democratically? After attending one of our trainings in Freedom at Work, one CEO, Linda, realized on her flight home that her website design and marketing agency needed to revisit and rewrite its core values to further support growth. She went back to its offices in Cedar Rapids, Iowa, and set up a democratic process by which each of her eighty employees could participate in identifying their core values.

The process happened in three rounds. Linda first invited everyone to write what they thought their core values should be on Post-it-Notes and stick them up on an office wall. She grouped the ideas into themes, then asked employees to vote on their top three core values. She tabulated the top-scoring values and put them out for one last vote.

The company's winning five core values, stated almost like a cheer, are:

- **Own it:** We're accountable to ourselves, each other, and our clients. We keep our promises.
- **Bring it:** We deliver exceptional service and value every day. We're aiming for Wow!
- **Push it:** We're always moving forward or learning from our mistakes.
- **Say it:** We've torn down the walls so ideas and information flow freely.
- **Unite!**

I loved walking around their offices in a hip renovated industrial building and seeing their core values painted on all the walls, as well as hearing them discussed at their regular town hall meetings.

Freedom-Centered Leaders understand that while Integrity may be difficult at times, it is the rock on which their Freedom-Centered Organization must be built in order to succeed.

## THE PROMISE OF INTEGRITY

Here's what Integrity will do for your team or organization:

**Integrity saves organizations money.** When individuals in an organization act without Integrity, it can hurt their reputation and contribute to a loss of customers, which both cost money. Practicing Integrity helps leaders avoid costly missteps.

**Integrity allows leaders to take the long view.** When leaders lack Integrity, they make decisions from a short-term, me-first perspective, which can damage an organization. Practicing Integrity helps leaders plan ahead and make smarter choices.

**Integrity helps everyone self-govern more effectively.** When everyone in an organization adheres to high ethical and moral standards, they are able to reduce organizational drama, which builds trust and allows the organization to operate more harmoniously. Integrity invites us to be better people overall.

**Integrity holds the entire democratic system together.** Even if an organization is practicing nine of the 10 Principles of Organizational Democracy, without leaders who operate with a commitment to Integrity, the entire democratic system will slowly erode and eventually collapse because of the immorality. Everyone must have a clear understanding of the expectations of Integrity in your Freedom-Centered Team or Organization, the consequences of violating ethical and moral standards, and how they can be given the opportunity to learn, grow, and improve.

## TOOLBOX

### TRANSFORMATIONAL PRACTICES IN INTEGRITY

#### Core Values | Beginner Level

How exactly can leaders guide and inspire the right kind of behavior within their Freedom-Centered Organization? It all starts with having core values. As we saw at the start of this chapter, one Freedom-Centered manufacturing firm prominently posts theirs in key communal areas of the company. They bring their core values to life in their hiring, internal training and curriculum, and promotions, and they use them to guide their business decisions. Their core values are embedded in their professional code of conduct and are even used when engaging with vendors. Every leader at the company is also expected to set the example of values-based behavior.

#### The Promises Pledge | Beginner Level

Most fear-based organizations don't have core values, or if they do, they are rarely used or discussed. But what if you took your core values and turned them into an actual pledge that your team members worked daily to uphold? One thirty-person digital advertising agency in Pennsylvania does just that with their "Promises Pledge," which applies to their management team, employees, partners, and even vendors. Here's what employees pledge to do:

- Watch each other's backs and help each other out
- Offer solutions, not just problems
- Meet our obligations on time or we will explain or negotiate in advance
- Be honest and forthright with information
- Approach our work and our challenges from a positive perspective
- Be open to new ideas and opinions
- Offer each other constructive feedback
- Catch people doing things right and praise and recognize their efforts
- Support each other when we vent and help guide each other back to a positive path
- Be sensitive, professional, and objective in our communications—not emotion-based
- Set clear expectations for each other
- Meet or exceed expectations
- Deal directly with each other when there are issues
- Won't take things personally
- Treat each other with respect
- Value each other's gifts and contributions
- Not lose sight of the human side of our business and our interactions

Employees are expected to hold themselves accountable to each of the promises of their pledge, which is also posted in the middle of their collaborative office space.

### Everyone Is Governed by the Same Standards | Beginner Level

One of the most egregious violations of the democratic principle of Integrity in fear-based organizations occurs when there is an "exception to the rule" and not everyone—particularly top leadership—is governed by the same standards. But at a Montana-based bakery chain, they have a deep commitment to applying their standards equally to everyone.

For example, an internal policy guides their decisions about where they allow new and existing bakery owners to locate new stores. They publish these policies on their intranet called the "Breadboard" so that the rules cannot change on a case-by-case basis. If a current or potential franchisee successfully proposes an exception to the rules, then they update their policies so that the change is visible to everyone and applies to all.

### Integrity at the Board Level | Beginner Level

Boards of directors of fear-based organizations can be rife with nepotism, cronyism, and corruption. But this large, multinational IT company based in India is committed to practicing Integrity regarding corporate governance at the board level. To meet obligations toward shareholders and other stake-holders, their standard is to create and adhere to a corporate culture of conscience, integrity, conscious-ness, transparency, and accountability for efficient and ethical conduct of their business. This is why six out of eight board members are independent, non-executive directors. The board has audit, compensation, shareholder, and employee stock-options allotment committees. The company is also certified by a Big Four Global Auditing Firm and has financials in line with both Indian and American GAAP standards.

### Put It on the Card | Intermediate Level

In fear-based organizations, employees must fill out a purchase order before they can buy anything. But at one online party supplier based in Budapest, Hungary, the CEO, Niki, trusts that her employees will have integrity and make smart decisions. For work-related expenses, her employees have full use of the company credit card without consulting her or anyone else first. She trusts that they won't buy the first airline ticket they see but will shop around for an inexpensive flight. She knows that they will choose to stay at a good-quality budget hotel instead of a five-star property. Even though they don't have to, she knows they will probably order pizza instead of going out for a big dinner. Consequently, if they truly need something, like a new chair, there is no purchase order to submit for approval. They just choose what they want and buy it. She trusts them to use their common sense and they always do. As she explains, "Giving employees freedom to make decisions and trust they will decide what's best saves time, money, and energy."

Additionally, when she goes on a long trip, she leaves the keys to her car so her employees can use it if needed. And what about that beach villa that's usually reserved just for the CEO and executive leaders? "They helped me get it, so why shouldn't I share it with them as well?" says Niki.

### A Safe Place for Whistleblowers | Intermediate Level

It's not enough just to have a standard of Integrity within a Freedom-Centered Organization; there must also be a safe way for internal whistleblowers to report breaches of Integrity *without* repercussions. That's why one Freedom-Centered company with 250 employees has what they call the "Leadership Board," which is a safe place that whistleblowers can turn to if needed. This is a group of peers that anyone can reach out to or confide in, during emergencies or not, should they experience or witness something that breaches the company code of conduct. If employees feel unable to handle the situation themselves, they can turn to the Leadership Board for help.

### Getting "Stoked" and Earning Values Medallions | Intermediate Level

This Canada-based warehousing and fulfillment company with 450 employees reinforces Integrity through their Stoked Recognition Program. They actively live their core values in their decision-making processes and regularly teach and demonstrate their core values by focusing on one each month. During the month, supervisors remind employees of what that core value means and its history and share examples of how it has been lived in the past. They then have a celebration where anyone can nominate a fellow employee they see going above and beyond in living one of their core values for a "Stoke." Supervisors then post approved Stokes on a main board in their warehouse facility for everyone to see and celebrate. Team members' Stokes are also recorded and can be redeemed for prizes.

Across the Pacific, at a small Agile training company based in New Zealand, each month they recognize how individuals are living the organization's four core values (Servant Leadership, Courage, Leadership, and Manaakitanga, a Maori word for hospitality) by giving out Values Medallions.

Their four core values appear on special silver medallions they had made, each of which has the core value on one side and a native bird of New Zealand on the other. They also have stickers made to look like the medallions, which people can collect and put onto their laptop skins. For the first round of giving out the medallions, their leadership team got together and picked someone who was specifically living each core value. Then, in a companywide meeting, they presented them with the Values

Medallion, told the story about how the individual was living that value, and gave them the story on a lovely card along with the sticker for their laptop.

The first four winners kept the Values Medallions for a month, and then awarded them to the next recipients. But instead of picking new winners individually, they collectively decided who they thought should be awarded the recognition. As this became a regular practice, the goal has been for each employee to eventually earn all of the Values Medallions while also gaining awareness of their core values.

## Design Roles to Advocate for
### Integrity | Advanced Level

What if you could literally design Integrity into an employee's role at your organization? One Ann Arbor, Michigan–based software company operationalizes Integrity by intentionally designing various employee roles *with specific purposes for which they advocate*, helping to ensure the highest levels of Integrity in their work internally and with clients.

For example, their developers advocate for the overall code, while their "High-Tech Anthropologists" advocate for excellent design. Their "Quality Advocates" advocate for total quality, and their Project Managers advocate for the client. Each role, and the purpose for which it advocates, carries *specific moral principles*. Collectively, this ensures they do the right thing for each other as well as for their clients and customers as they advocate from the perspective of their roles versus their personal prejudices.

### The Values Crew | Advanced Level

How do Freedom-Centered Organizations make sure their values are being upheld? Every few quarters at a Los Angeles tech company, they elect a dozen employees to form a Values Crew representing the interests of their entire team in their culture review meetings. The Values Crew ensures that their eight core values are being upheld in every area of their business.

Employees who believe that a value may be threatened by an impending policy decision can ask their representative—anonymously if they wish—to bring their concern before the Values Crew, where it is discussed and evaluated. If the Values Crew determines that a particular rule, policy, or action is not in alignment with their core values, then it's back to the drawing board for that particular initiative.

### Spiritual Wellness Groups | Advanced Level

Spirituality and religion are often vital channels for teaching integrity, morals, and ethics. But how can you bring them into the workplace? Many leaders have confided to me that they want to be able to openly share their spiritual views, but they are afraid it will come across as proselytizing, judgmental, or self-righteous. Is there a way to create a space for teams or organizations to talk about spirituality and religion?

At a digital asset management company, Matthew, the CEO, felt it was important to not only have committees on emotional, environmental, and physical wellness, but also to have a committee on spiritual wellness.

As a deeply religious person himself, he decided to start the committee with the purpose of "offering guidance for the well-being of the soul because work is but a fraction of the spiritual journey."

Here is how he explained it in an email to the entire company:

The most admired organization in the world takes a multidimensional approach to individual wellness, including the spiritual dimension. One definition of spirituality is, "the quality of being concerned with the human spirit or soul as opposed to material or physical things." When we gather to discuss spiritual wellness, we will start by leveraging the National Wellness Institute description of the spiritual dimension, which features the need for purpose and meaning . . .

While conversations about this topic may be frowned upon in a normal business environment, we are not in pursuit of normal. I believe we are capable of higher performance because of our holistic and multidimensional wellness pursuits . . .

In this forum, tolerance will be practiced through the ability to hear an opinion with which you strongly disagree (and may never agree), however, you are capable of listening.[3]

At each spiritual wellness committee meeting, the group grapples with questions such as, "What is spirituality?" and invites open discussion, striving to have appropriate representation from world religions and nonreligious spiritual perspectives. Every meeting opens with the following statement:

Thank you for participating in the spiritual wellness committee! An important reminder when discussing deeply-held beliefs: We are not seeking agreement, we are seeking openness and respect.

We need you to commit to the following:

1.  Openness: Maintain a level of openness to understand another individual's perspective, even if you disagree
2.  Respect: Be respectful to one another as you listen, be aware of your body language, word choice, tone, pitch
3.  Say Something: You are encouraged to remind others in this setting when they are not adhering to the openness and respect required for conversation.

The spiritual wellness committee meets once per month and shares ideas about how to promote spiritual wellness at work. The practice has given a constructive space for those who want to talk about the deeper moral and ethical, spiritual, or religious ideas that undergird a life of Integrity.

On the other side of the world, Razvan, the CEO of a small construction and real estate company in Târgovişte, Romania, also wanted to promote a healthy space for religious and spiritual dialogue, especially in a nation that was still recovering from decades of communism where no one was allowed to practice religion at all.

To that end, he created a monthly "Development Club" with a threefold purpose: to study the Bible, personal development books, and health and wellness. The club meets weekly and they rotate through the three areas. For example, they are reading the entire Bible through consecutively. They read a few chapters of the Bible each week and then come together to discuss it.

Anywhere from eight to twelve of their employees attend each week and the Development Club is open to everyone—including their vendors and the people who live in their apartment complexes. They have started to have more people come from outside the company, and, as Razvan explains, "I see the people around me becoming better people each week."[4]

START

# PRINCIPLE 3

## Dialogue and Listening

*He who is wise listens.*
—Anonymous—

Big changes were coming at a Los Angeles web hosting and cloud services provider. Its dynamic CEO had just resigned. With an important gap to fill, two of the company's founders stepped in as co-CEOs. Everyone had a lot of questions about how to best shape and grow the business.

The founders saw that they needed to restructure the company, taking a product-centric, top-to-bottom approach instead to better serve their millions of customers. But how would they communicate to nearly two hundred employees that their job functions, titles, and responsibilities were going to change—without creating more fear? The changes they were contemplating were disruptive, and if they didn't proceed carefully, the shifts might erode their Freedom-Centered Culture and harm the business.

So, instead of just telling people what the changes would be, they decided to commit considerable time communicating their reasons *behind* the changes to everyone in open and honest all-hands meetings, which often led to deep and thought-provoking one-on-one conversations. They listened to employees' concerns, worries, and fears. Through deep dialogue, senior management was able to determine where the goals of the business aligned with individual employees' professional interests and goals, arriving at job assignments that both met the needs of the organization and the needs of the employees who may have had reservations about the change. They also worked hard not to push roles on people that they weren't comfortable holding. In the end, their new structure was shaped entirely through Dialogue and Listening with their greatest asset—the people behind the company. Yes, this may be a cliché, but in this case it's true. Their co-CEO Dallas put it like this: "When employees are made to feel that they are valued and that their contributions matter, it's much easier for them to see and understand that they are crucial parts of a larger whole. It gives them a sense of ownership and they deliver their work with true pride that can't be manufactured by any other means. Democracy at work is good not just for employees, but for the overall health of the organization."

By listening instead of mandating, and collaborating rather than dictating, they were able to make the shift with a minimum number of disruptions. This led to a high level of employee engagement and top leadership now having a much better understanding of the needs of their employees and the business.

## WHAT ARE DIALOGUE AND LISTENING?

Dialogue and Listening are at work when each individual listens and engages in conversation in a way that deepens meaning and connection. Dialogue and Listening make up the third principle in the Start phase of designing a Freedom-Centered Organization because they help form the vital infrastructure of *trust and understanding* needed to develop and sustain a Freedom-Centered Culture. Dialogue and Listening provide the communication oil that keeps a team or organization running smoothly.

Dialogue and Listening also represent the *voice* element of the democratic framework, bringing freedom of expression into any democratic system.

The word *dialogue* comes from the Greek for "to speak, converse" and also means "legend." A legend is a story. When we engage in Dialogue and Listening, we listen with an open mind and heart to the stories that others are sharing and their different points of view. To build a Freedom-Centered Team or Organization, every individual must feel that they have an equal voice and feel heard, without being silenced or penalized simply because someone disagrees with them. Listening means honestly considering their point of view, rather than trying to beat them into submission with our rebuttal and opinion. It signals that we're willing to learn and consider another's perspective, even if we don't agree with it. Listening requires that we let go of willfulness, pride, self-righteousness, and defensiveness and consider what someone else has to share.

---

**Dialogue and Listening are at work when each individual listens and engages in conversation in a way that deepens meaning and connection.**

---

Fear-based teams or organizations don't have an environment of constructive dialogue and listening. Instead, the communication is usually a one-way, top-down monologue. Rather than having the difficult conversations that are needed for a healthy team, leaders and employees in fear-based organizations engage in either toxic exchanges, dysfunctional politeness, or a complete shutdown of differing points of view. People may know something is wrong, but everyone acts like everything is okay because there is no space for meaningful dialogue or listening. Additionally, employees know that speaking up and sharing their point of view is pointless and could spark retaliation, so they go silent. They operate in fear, which can lead to self-censorship, limiting ideas and discussion that might be helpful in solving a problem or further developing a leader. Additionally, if employees feel that there is not a safe place to authentically and honestly express themselves *without* penalty, it can make them resentful and angry and contribute to disengagement.

What does dysfunctional communication cost an organization? One study by VitalSmarts published in *Harvard Business Review* surveyed 1,025 employees and managers and asked them about a situation where they had a concern or issue at work, but never said anything. The average employee wasted a total of seven days ruminating about the problem, complaining to others, doing unnecessary work, or getting angry instead of speaking up about the situation. Surprisingly, 40 percent of those surveyed admitted to wasting two weeks or more engaging in this kind of unproductive behavior. And what does this silence do to an organization's bottom line? The researchers found the estimated cost of dysfunctional politeness is $7,500 to $50,000 per person. So, a lack of Dialogue and Listening does more than damage relationships and lower engagement—it upends deadlines, strains budgets, increases turnover, and destroys the overall organizational culture.[1]

| FEAR-BASED ORGANIZATIONS WITHOUT DIALOGUE AND LISTENING PRACTICE: | FREEDOM-CENTERED ORGANIZATIONS WITH DIALOGUE AND LISTENING PRACTICE: |
| --- | --- |
| Debate | Dialogue and discussion |
| Level 1 and 2 listening | Level 3 and 4 listening |
| One-way conversations | Two-way conversations |
| Censorship | Free expression |
| Shallow conversations | Deep and meaningful conversations |

Dialogue and Listening provide a solid foundation for inspiring trust, respect, and full engagement into your team while minimizing fear.

## THE FOUR LEVELS OF LISTENING

Leaders simply cannot practice healthy organizational democracy—and engage in the robust conversations that inevitably come with it—if they don't have the Dialogue and Listening skills required. But how do you learn to be a better listener? At WorldBlu, we've found it begins with teaching people the Four Levels of Listening.[2]

Level 1 listening is simply downloading information. It's when we listen to each other at a transactional level, gathering basic data (who, what, when, where). This is the average listener's level. The listener isn't open; instead, they are listening to reconfirm old opinions and judgments and hear what the speaker has to say in general—and often, they aren't paying much attention anyway. We all know what it's like to try to talk with someone while they scroll through their phone, barely looking at you and grunting replies. During one of our trainings, I once had a client say to me, "This is how all of the communication is at my company. I didn't even know there was another level of listening!"

Level 2 listening is factual listening, when one individual is listening to the other with an open mind. This is a good listener's level. They listen to confirm new data and information and analyze facts to make meaning. They might share common experiences, ideas, or feelings infused with gentle, noninvasive questioning (how, why). More than just grunting their replies, the listener is giving audible *and* visual attention to the individual talking.

Level 3 listening is empathetic and active listening, when both people have an open mind and an open heart and are connecting on a deep and compassionate level. These are the skills of excellent listeners who make each other feel emotionally and spiritually safe so they can open up in a meaningful way, taking the conversation to the next level of insight and understanding. Level 3 listeners do this by acknowledging the other's viewpoint, the way they feel, or why they made the decision they did. They strive to see a situation through another individual's eyes, recognizing why the other is speaking and *why* the topic is significant to them. They allow the speaker to breathe and pause between ideas. Often, the listener will paraphrase to keep the focus on the other individual and not shift it back to themselves by comparing or injecting their own experience into the conversation.

Last, Level 4 listening is generative listening, listening for the future that wants to emerge. It is the realm of masterful listeners. Everyone in the conversation has an open mind and heart and is willing to grow, with no need to steer the conversation toward the outcome they want. They are willing to leave the known for the unknown, promoting the development of new ideas and exploring new views together. On this level, everyone is listening to more than just the words—they are also listening to their intuition or any divine guidance that comes to them through the conversation. There may be lots of silence; listeners are not rushing to talk or fill in the gaps, instead exchanging patient, purposeful, and appropriately timed questions and responses. This is all-in listening, where each individual is entirely focused on what is being said, without mental or physical distractions. Amazing breakthroughs, healing, and connections can happen at this level.

I love to demonstrate the difference between the levels in our live trainings. I often invite a willing participant to sit up at the front of the room with me. First, we model a Level 1 listening conversation. I try to engage them in a deep topic but do a horrible job listening, playing with my phone, my shoes, my hair—anything. You can actually feel the discomfort in the room as the other participants watch. The discomfort is a recognition that they have been listened to—and have listened to others in the past—on this shallow, transactional level. After the conversation, I then ask both the participant and the audience how a Level 1 conversation made them feel. Unsurprisingly, they say it made them feel "horrible" or "uncomfortable"—at times, people have even said "angry."

I then model a Level 4 listening conversation with the same participant. The tone is visibly different, and despite an audience, I've often had the participant

| LISTENING LEVEL | CHARACTERISTICS |
|---|---|
| **Listening Level 1:** **Average Listener** Listening from Habits | Transactional listening; rushed, interrupting Questions are focused only on gathering basic information Not open-minded Only audible listening |
| **Listening Level 2:** **Good Listener** Listening from Outside of Oneself | Factual listening; analyzing data to make meaning Sharing experiences, ideas, or feelings Gentle questioning; reflective listening to check for accuracy Open-minded Audible and visual listening |
| **Listening Level 3:** **Excellent Listener** Listening from Within | Empathic listening; person feels emotionally safe Authentic questions and responses; connecting emotionally; paraphrasing ideas; keeping the focus on the other person Open mind and heart Audible, visual, mental and physical listening |
| **Listening Level 4:** **Masterful Listener** Listening from Source/God/The Divine/Universe/etc. | Generative listening; letting new ideas emerge Patient, purposeful, and appropriately timed questions and responses; no interruptions Open mind, heart, and will Audible, visual, mental, physical, and intuitive listening |

*Chart developed based on concepts from WorldBlu, The Presencing Institute, and the Educare Unlearning Institute.*

tell me later that they totally forgot they were being watched and truly opened up because they felt so heard, supported, and safe. Again, afterward, as we debrief the conversation, it's incredible how those watching said even *they* felt heard, respected, and embraced.

I recall on one occasion, after teaching the Four Levels of Listening to a group of top leaders at a training in California, I decided to try an experiment. It was in the afternoon right after lunch, and I could sense that people were feeling a bit unfocused. As we started the training back up, for the first time, I was inspired to ask everyone to please listen to me at a Level 4. I wondered how it would feel to ask a group, and not just the individual I was talking with in a conversation, to do this. Much to my surprise, I instantly felt a profound focused energy in the room. Everyone was suddenly locked into what I was saying, and for me as a speaker, it felt energizing and engaging.

It is vital that as Freedom-Centered Leaders, we consciously learn and practice listening at Level 4 as much as possible and model it for those on our team. Leaders often tell me they don't have time to listen at Level 4. But the reality is that you don't have time *not* to listen at Level 4, because not listening at that level means that you're missing crucial pieces of information to help your team and business grow. Listening at Level 4 is not something you do; it is *a way of being*. Yes, it takes practice, but when you develop the habit of listening at this level as much as possible, you don't need to take time to tune your instrument; you are already in tune and are ready to have the deeper conversations that are required of high-performing leaders.

## THE PROMISE OF DIALOGUE AND LISTENING

The principle of Dialogue and Listening contributes several key ingredients to building a Freedom-Centered Team or Organization:

**Dialogue and Listening develop harmonious, higher-performing teams.** Unsurprisingly, research shows that teams that communicate better perform better. In his article "The New Science of Building Great Teams," Alex "Sandy" Pentland, the director of MIT's Human Dynamics Laboratory and the MIT Media Lab Entrepreneurship Program, collected data measuring patterns of communication and found that successful teams share several defining characteristics. To quote the article:

1. Everyone on the team talks and listens in roughly equal measure, keeping contributions short and to the point.
2. Members face one another, and their conversations and gestures are energetic.
3. Members connect directly with one another—not just with the team leader.
4. Members carry on back-channel or side conversations within the team.
5. Members periodically break, go exploring outside the team, and bring information back.[3]

Without authentic, ongoing, real-time, and direct conversations where everyone can freely express themselves and listen to each other, a team isn't in harmony, which means it can't perform at its peak.

**Dialogue and Listening exchange the fear of not feeling heard for the freedom of expressing your voice.** In fear-based organizations, individuals constantly feel silenced and shut out. But in Freedom-Centered Organizations, the practice of Dialogue and Listening says, "I see you. You have value. Your voice matters." This invites more engagement because employees feel included in the conversation, which invites better ideas, more innovation, and progress. It also engenders more trust throughout the entire organization.

**Dialogue and Listening develop an Ubuntu spirit and shared understanding.** In fear-based organizations, everyone is siloed off without a lot of collective insight or wisdom. But in Freedom-Centered Organizations, where there are authentic and meaningful conversations happening, a shared wisdom and collective Ubuntu consciousness develops that allows everyone to perform at a higher level. This shared spirit fosters a deeper sense of trust and understanding, which means that fewer policies, rules, and bureaucracy are needed, moving the team forward swiftly and cohesively.

## HOW TO SUCCESSFULLY IMPLEMENT DIALOGUE AND LISTENING IN YOUR TEAM

As you think about how to bring more Dialogue and Listening into your team, consider these tips for implementing it successfully.

1. **Develop shared standards for constructive communication.** Have a clear and mutual understanding of what healthy dialogue and listening skills look like in your organization and constructive, non-punitive ways to address it if those standards are infringed. Make sure there is a way to raise a red flag if a conversation is about to or has become harmful and toxic.

2. **Make sure leaders model healthy dialogue and listening skills.** Freedom-Centered Leaders should lead by example in this respect. Their leadership should help create a healthy environment that makes everyone feel psychologically safe to express their point of view.

3. **Have ongoing training for success.** Regular training in healthy dialogue and listening skills should be available for everyone in areas

such as the Four Levels of Listening and how to have difficult conversations. For example, a twenty-person social media consultancy in Brighton, England, created monthly communication workshops on a range of topics so all team members could learn and practice effective communication skills. "We also created a shared vocabulary about communication—feedback, respect, empathy, and congruence—that has enabled us to better interact with one another and work as a team," explained their cofounder and CEO, Will.

4. **Create a learning environment rather than a punitive one.** We live in a time of intolerance worldwide as it relates to free speech. However, in healthy Freedom-Centered Teams and Organizations, there must be a space for everyone to be able to share their point of view in a professional manner, even and *especially* if those views are divergent. Therefore, it is imperative that employees are not censored, ostracized, belittled, humiliated, scolded, or fired if they cross a communication line that offends someone else. Instantly firing someone simply because they've said something that offended someone else's worldview—often unintentionally—is not democracy; it is dictatorship.

## TOOLBOX

### TRANSFORMATIONAL PRACTICES IN DIALOGUE AND LISTENING

#### Frank, Open, and Honest Conversations, and a Team Charter | Beginner Level

How do you make sure you're having healthy, fear-free conversations? The employee-owners at one solar-electric company in Boulder, Colorado, practice Frank, Open, and Honest Conversation, or "FOH" as they like to call it. The practice establishes ground rules for discussion and a shared standard of communication both internally and externally. "We practice FOH," explains their CEO, Blake, "because it elevates the quality of our interactions and therefore our work. We enjoy working together because we have this shared standard for our communications." The employee-owners of the company encourage each other to share their views honestly, even when it isn't easy, and listen to each other with an open mind, holding themselves to a higher standard of professional communication.

Another example comes from a US- and Canada-based warehousing and fulfillment company with 450 employees. They have created a team charter with guidelines for respectful conversations. These guidelines include trust, conflict, commitment, accountability, and results. Their charter gives their team members permission to feel like they can bring up new ideas or challenge each other.

### The 10-Word Rule | Beginner Level

What if you want to promote healthy dialogue and listening skills in a Freedom-Centered Organization, but you know that at some point, someone might cross a line and cause offense? The Dillon, Montana–based bakery chain found a solution called the 10-Word Rule. "We practice open communication, yet we recognize that not all conversations are appropriate," explains their CEO, Mike. "While we believe in open conversations and questions, some things can be inappropriate, which is why we created the 10-Word Rule. Anyone can say anything they want, whenever they want to, and others in the conversation have the right to call 'ten' when they deem the conversation is within ten words of breaking a trust."

### Daily Huddles | Beginner Level

Does practicing Dialogue and Listening always have to take a long time? Is there a way leaders and employees can have quick check-ins with each other that are still valuable? Yes, and here's how: Each day, all one hundred employees at a Vancouver-based junk removal company participate in a seven-minute Daily Huddle. The huddles provide a forum for people to share successes, discuss financials, and identify obstacles. The meetings are also video-streamed to the company's 155 franchise locations in Canada, the US, and Australia.

## Circles of Change | Intermediate Level

How do you teach dialogue and listening skills in a way that sticks? At an educational nonprofit based in Port-au-Prince, Haiti, they teach the principle of Dialogue and Listening through a practice called "Circles of Change."

Circles of Change is a six-month, two-hours-per-week seminar that helps leaders and coworkers develop their skills in dialogue, listening, and collaborative leadership. Everyone meets as a large group and reads a thought-provoking text together. Then, they break up into groups of three and reflect on what they found interesting in the text, using the Circles of Change method. Eventually, they gather back into a single group to share their thoughts.

During the process, they are asked to pay attention to group dynamics. Are some people talking while others are silent? Are some people just preaching their convictions while others bite their tongue? Some participants might be afraid to share their thoughts, but through the Circles of Change training, individuals are taught to recognize and respond to these situations by using phrases such as, "I sense you're wanting to say something," to create an opening for someone who might be too shy to express themselves. These tools create a culture in which all voices are listened to and valued. As their executive director, John, explains, "Over time, the group discovers the profound connections that can happen with true dialogue. They discover mutual understanding and the depth of authentic relationships that can occur."

## Town Hall Meetings | Intermediate Level

Another powerful way to practice Dialogue and Listening is through town hall meetings. At this multinational healthcare company, they have regular, live and virtual town hall meetings in which the entire global workforce is invited to ask the CEO and executive leadership team any question they'd like in a real-time, in-person format.

I experienced one of these meetings in Nashville one year at their "Villagewide" annual event. For an hour, I watched as their CEO ran through a ballroom filled with three thousand of their employee "teammates" fielding questions while the president, chief medical officer, and head of human resources sat onstage and answered questions as well. More than just hosting a cursory session, senior leadership was honest and humble about listening to challenges and issues that were voiced. If they didn't know the answer, they said they would look into it and transparently post their answer for everyone to see. For example, an issue about benefits came up and several people in the audience began grumbling about it to each other. This made the CEO take note and realize how important the issue was to everyone. He asked, "Is this an issue for many of you?"

The audience replied, "Yes!"

"Then we will look into it more and get you all an answer," he replied.

Dialogue and Listening are not about quick answers; they're about communicating in a way that surfaces and addresses issues and solves them rather than ignoring or covering them up.

### One on Ones | Intermediate Level

In fear-based organizations, employees do not feel seen and heard. Instead, they often feel like cogs in a machine, disposable and unvalued. Meeting with a boss or manager can feel tedious at best and belittling at worst. But what if your manager actually cared about you? Well, a multinational publishing company focused on personal growth based in Estonia instituted a transformational practice called "One on Ones" where every single manager is required to meet with each of their direct reports at least once a month *only* to talk about the employee's life—nothing else. Managers take a sincere interest in what their colleague is thinking and feeling, their state of well-being, and any suggestions or feedback they might have for the organization. Any feedback is then shared (without divulging any sensitive information or betraying the employee's confidence) in the manager's weekly meetings so that any supportive actions can be taken.

### World Cafés | Intermediate Level

Leaders are often looking for methods to encourage healthy conversations that can spark new ideas, build trust, and deepen connections. At one nonprofit educational organization in Laval, Quebec, Canada, they achieve this goal using a method called World Café.

A World Café practice begins with breaking everyone into groups of no more than five people with one scribe. Everyone is asked the same question and given a certain amount of time to answer it, with the scribe writing down key points. When time is up, everyone but the scribe moves to a new table with a new question that everyone answers. Before the new question starts, the scribes share what they wrote down from the previous session while everyone listens. This is repeated one more time, for a total of three sessions. The method promotes cross-pollination of ideas with people who might not normally have regular or extended opportunities to dialogue with each other. After the three sessions are done, everyone gathers to share key points from the various groups.

### CEO Facetime | Advanced Level

Fear-based leaders often hide in their offices, while Freedom-Centered Leaders do their best to get out and really listen to and connect with their colleagues, which can make a huge difference in helping employees feel seen and understood. Vishen, the CEO of a 250-person company, blocks out two and a half hours every week to meet with five different teams so that each gets its one-to-one "CEO Facetime" with him. He moves from one team to the next, with only a five-minute break between each one. The meetings are fun and relaxed, and the purpose is to share ideas and build a culture of Dialogue and Listening. The CEO also takes ideas from each team to the next, connecting the dots on ideas, resources, and assets, which supercharges innovation.

Since implementing CEO Facetime, a number of things happened: 95 percent of the employees now meet with the CEO at least once a week, and innovation has accelerated, with some of its fastest growth in new projects and new ideas that have boosted profitability and revenue.

### Level 4 Meetings | Advanced Level

One of the issues that elicits a collective groan in most organizations is endlessly long and draining meetings. However, at this global management consultancy based in London, with members of the team spread out across the world, they have figured out how to have meetings that aren't filled with shallow and frustrating interactions, because Level 4 listening is a very real part of it.

They start their meetings getting everyone centered by giving a few minutes of silence. During their meetings, which are usually a mix of in-person and virtual, everyone can be quiet, pray or meditate if they choose, and get mentally ready. Often everyone is rushing from one meeting to the next, so providing these few minutes of grounding silence invites people to shift into Level 4 listening.

Next, they do a check-in. Each individual has the opportunity to share what has happened to them that day. Often, this is something that is top of mind and outside of the scope of the meeting. This gives the other participants a greater understanding of each person's mindset and the circumstances everyone is dealing with, generating greater understanding and empathy.

Last, each meeting ends with a checkout. This gives everyone the opportunity to say what they valued from the meeting and provide direct feedback to help improve future meetings. They have found that when everyone can do their best to shift into a Level 4 listening level, it accelerates shared understanding and decision-making, reducing the length and frequency of meetings.

### Brutal Honesty Sessions | Advanced Level

One of the most challenging things for top leaders is having direct and clear communications with their colleagues and employees, modeling Dialogue and Listening in a way that feels authentic, straightforward, and honest. At a personal growth company with 250 employees, they recognize that authentic conversation starts at the top. Each week, the CEO conducts a transformational practice called "Brutal Honesty Sessions" during which employees may anonymously ask the CEO any question they want. The CEO must then answer them publicly during the company-wide meeting. Sometimes, the questions are difficult and even painful, but he is committed to answering them all openly and authentically. As a result, Brutal Honesty Sessions have contributed to a climate of healthy dialogue, deep listening, and trust, which has been vital to the company, particularly during times of challenge or accelerated growth.

START

# PRINCIPLE 4

# Transparency

*Truth never damages a cause that is just.*
—Mahatma Gandhi—

A small advertising agency in Austin, Texas, hit a crisis point one February day. They'd just received a call that their company's entire savings—enough to cover two years of operations without a dime of additional customer revenue—had vanished overnight.

It was a tumultuous time in the banking industry, and their bank had just been seized by the US Securities and Exchange Commission. There was $19 billion missing from the bank, including the company's hard-earned savings. They now had no money for payroll, to cover their office rent and overhead, or to pay their suppliers.

However, what should have forced them to close their doors or set them back several years turned out to be just a blip. Why wasn't the impact more severe? They attributed this 100 percent to their democratic organizational model and their practices in Transparency.

## WHAT IS TRANSPARENCY?

Transparency is at work when ideas and information are openly and responsibly shared. Transparency is the last democratic principle in the Start phase because it continues to lay a solid groundwork on which to build a highly successful Freedom-Centered Team or Organization. Transparency is also one of the four principles that is a driver of a democratic system. Transparency is the *light of truth*, communicating the accurate and timely information so vitally needed to operate and lead a team democratically. Transparency of information is what gives real power to the people so that they can confidently make decisions, act in a prompt and appropriate manner, and continue to chart a path of growth. With Transparency, the trust that is so vital to the long-term success of a distinctly Freedom-Centered Team or Organization is established and maintained. Once the principles of Purpose and Vision, Integrity, and Dialogue and Listening are instituted, an organization is ready to implement increased levels of responsible Transparency.

---

**Transparency is at work when ideas and information are openly and responsibly shared.**

---

In fear-based teams or organizations, leaders use a lack of Transparency and secrecy to dodge personal accountability, control the narrative, and keep an upper hand over their employees, perpetuating their control-based culture while daily ratcheting up the levels of fear. They know that keeping their employees in the dark makes them easier to control and manipulate, preventing them from making well-informed decisions that might benefit the entire organization.

When employees don't have complete information or understand the full picture, they can become fearful, which can make them angry, reactionary, or easier to sway. But when employees have access to the light of Transparency, they are well informed, making it much harder to control and silence them. They are empowered and equipped with what they need to thrive, make smarter choices, and contribute meaningfully. They are equipped with the information they need to have an intelligent voice.

| FEAR-BASED ORGANIZATIONS WITHOUT TRANSPARENCY BELIEVE: | FREEDOM-CENTERED ORGANIZATIONS WITH TRANSPARENCY BELIEVE: |
|---|---|
| Top leaders should act like a secret society | Top leaders should be open and authentic |
| Employees aren't smart enough to handle the truth | Employees are smart enough to handle the truth |
| Employees will use information to revolt | Employees will use information to make better decisions |
| Transparency breeds distrust | Transparency breeds trust |
| Incomplete, biased, or manipulated information is fine | Clear, accurate, and timely information is best |

The Austin ad agency used open-book management to let their team see their financial position in real time so that together, they could address the massive financial setback each day and come up with solutions. Over time, they found ways to make up the lost revenue and navigate the challenges with surprisingly little impact on their business. They didn't lose a single member of their team, and just one year later, the company was healthier than it had ever been before.

## THE PROMISE OF TRANSPARENCY

Transparency is a vital principle to designing a Freedom-Centered Culture within your team or organization because it delivers on several key things:

**Transparency makes your workforce smarter.** When accurate information is shared in context with employees on a regular, if not real-time, basis, everyone can make smarter and faster democratic decisions. Leaders must also educate their employees to understand exactly what the information means to them. For example, I remember sitting in a training at the internal university of a Denver-based, publicly traded healthcare company with more than 52,000 employees. The company educated "teammates" to understand the finances, strategies, and ways decisions were made. The Freedom-Centered Leaders there understood that by increasing their employees' collective intelligence through the practice of Transparency, they decreased the costs associated with poor decision-making, thus improving overall performance.

**Transparency helps reduce fear and confusion.** When employees don't know the truth within their organization, they are filled with fear and confusion, which perpetuates gossip, backstabbing, fiefdoms, and politicking. Knowing the truth gives employees a greater feeling of freedom and self-determination.

**Transparency builds massive trust.** Many leaders ask for more trust from their employees without giving them the information they need to build that trust. But when Transparency of information empowers employees to see that good and timely decisions are being made and they are being treated fairly, it increases trust and eliminates the "us vs. them" divide.

**Transparency decentralizes power to your people to make better decisions.** The old adage "Information is power" is so true, which is why fear-based leaders are scared to give their employees accurate and timely information about what is actually happening in their organization. Doing so takes control away from the top of an organizational hierarchy and ultimately decentralizes it through-out an organization to the people. Yet granting access to relevant information by increasing an organization's level of transparency can shift power from a small group at the top to everyone, enabling employees to make better deci-sions. Leaders need not be afraid to do this and must understand the long-term benefits of a responsible level of transparency for the organization.

**Transparency shifts employees from "renters" to citizens.** If leaders aren't giving their employees accurate and timely Transparency of information, I can guarantee they are just renters rather than owners, costing your company all of the benefits that it could be enjoying with employee-citizens who think and act with an ownership mentality. With the democratic principle of Transparency at work, employees have what they need to more fully participate, cultivating greater ownership in the success of the team.

**Transparency contributes to a more ethical work environment.** The best way to help leaders and employees be honest and ethical isn't more rules, pol-icies, or micromanagement—it's increased transparency. When everyone can see the real numbers, it's harder for bad actors to manipulate or steal from the organization. Also, sharing financial numbers and other relevant strategic information helps everyone up their game. Transparency helps everyone be more ethical and trustworthy.

**Transparency means you don't need as much hierarchy and bureaucracy.**
Hierarchy exists largely because of how information is distributed within an
organization. Traditionally those who are "in the know" are atop the organizational ladder, and those who are on a "need-to-know" basis are on its bottom
rungs. While some hierarchy can be helpful even in the most democratic organizations, when information flow is transparent and decentralized, unnecessary
and wasteful levels of bureau-crazy are exchanged for increased self-management.

**Transparency creates organizational alignment.** When everyone, regardless
of position or title, has access to the same relevant and timely information, leaders can rapidly create a greater level of organizational alignment. All employees
will see how they are part of a bigger picture. They will also understand specifically how their decisions impact the whole.

## HOW TO SUCCESSFULLY IMPLEMENT TRANSPARENCY

Freedom-Centered Organizations transparently share information with their
employees in areas such as the company's financial health, strategy, goals,
advancement opportunities, salaries, hiring and firing practices, and anything
else that impacts their ability to make great decisions. Aside from legal restric-
tions on what can and cannot be shared, is there anything else that should
not be transparently shared with those on your team? In general, if sharing
something will do harm, break a trust, or be unkind to others, this is a good
standard for whether to share something or not.

There are many more areas where we as leaders should be more transparent
with their colleagues and team members than not, including the following:

- the financial health of your company, including profit and loss, sales,
  revenue, and spending
- salary ranges
- criteria for hiring, firing, and promotions
- decision-making processes
- strategy
- meeting minutes, including board minutes
- top-level meetings, including the executive team and board
- challenges and mistakes made
- employee morale levels

- customer service indicators
- turnover numbers

What's the best way to roll out more Transparency within your team organization? Here are a few key tips:

1. **Share real-time information to inform action.** Real-time or "smart" information is accurate and timely enough for your employees to act on it in meaningful ways. As much as possible, share information openly, in-person or virtually, regularly (even daily), and ensure it is relatable to employees' individual goals as well as the collective performance metrics of the organization. Many technologies can help you automate this process.

2. **Provide context for making transparency meaningful.** It's not enough for leaders just to be transparent; they must also provide *context* for the ideas and information they share so that Transparency creates real value for employees. Share information in a context that feels responsible and respectful, not reckless.

3. **Open up about the good, the bad, and the ugly.** If leaders only share good news, then the practice of Transparency feels inauthentic. While this can be difficult at times—as leaders, our natural inclination is to hide the "bad"—sharing news responsibly in a context where employees can take action is critical to growing and maintaining an environment of trust and respect. For example, at a twenty-person computer training company in London, they have a "no secrets" policy so that everything is out in the open.

## TOOLBOX

## TRANSFORMATIONAL PRACTICES IN TRANSPARENCY

### Open Office | Beginner Level

While an open office plan might not be the right idea for every company, this sixty-person software development company loves keeping things transparent for everyone to see what's going on in its 18,000-square-foot office building in Michigan. Collaboration between coworkers and clients occurs in full view of everyone, with project plans spread across tables for anyone to analyze and comment on. Visual tools, such as open-book management score-boards and work authorization boards, are posted for all to see as they walk around the open and bright office space.

### Fireside Chats and Lunch + Learns | Beginner Level

This digital asset management company has found a way to address communication challenges with more open conversations. They have implemented several methods for knowledge and idea sharing, including Fireside Chats, Lunch + Learns, new product idea presentations, Hackathons, and Sprint Presentations.

For example, regular Fireside Chats address a variety of topics, from customer satisfaction to changes in organizational structure to addressing sexual harassment issues. Team members also exper-iment with new technologies and share their updates at Lunch + Learn sessions, while product managers and developers share results during Sprint Presenta-tions. These methods support free-flowing ideas, shared knowledge, and continual learning.

### CEO Dashboards | Beginner Level

A California-based employee recognition company practices open information with "CEO Dashboards" that share real-time company information with every-one. They also have committed to communicating both good and bad news transparently. By embracing real-time communication as much as possible, they believe they can address and resolve problems as soon as they arise, rather than having them linger.

As their founder, Razor, explained to me, "People are the most valuable resource any company has and treating them as such is fundamental to busi-ness success. Democracy in the workplace is about recognizing employees for their contributions, providing the right tools and trusting that they will deliver, and developing mutual relationships that benefit the individual and the organization. We practice transparent, two-way communication that empowers employees to play a larger role within the organization and have a voice in shaping our future, which continues to generate innovation, excellence, and growth."

### Open-Book Management | Intermediate Level

Open-book management, a now well-known management method, was developed in 1993 by John Case of *Inc.* magazine. A Colorado-based artisan brewing company with seven hundred employees decided to open their books early on, when leaders asked their workers what percentage of every incoming dollar they thought was profit. When they answered around 50 percent, the leadership team decided that financial literacy training was desperately needed. Today, there are financial classes and ongoing training at each monthly all-staff meeting. Anyone in the packaging department, for example, can look at how the branding department allocates its spending. Workers are also taught how to read profit-and-loss reports, and the organization conducts a coworker-led "ESOP 101" class for all new employee-owners.

The company's cofounder, Kim, explains why they believe so much in practicing Transparency: "We practice open-book management and engage all coworkers in our annual strategic planning. We encourage open and honest communications throughout the organization. You can question, prod, and disagree with decisions, which makes for a robust planning process. We feel Transparency fosters trust and engagement, while allowing people to bring their true best selves to work every day."

### Open Town Halls | Intermediate Level

Some Freedom-Centered Organizations believe that Transparency isn't just an internal thing—it can also be applied externally with their clients and vendors. While many of us have heard about town hall meetings, this Las Vegas–based online retailer livestreams their online meetings for anyone—*inside the company and out*—to watch. I recall watching one town hall meeting while sitting with my colleague at her kitchen table outside of London. If anything that was extremely confidential came up that needed to stay internal, they simply paused the external viewers' stream. Otherwise, everything was open and transparent to customers, vendors, and even competitors.

## Culture Book | Intermediate Level

How willing is your organization to share with the world what your culture is like? One online retailer publishes an annual "Culture Book." They collect short essays from their 1,700 employees on the subject of the company's culture and then publish them—unedited—in a book that the CEO distributes to everyone. Each year, all employees, both new and old, contribute a fresh essay to the book, which has grown to 480 pages. Their CEO uses it not only to get employees thinking about the meaning of their work, but also to show the outside world what they have built together.

## Rights and Responsibilities | Advanced Level

How do you make sure that employees have the right to speak freely and openly within an organization, especially if what they have to say isn't what the leaders want to hear or have widely shared? This Massachusetts-based fair trade food cooperative created a worker-owners list of Rights and Responsibilities, which was written and approved by their 150 worker-owners themselves and which only they may amend. The document states that all worker-owners have the following free-speech rights:

- the right to speak at worker-owner meetings
- the right to propose agenda items
- the right to publicly raise issues and express opinions in co-op forums and communication channels
- the right to contribute to coworker annual evaluations

### Open Up to Competitors | Advanced Level

Leaders at this Estonia-based personal growth publishing company asked themselves a key question one day: If they were *really* committed to achieving their vision of touching a billion lives, and if that vision were more important to them than just profit, then why not stop thinking of their competitors purely as competitors and open up to them about the company's ideas? As their CEO put it, "What if we shared our best thinking with our competitors so that we can fulfill our mission *together*?"

This led to a project where they started a community and a blog to share their best practices with their competitors. Now, any of their competitors can go to their website and learn about the hottest ideas they're currently exploring in management, operations, marketing, culture, and systems. As the proverb says, "iron sharpens iron," meaning that by helping their competitors be better, this would help them improve as well.

### Open Board Meetings | Advanced Level

A twenty-five-person social media consultancy in Brighton, England, offers two open guest seats at their company board meetings, which all employees are invited to come and take. Having these open seats avoids any feelings of secrecy at the board level and encourages employees to participate in running the business. It also prevents the board from becoming removed from the employees and their issues and concerns. Often, the most valuable contributions and questions come from the employees in the guest seats.

### Open Salary Ranges | Advanced Level

Leaders at one publicly traded San Diego manufacturing company decided to disclose salary ranges to their hundreds of employees across over two dozen countries. Since they were already practicing organizational democracy, the trust, communication skills, and high level of integrity were already in place for them to open up the books even more by fully disclosing salary ranges. However, being a Freedom-Centered Organization, they first identified pay inequities, which they corrected in an open and honest manner.

Next, as Stan, their vice president of global organization development, explained to me, they set about the complex task of deciding what their market-based salary ranges would be and assigning the proper range for each job description. Under US law, employers aren't allowed to talk directly with other companies about how much they pay their employees for similar work because that might artificially fix what people are paid. So, instead, they participate in commercial compensation surveys with other companies to get a benchmark, as is customary for most employers. They also turned to the Hay System (now Korn Ferry), a job valuation method developed in the 1950s as a reliable way for leaders to gauge what the marketplace is paying people. From there, they made their best judgment call to determine the range for each position.

After they determined the ranges and wrote hundreds of job descriptions, it was then time to educate their employees about the open salary–range system, starting at the top. Through a series of live workshops with audiovisual aids, handouts, and group interactions, mixed in with principles of adult learning, leaders learned how to understand and then speak intelligently about the open salary–range system.

"Trust is all about transparency," Stan shared with me. "We did this because if people are treated like property or 'human capital' they won't have a sense of personal accountability and personal freedom, which is what we want to foster here. We wanted to be able to tell people everything, and not just some things. It's because we are honest and open that we have sustained a 93 percent engagement rate for many years. And if we didn't have an engaged workforce, we would not be able to respond to the inevitable highs and lows of business."

When I asked Stan why they don't share specific salaries and instead just share the salary ranges, he said, "I don't think it's our place to share an employee's specific salary. We respect an individual's privacy. If they want to do that, it's their choice."

With open salary ranges and access to all job descriptions, team members now have the freedom to choose the direction they want their career to move in, equipped with the information they need to make it happen, which gives them the opportunity to take even greater control of their future.

# SCALE

---

Growth is never by mere chance; it is the
result of forces working together.
—James Cash Penney—

# PRINCIPLE 5

# Accountability

*Accountability is essential to personal growth,
as well as team growth.*
—Pat Summitt—

There it was on the wall, right in the middle of it all. I was visiting one of our client organizations in San Diego, a publicly traded, manufacturing company with a market cap of $2 billion and more than 530 employees worldwide. As I got to the top of the stairs, my eyes immediately landed on these words:

> I am responsible for taking action, asking questions, getting answers, and making decisions. I won't wait for someone to tell me. If I need to know, I'm responsible for asking. I have no right to be upset that I didn't get this sooner. And if I'm doing something that I shouldn't, that others should know about, I'm responsible for telling them.

Those powerful words are the company's Accountability pledge. But to understand how it practices the democratic principle of Accountability at this WorldBlu certified Freedom-Centered Organization, you must first understand how it handles failure.

"When I became the CEO, we had an okay culture, but it was punitive, as many corporate cultures are," its CEO, Garry, explained to me. "I realized that before I could take the culture to the next level, I had to get rid of the fear of failure."

When workplaces take steps to mitigate or remove their employees' fear of being shamed or unfair punishment for making an honest mistake, it becomes easier for individuals to be accountable. "We had to remove the fear of Accountability before we could introduce the pledge," Garry explains. That's when Garry landed on the phrase "Learning Moments"—what we often label "mistakes"—to take away the sting and stigma of failure that can happen all too easily in the workplace. "When we created Learning Moments, the culture really started to shift dramatically." (Learning Moments are also a wonderful example of another democratic principle, Reflection and Evaluation—more on that in Principle 10.)

At this publicly traded company, with high-stakes Accountability to their shareholders, they realized the bedrock of Accountability to each other and the company started with seeing themselves as a "tribe" rather than a team. "Everyone wants to feel that they belong to something," shares Garry. "That's why we call ourselves a tribe. And one of the first attributes of a tribe is being responsible or accountable to someone else.

"We worked out a long time ago that micromanagement wasn't scalable. So, if we were to succeed as an organization across 176 countries where our clients live, we better be clear on what a good outcome looks like," Garry shared with a rapt audience at one of our annual WorldBlu Freedom at Work summits. "Most organizations fall down on Accountability because, number one, they don't make it clear what a good outcome looks like."

So how do they bring all of this together to create a culture of Accountability throughout the entire organization? By painting their pledge on the wall in the corporate headquarters and in their offices around the world so their 530 employees will see it every day. Then, each tribe member takes the pledge and is held accountable to living the pledge's principles.

Whenever a situation comes up where a tribe member is not being accountable for their actions, making excuses, or self-justifying, their colleagues invoke the pledge. "There are times in meetings where I hear my fellow tribe members say, 'I am invoking the pledge right now to hold each other accountable,'" Garry shares with a smile.

Freedom in our workplaces can only work with Accountability at the helm. Without it, fear and confusion ensue because people don't know for what and to whom they are accountable. "Fear is the most disabling emotion we have," explains Garry. "When you don't have clear Accountability, it creates a lot of fear."

## WHAT IS ACCOUNTABILITY?

Accountability is at work when each individual and the organization are responsible to each other for their actions. Accountability starts with leaders being accountable to themselves first for their actions and behaviors. If leaders can't be accountable to themselves first, they can't expect others to be accountable, either. In the words of Thomas Paine, "A body of men, holding themselves accountable to nobody, ought not to be trusted by anybody."

Accountability, one of the four drivers of a democratic system, is the first principle in the Scale phase of the 10 Principles of Organizational Democracy because you cannot scale and grow a Freedom-Centered Organization without the backbone of clear Accountability living in each individual and the team. Without Accountability, a democratic system lacks the teeth it needs to be successful, resulting in anarchy or a free-for-all attitude that leaves employees feeling disempowered and confused. While it may seem paradoxical, freedom is only possible when you have an individual and collective sense of responsibility to yourself and to each other.

---

**Accountability is at work when each individual and the organization are responsible to each other for their actions.**

---

Freedom-Centered Leaders understand that Accountability can be difficult to practice at times, but the rewards are worth the short-term struggles. Accountability builds trust and empowers leaders to set healthy boundaries.

When everyone knows for what and to whom they are accountable, it brings clarity to murky waters so leaders can act confidently. It can also mean, at times, upsetting people. Freedom-Centered Leaders understand this and aren't afraid to hold people accountable, not out of blame, but in a way that liberates everyone to rise to a higher level of performance and self-worth.

By contrast, fear-based organizations lack clear accountability, compounding confusion, disengagement, and resentment in an already toxic environment. In addition, fear-based leaders rarely take personal accountability because it often exposes them as a fraud. Ethical breaches, cover-ups, and scandals, all arising from a lack of personal accountability, exacerbate a culture of fear and blame. Failure to live the democratic principle of Accountability also leads to short-term thinking and reactionary decisions by leaders. This lack of Accountability degrades integrity throughout an organization, hurting employees, shareholders, the company's reputation, and its bottom line. In organizations with accountability-free zones, nothing worthwhile gets done, infighting and fiefdoms are the norm, and the fog of self-centeredness rests on everyone.

| FEAR-BASED ORGANIZATIONS WITHOUT ACCOUNTABILITY BELIEVE: | FREEDOM-CENTERED ORGANIZATIONS WITH ACCOUNTABILITY BELIEVE: |
| --- | --- |
| *They* are responsible | *I* am responsible |
| Blame others for your mistakes | Own your learning moments |
| Discipline is hard | Discipline leads to excellence |
| Employees are dependent children | Employees are interdependent adults |
| You are a victim | You have agency |

When we are governed by freedom rather than fear, we design workplaces that operationalize the principle of Accountability, liberating individuals to take the actions needed to move the organization forward.

## THE PROMISE OF ACCOUNTABILITY

Here are a few of the promises that Accountability can deliver to your team or organization.

**Accountability cultivates an ownership mentality rather than a victim mentality.** It replaces the "us vs. them" divide that can exist between teams and leaders with a shared spirit of Accountability. An ownership rather than victim mentality also leads to real and lasting engagement. (That's why Garry's company has a 93 percent engagement rate.)

**Accountability develops leaders with higher self-worth.** Low self-worth leaders lack personal Accountability, always blaming others for their mistakes, inaction, or incompetence. Practicing personal Accountability helps leaders mature, cultivates moral courage, and increases inner joy. And when an organization has incorporated systems and processes of Accountability into the way they work, it naturally helps everyone develop a higher level of self-worth.

**Accountability increases the speed of execution and performance.** When everyone knows to whom and for what they are clearly accountable, it eliminates confusion and increases the speed of execution, boosting individual and team performance.

## HOW TO SUCCESSFULLY IMPLEMENT ACCOUNTABILITY IN YOUR ORGANIZATION

As you think about how to bring more Accountability into your organization, consider these tips for implementing Accountability successfully:

1. **Model it at the top.** Your top leaders *must* model accountability; otherwise, employees will see it as blaming and scapegoating.

2. **Practice individual and collective accountability.** There must be personal as well as collective Accountability to upholding your team's or organization's purpose, vision, and goals.

3. **No hypocrisy.** We all know what it's like to see a leader unfairly admonishing an employee when they themselves have not been accountable for something. This is highly hypocritical and destroys trust, breeds resentment, and undermines a democratic system.

4. **Make it clear.** Who is accountable to whom and for what must be extremely clear on every project and team.

5. **Stop the blame game.** Leaders must ensure that everyone feels comfortable sharing if they make a mistake, fail, or have a "learning moment" so that they are more willing to take accountability.

6. **Peer-to-peer accountability.** Legendary American basketball player Joe Dumars once said, "On good teams, coaches hold players accountable. On great teams, players hold players accountable." Accountability practices should allow employees to hold leaders accountable and leaders to hold employees accountable.

## TRANSFORMATIONAL PRACTICES IN ACCOUNTABILITY

### Achievements and Objectives | Beginner Level

How can organizational leaders make it clearer who is accountable to whom and by when so that there is less confusion and more alignment? A Virginia-based telecom company instituted a process called "As and Os," short for Achievements and Objectives. Each Monday, all employees send out a detailed list of their achievements from the previous week and their objectives for the coming week. In addition, at their Monday morning all-hands meeting, each employee shares their top three As and Os so everyone is aware of what people are working on and for what they are accountable.

### Accountable Tracking | Beginner Level

One of the biggest challenges for nonprofit organizations is establishing and maintaining public trust so donors will continue to give. So at a small nonprofit educational organization in Canada, they adopted accounting mechanisms to track every dollar and project in which they were engaged. Since they rely heavily on contributions from the general public, they believed it is their moral responsibility not just to *be* accountable, but to *show* others that they are accountable as well.

### An Accountability Pledge | Beginner Level

Most organizations fail miserably when it comes to holding leaders and employees accountable for their behavior in a healthy way, which only exacerbates cultures of fear and mistrust. But, as described in this chapter, one large manufacturing company instituted a transformational Accountability pledge, which is displayed on the wall in all of its offices around the world. Every employee takes the pledge, which begins: "I am responsible for taking action, asking questions, getting answers, and making decisions . . ." If someone feels that a fellow employee or leader is not being accountable, they can invoke the pledge at any time.

## Model It at the Top | Intermediate Level

How often are leaders at the top of an organization truly held accountable by their employees for their behavior or performance? Almost never. But each year at this large healthcare company, all 52,000 employees score their CEO, or "Mayor" as he likes to be called, on how well he is living the company's seven core values, one of which is Accountability. His scores are then sent to the board of directors. The CEO himself also presents his scores in front of three thousand of the company's top leaders at their annual "Villagewide" conference.

I've had the honor of attending several of these Villagewide conferences and watched their Mayor, with great humility and transparency, show his core value scores to his employees. Some of his scores were high; in other areas, he was struggling. He spoke openly about what he was doing to improve in each value. By modeling personal accountability in front of all of his employees, he built trust and inspired personal accountability in them as well.

As the CEO-Mayor explained to me, "To us, Accountability means we don't say, 'it's not my fault' or 'it's not my job.' We take responsibility for meeting our commitments—our personal ones as well as those of the entire organization. We take ownership of the results."

## Reciprocal Accountability | Intermediate Level

What if there was mutual accountability between an organization and its customers? At a forward-thinking, nonprofit primary school in Haiti that serves extremely underprivileged children, that's exactly the standard they have created. Understanding how important parental involvement is to children's school experience, all parents sign an annual agreement with the school that clearly spells out what they can expect from the school and what the school expects from them, including four hours each week of service work. The four hours of weekly service that parents are required to give as part of their contribution to the life of the school nurtures Accountability among the staff and parents who are part of the school community.

### Objectives and Key Results | Intermediate Level

What's the best way to help employees be accountable both personally and to the organization? Many organizations use Objectives and Key Results, or OKRs. At this software development service company in Hermosillo, Sonora, Mexico, the team at large defines the company's five-year vision, and then at the end of every year, the whole company participates in defining the goals for the following year. Employees align their personal OKRs to their company-wide vision and goals. Then, through their 360-degree assessment process, employees are accountable to their teams and report results on their previous assessments and challenges every six to eight months. While they self-manage and don't have bosses, they do have teams to which they are responsible for their part in the overall team's performance.

### The Get Upgraded Plan | Intermediate Level

It's one thing to have methods that help leaders and employees be accountable for their work, but what happens when they aren't? With the "Get Upgraded" plan, team members at this Penang, Malaysia—based, infographic-platform company are held accountable for results, especially if they have not been performing well or have been causing problems within their team. As part of the process, team leaders use a "GROW" framework (Goal, Reality, Options, and Willingness) to guide conversations with team members, explaining the criteria on which they have been evaluated. They then collaborate on a plan that will upgrade performance within one to three months.

### Positive Pairing | Advanced Level

One of the best ways to practice Accountability is to have a buddy who helps you do it. This Michigan-based software development company operational-izes Accountability by using processes that promote teamwork and interdependence.

All team members work in pairs, rather than individually, developing and coding for the client. This looks like two developers on one computer sup-porting each other with the coding. The pairs rotate weekly and are focused on adding client value through this unique pairing method.

### Bottom-Up Accountability | Advanced Level

With Bottom-Up Accountability, Philip, the CEO of a San Francisco–based virtual reality platform company, is held accountable to a clear performance benchmark. With regular surveying against key metrics that are important to their organization, employees are anonymously asked how well he is doing. His overall scores must stay above the bench-mark line they have set for him to retain his position as CEO. If he dips below this benchmark *and* his scores are trending down-ward, the employees have grounds for asking him to resign.

### Baseball Accountability | Advanced Level

From the beginning, this sixty-person software development company has never had an organiza-tional chart. They report to each other, often using the analogy of a baseball team. The pitcher doesn't report to the catcher. The first baseman doesn't report to the center fielder. Each member of the team understands their role and the relationship this role has to other roles on the team. They all report to each other, periodically stepping outside of their roles to help teammates who may be struggling.

During a tour of their offices for a group of visiting CEOs, someone asked their cofounder, Rich, who their employees thought they were accountable to. Rich paused for a second and then, in a common tradition within their culture, he shouted out to everyone, "Hey, team!"

Everyone instantly stopped working and shouted back, "Hey, Rich!"

And then Rich asked, "Who are you all accountable to?"

Everyone started looking around the large office space at each other and then, rather than pointing at Rich, they pointed at each other.

"Thank you!" he replied. The CEO who had asked the question looked at him with awe. Like a top baseball team, these high-performing employees know they're accountable to each other.

# PRINCIPLE 6

## Decentralization

*The people are the only legitimate fountain of power.*
—James Madison—

"I think we need to slow down a bit on the decrescendo," offered the flute player. "Then it helps set the mood for the next section's tempo change better." There was a low murmur of agreement as thirty-five musicians whipped out their pencils and made notes in their music. Then, with a nod, they all picked their instruments back up and, though there was no conductor to guide the group through the change, played the piece flawlessly.

It was a beautiful spring day, and I had the privilege of sitting in a small, charming theater in Napa Valley, California, watching a Grammy Award–winning chamber orchestra rehearse. Though the show was just hours away, the group was still making changes to perfect its performance. What was so unique about this New York City–based orchestra? It wasn't just that they had produced thirty-four original commissions and over seventy albums. It was that, since their founding in 1972, they have been an entirely *conductorless* orchestra.

I had first heard this legendary group perform at the acoustically superb Music Center at Strathmore, outside of Washington, DC, the year before. At the last minute, I discovered they were in town, and I was able to get tickets for some friends and me in the very last row of the upper balcony. Having been a flute player in a nationally ranked high school band with a benevolent dictator for a conductor, I was curious to watch how a decentralized leadership model could actually work in this unique workplace context.

Within minutes of the first note being played, even while sitting what seemed like miles away from the stage, the hairs on my arms stood up. One of my friends turned to me with wide eyes and simply said, "Wow." As the complex music flowed forth, I felt like we were experiencing the power of one harmonious team consciousness at work. After each piece, the musicians stood up, exited the stage, and then walked back on, sitting in different seats for the next piece, indicating a rotation of leadership.

The entire show was flawless. I found myself pondering a game-changing question: If an orchestra can perform at such a brilliant level *without* a conductor, do organizations really need CEOs? After all, where should power be held? And can that power and leadership regularly be rotated or shared?

I had to know more about exactly how this democratic process worked, and how they had sustained such a high level of excellence for so many years. That's how, later that year, back in New York City, I found myself walking around the chamber orchestra's headquarters on Riverside Drive, interviewing their executive director, Graham, about their process.

Graham explained to me that for each piece of music, a small core group of musicians is selected to rehearse the piece and decide how it should be performed. This core group then meets with the entire orchestra and shares how they think the piece should be played. Everything is up for discussion, suggestions, constructive criticism, and debate. In the end, the group eventually reaches a consensus. Throughout the process, the musicians learn not only about expressing themselves with their instruments, but also about developing the confidence and communication skills necessary to express their voice and point of view to a highly sophisticated group of intelligent and experienced musicians.

In the chamber orchestra, two-way communication is expected, fostered, and reinforced. Power is also shared. There is open and constructive feedback, even from a violinist to a flutist. Most orchestras have a conductor who makes all the decisions and egocentrically discourages the suggestions of their musicians. Traditionally, musicians are organized and seated in a fixed hierarchy, with first- and second-chair players, indicating their ranking as a musician. Not here—no conductor, no hierarchy. The musicians also freely express themselves to one another in a professional manner, so resentments and feuds rarely have an opportunity to develop. The result is an environment where all the members of the orchestra are focused on one thing: producing the best music possible.

"What's incredible about the process," Graham explained to me, "is that the musicians will spend so much time talking with each other about the piece, listening to various perspectives and examining, down to the detail, why a piece should be played a specific way, that they develop a shared understanding about a musical selection. They can then take the same piece of music out again years later and they will play it even better than at their last performance. I've experienced it before. It's magical."

This process of ongoing dialogue and listening is what they have used to sustain and advance their highly refined model of organizational democracy for over four decades. When they walk onstage, they are accountable to each other, not a conductor. In a mark of their excellence, they've worked with world-class musicians such as Yo-Yo Ma and Renée Fleming, had their democratic model studied by Harvard and Stanford universities, and performed for major multinational corporations such as Mitsubishi so that they, too, might learn about how leadership in a decentralized, democratic context could transform their organizations.

Without a conductor, it's easy to ask what holds the orchestra together. Isn't that the job of a leader? But the shared commitment to a democratic leadership philosophy—along with clear purpose, vision, and values—is the glue that holds decentralized organizations together.

## WHAT IS DECENTRALIZATION?

Decentralization is at work when power is appropriately shared throughout an organization. Decentralization is one of the four vital, driving principles of organizational democracy because it is the "power to the people" principle. Decentralization is in the Scale phase because without understanding how to decentralize power appropriately, a CEO or leader will never be able to scale his or her team or organization.

What exactly should be decentralized? Leaders must decentralize decision-making, information, power, and ownership as much as possible throughout their teams or organizations through democratically designed systems and processes.

## Decentralization is at work when power is appropriately shared throughout an organization.

When I tell people that I teach top leaders how to lead their companies with freedom and organizational democracy, I often get the wide-eyed question "Does that mean there is no top leader or CEO?" I find the cognitive dissonance amusing. We have a president or prime minister when it comes to democracy in a political context; why wouldn't we still have a CEO or top leader when it comes to democracy in an *organizational* context? Yes, you can still have a top leader in a Freedom-Centered Organization. As in other democratic organizations, you can even have co-CEOs, a governing council, or another creative model of decentralized leadership. Or, like the chamber orchestra, you can regularly rotate who the core leadership team is.

It's interesting to ask, however, what the role of a CEO (or equivalent) should be in a Freedom-Centered Organization. How much power should they *centralize* and how much should they *decentralize*? Someone who has thought about this deeply is Vineet, the CEO of the IT company I introduced in Part I. According to Vineet, the best way to improve the performance of your company is to get rid of the CEO. "I don't mean literally kick him or her out the door," he explains. "I mean jettison the *idea* that the CEO should be the supreme corporate leader."

Vineet explains that in today's global, fast-paced, and hyper-connected world, no one individual can fulfill all of the roles traditionally assigned to a CEO. Vineet describes a CEO's roles as:

- **Creator of Value.** The CEO alchemizes all the company's ingredients into gold.

- **Answer Machine.** The CEO is asked all the questions and knows all the answers.

- **Strategy Wizard.** The CEO predicts the future and formulates a grand plan for the organization.

- **Approval Granter.** The CEO reviews all business plans, determines their value, and divides up the resource pie among them.

- **Performance Reviewer.** The CEO acts as teacher and mentor to hundreds of senior managers.

Vineet further explains that when a CEO plays the role of "Supreme Leader," they rob fellow employees of leadership initiative and stifle creativity. They keep employees from having to discover their *own* answers, strategies, and plans, and assessing their own performance. The "Supreme CEO" turns employees into minions and automatons.

So, what can Freedom-Centered CEOs do instead? At Vineet's company, they stopped acting like the CEO had to have the answer to *every* question and instead developed a portal that enabled everyone to ask questions of each other. As I mentioned in Part I, they did everything they could to enable employees to create the most value. Peers now review each other's business ideas. Managers come up with their annual plans and post them on a company intranet for everyone to review, improving the quality, integrity, and executability of their strategies through feedback and refinement.

The result of this level of decentralization has been a massive increase to their revenue growth and share price, a greater ability to attract and retain top talent, and numerous accolades. Vineet says, "We are making progress in transforming the role of the CEO and transferring the responsibility for change to employees, as are other companies around the world. Until that day comes, we will have to get along with a CEO who is willing to admit he doesn't know very much, answers as few questions as possible, and is always asking for help—but whose company is growing and thriving."[1]

In fear-based organizations, however, power, decision-making, information, and ownership aren't decentralized—they are concentrated at the top, in the hands of the few. Fear-based organizations are characterized by hierarchy, top-down communication, longer decision-making times, inflexibility, and layers of bureaucracy.

Centralization of power can create a kind of corporate caste system that encourages a mentality of "do what you're told" subordination. This hands-on, rigid command-and-control structure reinforces paternalism rather than peer-to-peer, adult relationships. It creates a climate of positional power, rather than merit-based authority, rankism rather than leadership, and "it's not my department" excuses rather than genuine accountability. Centralization can also more easily hide fraud and corruption. Centralized organizational design has become an outdated way of organizing people in an increasingly complex, networked, and interconnected world.

I was once invited to speak at the United States Naval Academy's annual leadership conference, which gathered the top military students from every US

| FEAR-BASED ORGANIZATIONS WITHOUT DECENTRALIZATION HAVE: | FREEDOM-CENTERED ORGANIZATIONS WITH DECENTRALIZATION HAVE: |
|---|---|
| A pyramid structure | A democratic system |
| Paternalistic relationships | Adult relationships |
| Fixed leadership | Rotating leadership |
| Red tape and bureaucracy | Minimal bureaucracy |
| Power at the top | Power to the people |

military academy. The conference organizers wanted me to talk about the effectiveness of decentralized and democratically designed teams and organizations, compared to centralized command-and-control models.

As you can imagine, I was a bit nervous because I was concerned that the students might think I was about to challenge what has arguably been the US military's very effective command-and-control style of leadership. I also have great respect for our military and anyone who fights for and works to preserve freedom. So, I did my research and was pleased to learn about Michael Abrashoff, a graduate of the US Naval Academy and the captain of the USS *Benfold*, who turned around one of the worst ships in the fleet by leading it with a highly decentralized and more democratic model of leadership. He tells his story in the best-selling book *It's Your Ship: Management Techniques from the Best Damn Ship in the Navy.*

I took the stage and explained the benefits of a democratic model of leadership compared with a highly centralized system. I shared the successes of the USS *Benfold* and what it might mean for them as leaders. The students sat in stunned silence. Apparently, I had just shared an alternative view on leadership that they weren't fully aware of yet! I then opened it up to a question-and-answer session. One student stood up and asked, politely but incredulously, "Ms. Fenton, are you saying that command-and-control leadership is bad?!" I heard echoes of that question throughout the questioning period—it felt as though every student wanted to know the same thing.

Naturally, there are times when centralization is a good thing. In the heat of battle, it's not the time to question things or take a vote—a commander needs to be able to give orders from available intelligence, along with their experience and wisdom, and know that they are being carried out. However, as I explained to the students, while as leaders we may like to think that running our organizations is a life-or-death battle each day, let's be honest—it's usually not. In fear-based situations, most leaders' natural inclination is to centralize and consolidate power. More times than not, however, leaders must resist this urge. As we've been exploring, if a robust and healthy democratic system is in place, leaders should be able to achieve their goals by giving power to their people to solve the problems quickly and intelligently, because they are a trusted, educated, and informed team that is competent in solving the problems it faces.

The struggle between Decentralization and centralization has been a defining element of democracy throughout the centuries. Every Freedom-Centered Team or Organization must work out their right mix; there is no perfect ratio or formula. However, the quality of decentralized decisions is *proportional* to the education of a team's democratic citizens, which is why leaders must do their best to make sure information is accurate, factual, and contextual so that everyone can make smarter and faster decisions.

After I finished answering the students' questions, several different professors, themselves all decorated military leaders, stood up and admonished the students for their shortsighted questions and defense of the outdated and underperforming centralized model of command-and-control leadership. One professor got up and said, "You need to listen to what Ms. Fenton has to say because this is the future of our military."

In the words of the celebrated and decorated commanding general of the US Air Force Tactical Air Command, Wilbur L. Creech, "Many people believe that decentralization means loss of control. That's simply not true. You can improve control if you look at control as the control of events and *not* people. Then, the more people you have controlling events . . . the more control you have within the organization, by definition."

## THE PROMISE OF DECENTRALIZATION

Decentralization delivers on many promises that help Freedom-Centered Leaders grow their people and scale their organizations more effectively.

**Decentralization makes your organization more agile and competitive.** A decentralized organization is able to pivot and respond more quickly to changes in the market, laws, consumer tastes, and challenges compared to hierarchical, centralized companies.

**Decentralized organizations are more stable than centralized ones.** Centralized systems are overly dependent on one individual at the top calling the shots on everything. Remove them, and the entire system can collapse. Decentralized organizations have more broadly distributed leadership, making them more stable when there are leadership changes.

**Decentralized organizations develop leaders rather than blind followers.** When power is decentralized to the people of an organization, they become better communicators, more critical thinkers, more personally accountable, and more confident. Decentralization also helps develop a wiser, more team-oriented (or Ubuntu!) consciousness that allows an organization to move faster.

**Decentralized organizations are harder to corrupt.** Whereas centralized systems are easier to corrupt and manipulate, decentralized institutions resist these threats because there is no key center.

**Decentralizing means more speed and efficiency.** In fear-based organizations, all decisions must be made by the top, creating massive bottlenecks that slow everything down. In decentralized organizations, decision-making is distributed, making them more efficient with fewer people waiting to get their orders from the top.

There are two key areas where leaders need to take a close look at implementing decentralization: *decision-making* and *ownership*.

## DECENTRALIZED DECISION-MAKING

A key practice of Decentralization is democratic decision-making. As I've traveled around the world talking about organizational democracy, some leaders have asked me if this means no decision is ever made or that everything must be voted on. No, of course not! So, who makes the decisions in a team or organization and who gets the final say? And how does the decision-making process happen?

Decisions should be made by those with the most information about the situation and who will be impacted by the decision within the boundaries of an agreed-upon decision-making matrix. In a Freedom-Centered Organization, there are three major types of democratic decision-making methods:

**Majority rule:** This is usually the first thing people think of when they hear the word *democracy*, and we all know how this method works: the individual or issue that gets the majority of the votes wins. It's familiar, effective, and can provide swift results—but it also means that a single vote can carry the decision, and many of the people who voted may be unhappy with the outcome. The other two methods address this.

**Consent:** Often overlooked, this is when those in the minority of a decision give their willing consent and *do not object* to the decision of the majority,[2] pledging not to sabotage it.

**Consensus:** In this type of decision-making, everyone agrees with a decision. Now, I understand that when someone says the word *consensus*, it can conjure a groan from leaders who think that it will slow or water down the process—and, in fairness, they're partially right. In the short term, it can take longer to reach a decision. But once objections are discussed and worked through fairly, the choice can be implemented faster because everyone is behind it. And consensus-based decisions don't have to be compromises. A stronger, better option can—and often does!—emerge from this deep dialogue and listening.

Freedom-Centered Leaders and their teams need to decide what decision-making method they want to use and for what types of decisions. Some great examples of how to do this are included in the Transformational Practices section on pages 168–171.

## DECENTRALIZED OWNERSHIP

There are several models of decentralized ownership, from employee ownership to employee stock ownership plans (ESOPs) to worker cooperatives (also known as co-ops). While not all organizations are in a position to decentralize ownership due to their size or revenue, national laws, or other factors, decentralizing ownership in order to create the conditions where a team can win (or lose!) together can be highly effective. It is a powerful way to motivate employees while creating a shared sense of accountability and responsibility for the overall success of the organization. I share examples of how to do this in the Transformational Practices section on pages 171–174.

## TOOLBOX —————————————————————————

## TRANSFORMATIONAL PRACTICES IN DECENTRALIZATION

### Decision Matrix | Beginner Level

Organizations and teams need clear processes and guidelines for making smart, strategic, and non-reactionary decisions together. At a product-software-development company based in Mexico, they have a Decision Matrix that guides their decision-making process. When any member of the organization identifies a problem that needs to be solved, they call for others to join in a collective effort to resolve the issue through their "Leadership Teams." The Leadership Teams then use their Decision Matrix to define what types of problems require what types of solutions. The Decision Matrix outlines the types of decisions to be made and who should make them.

Another example for how to make democratic decisions comes from a Massachusetts-based cooperative. They have a "Governance Matrix" that breaks down key areas where decisions need to be made, such as financial, personnel, corporate organization, and operations. Under each category are the key decisions, and next to it is an index that says whether the executive director, board of directors, worker-owners, or management council is the "Decision-Maker," the "Ratifier," or if their "Input" is required, making it very clear who is responsible for which decisions and why. Their matrix also spells out where you can go if you need more input before making a decision.

Last, at the San Diego–based manufacturing company, their nine-step "Decision-Making Process" hangs on the wall in every meeting room. In their words:

1. Clarify the issue.
2. Gather the facts—don't rely on assumptions.
3. Refuse to be pressured into a decision.
4. Ask what risks are involved.

5. Get good counsel.
6. How will this decision affect those involved?
7. Try to determine the results of your decision in 5 years, 10 years, or 15 years.
8. Questions to honestly answer: Is it the right thing to do? Is it immoral, is it unethical, is my heart at peace?
9. Be wary of advice from those who don't have to deal with the consequences.

Practicing democratic decision-making doesn't need to be difficult or clunky, or take a long time, when you are clear about your decision-making criteria, who should make what decision when, and the style of decision-making you want to use. Doing this in a way that is clear, fair, and decentralized will deepen team spirit, trust, and understanding.

## Decision-Making Through a Majority Vote | Beginner Level

For the past sixty years, this Montreal-based business membership organization with over 48,000 student members in 126 countries has used a majority vote to decide who their new international president and executive team will be for the upcoming year. Through a series of votes cast throughout the organization, several candidates earn enough votes to make it to the final round. Each candidate shares their vision, strategies, and plans. After the speeches, the national presidents of all member countries cast their votes for the new, international president, elected through a majority vote. The outgoing president trains the new one, with the support of everyone in the organization. They believe that rotating their president and leadership team has made them more adaptable to changes in the marketplace and world.

## Decision-Making Through Consensus | Beginner Level

This jet engine builder based in Durham, North Carolina, makes most of its decisions using consensus. It's part of a multinational public company; this division has 370 employees. The jet engines that power Air Force One and most of the commercial airplanes that you and I fly on are made at this plant. Its work is extremely complex and detailed, and it must be done *perfectly*.

The plant has a stellar reputation for its jet engines and is superbly efficient. Operating from the basis of organizational democracy, the plant workers and just one plant manager, Chuck, follow an A-B-C decision-making process. Here's how it works.

They have three types of decisions. "A" decisions are made unilaterally by the plant manager and occur less than a dozen times a year. "B" decisions are made by the plant manager after consulting with those whom it will affect. "C" decisions are made through consensus by those who are directly involved and will be most affected.

| TYPE OF DECISION | HOW THE DECISION IS MADE |
|---|---|
| "A" Decision | Unilaterally by the plant manager. Only 10–12 decisions made this way annually. |
| "B" Decision | By the plant manager, but with input from those affected. |
| "C" Decision | Through consensus by those directly involved and affected. With consensus, the plant manager's opinion carries no more weight than anyone else. Most decisions are made by consensus. |

Consensus or "C" decisions are the most common kind of decisions at the division, so much so that they actually call it "consensing." They've been running the plant this way for nearly fifteen years, and it seems to be working very well—with positive results that impact almost everyone's lives.[3]

### Decision-Making Through Consent | Beginner Level

At this employee-owned solar energy company, most decisions were made by consensus. But once they grew to twenty employees, they switched to operating by consent. A single thumbs-down would table an issue, but employees could also abstain from voting. At thirty-five employees, the company then established a super-majority threshold of 60 percent, with questions attaining the magnitude of a possible sale requiring consent from two-thirds of the staff. Today, with 165 employees, this model continues to be their best choice for decentralized decision-making.

## Vote-o-Rama | Beginner Level

The maker of a San Francisco–based online virtual reality platform determines some of its key decisions through their decentralized voting practice called "Vote-o-Rama." Any employee can submit an idea for the business to everyone through their internal communications platform and then employees can vote on whether they think it's a good idea or not.

For example, Ramzi, the office coordinator, had an idea to make the image on the company's website homepage a membership-page link. He posted the idea on Vote-o-Rama, people thought it was a good one and voted for it, and then the company acted on it. As a result, membership sign-ups increased by 10 percent, resulting in a $3 million increase in revenues.

## Localized Leadership | Intermediate Level

It can be easy to think about how to decentralize power in smaller organizations, but what about in large, multinational, Fortune 500 organizations? In one such healthcare company, local leadership teams manage each area of the company independently and are responsible for creatively meeting and maintaining the company's strategic goals. The company has no central authority but is divided into five regional groups that make both decentralized decisions (e.g., picking their own team names and designing their own logos) and more strategic decisions at the local level. Each area's team decides how best to achieve its goals according to their local market.

### Power to the Edge | Intermediate Level

When this Wisconsin-based digital asset management company opened its first UK office, they found that the local business culture didn't fully align with their Freedom-Centered Organization's culture back in the US. Specifically, their UK colleagues were more reluctant to speak freely and directly. This reticence created fear and uncertainty for the US team working with them.

In response, they developed "Power to the Edge" (inspired by the book of the same name), creating a freedom-centered decision-making framework that calls for 80 percent of decisions to be made at the "edge" of the organization by their employees, including those from other countries where hierarchy runs strong. Power to the Edge helps the team members find a voice and make decisions independently. "This decision-making framework encourages accountability by asking decision-makers to consider who is impacted by the decision," explains their CEO, Matthew. "The process leads employees to be accountable to themselves, to their team, and to our organization."

### Freedom Franchises | Advanced Level

While most franchised companies control every element to ensure uniformity of product, this Dillon, Montana–based bakery chain eschews the cookie-cutter approach and instead has over 230 "Freedom Franchise" retail stores across the US. They only have two rules that franchisees must follow. One, franchisees must only use company-approved wheat. Two, franchisees can only build stores in areas approved by the head office. Everything else, from their menus to the look of the store, is determined by the franchisee.

### Co-CEOs | Advanced Level

Most organizations have one CEO, but what if you could have two? A nonprofit educational institute in Tel Aviv, Israel, did just that. They began by creating a process for a CEO selection. A committee of employees and managers discussed and planned the participatory model, in which a representative team of employees and managers elect the institute's CEOs. Employee representatives were voted in by the employee assembly, and a team of six launched a professional and transparent selection process. In the end, they decided on a co-CEO model with the position filled by both a man and a woman in order to decentralize power and recognize different perspectives.

### Democratic Ownership Through ESOPs, Co-ops, and Shared Ownership | Advanced Level

Traditionally, for-profit companies are owned by one person or a small group. If they are public, shareholders are the owners. But many Freedom-Centered Organizations have decentralized, democratic ownership, where the employees themselves own the company.

At a solar energy company in Colorado, in order to encourage team members to think and plan long-term, they established a restricted employee stock ownership plan (ESOP), allowing everyone to buy stock from their first day of employment, effectively becoming co-owners. Having employees actually buy the stock, instead of offering stock options or gift stocks, ensures team members take greater ownership in the company. According to CEO and cofounder Blake "We want to share all aspects of ownership, a true *experience* of ownership, not just the rewards, the profits, and the good stuff. We also want to share the risks and the responsibility, and we think that is only possible when people are putting money on the line."

Another decentralized ownership model, a co-op, is used at a Massachusetts-based fair trade company. Each of the 150 worker-owners has an equal stake in the company and an equal vote—regardless of their position or title.

After one year of service, all employees are eligible to become owners in the cooperative. At that time, they each buy one and only one share of Class A voting stock. Regardless of their rank or seniority, they will always have *only* one vote in matters presented to the body of worker-owners.

The company's board vice chair, Rodney, explains, "Some may ask us why we've brought democracy into the workplace. To them we ask, 'Why have you kept it out?' Democracy, wherever it can take hold, does not need to be rationalized. As proclaimed in the Declaration of Independence, *these rights are*

*'self-evident.'* Ultimately, we think democracy is important *inside* the workplace largely for the same reasons Americans cherish democracy *outside* the workplace."

Democratic ownership isn't just limited to companies—it can be applied to sports franchises, too. While most soccer clubs are privately owned, one in Lewes, England, has taken a different approach to ownership—anyone can buy a share! They now have nine hundred owners worldwide who all own a part of the team—a maximum of one share each. The rights and opportunities afforded to each owner are outlined in the club's constitution, which also details the guiding principles of the club and how it should operate.

SCALE

# PRINCIPLE 7

---

# Individual and Collective

*An individual has not started living until he can
rise above the narrow confines of his individualistic
concerns to the broader concerns of all humanity.*
–MARTIN LUTHER KING JR.–

ven at the most exemplary WorldBlu certified Freedom-Centered Organizations, one fear can be difficult to overcome: the fear of change. I've seen
the worried looks in the eyes of employees around the world. They tell me
they love their freedom, their company, and their Freedom-Centered CEO,
but they wonder: What will happen when their CEO leaves, retires, or sells the
business? What will happen when a new CEO takes over, or a new investor or
board member joins the firm? Will that new leader also value the principles of
freedom and organizational democracy on which the company is built? Or will
they change their Freedom-Centered Design and revert to a more dictatorial
command-and-control structure?

It is not difficult to imagine this scenario. In fact, I've seen it. Many Freedom-Centered CEOs have built visionary, democratic companies only to have all of their hard work destroyed by investors, shareholders, or boards of directors who wonder when the CEO will "grow up" and run the company "like an adult"—meaning, like a dictator. (More on how not to accidentally destroy your Freedom-Centered Organization on page 225.)

I recall the CEO of a widely admired, multibillion-dollar WorldBlu certified Freedom-Centered Organization explaining how he *had* to sell his business to a huge multinational company to get his investors, who didn't understand Freedom at Work, off his back so he could run it in a democratic way. He had a good relationship with the purchasing company's CEO, who promised him he could retain the business's democratic design. That sadly changed, however, and the Freedom-Centered CEO was eventually pushed out of his own organization. Then the top leadership team that built their culture was removed while the new owners rapidly dismantled their democratic culture—despite all its success. Now, the company culture is just a shell of what it used to be.

Many of the companies we've certified that have needed a cash infusion to grow have had to sacrifice their democratic culture for shortsighted, uninspired, or even greedy investors who lacked an enlightened view of how to build and maintain a high-performing organization. As a result, they had to redesign the company using a more traditional, hierarchical model while the employees who stayed on wrestled with the sorrow of relinquishing something that was once truly great.

When I first began this work, I had not thought much about turnover, merger, or acquisition issues once a Freedom-Centered CEO left or sold their company. Then I met Rodney, who helped me see things much differently.

First, a quick aside on civics. In the United States, we have a Constitution and Bill of Rights, which are considered the guiding documents and laws of our nation. These documents outline our democratic leadership, governance structures, and foundational rights, and inform and guide subsequent laws. The *principles* they enshrine—rather than a *person*—are what govern us. They are supreme and cannot be overthrown or abolished by a change in leadership of our country. The leaders of our nation, our military, and millions of civil servants all take a solemn oath to uphold not what a *president* might want, but what our *Constitution* guarantees for our nation. This is how we ensure that our citizens' rights cannot be overthrown or taken away at the whim of a political, corporate, social, or religious leader.

But what about our organizations? Wouldn't it also be important for everyone within a Freedom-Centered Organization to *also* have their democratic "rights" guaranteed? And if not, *why* not?

Here's where Rodney's company comes in. He was the vice chair of the board of directors of a WorldBlu certified co-op. He explained to me that around 2005, the eighty-five worker-owners of their co-op agreed that it was imperative to clearly identify the rights they already had within the company, but that were scattered (almost hidden!) within their bylaws—as is true at many cooperatives. Further, they needed to identify any cherished rights that lived as strong traditions, but had never been codified in writing. They carefully reviewed their legal documents, history, and customs. Then they asked, "What other rights might we need to *sustain* our democratic practices?" and "What is *required* of every worker-owner?"

The result was a new "Rights and Responsibilities" document, which, when combined with the co-op's bylaws, functions somewhat like the US Bill of Rights when paired with the Constitution. Together the two documents make it clear that they have democratic systems, processes, and practices in place, so that if a new CEO or manager is hired, the employees' rights and opportunities cannot be diminished or taken away without their agreement.

For example, this document includes the right to financial participation in the form of a portion of the cooperative's profits; the right to free speech; the right to educational opportunities; and the right to vote on issues such as new co-op members, board candidates, and whether they should add, delete, or amend a bylaw. They also have the right to run for office within the organization and the right to access accurate information, such as company financial information; any strategic plans; all staff, board, and worker-owner meeting minutes; and all of their governance documents.

These rights, coupled with the bylaws and other foundational documents, give the worker-owners of this now $80 million company assurance that the democratic organization they have built cannot be overthrown by a newly arrived fear-based leader. Just imagine how this reduces fear in the organization and creates a sense of stability, deep trust, and an Ubuntu spirit. These Constitution-like legal documents encapsulate the balance of the individual's needs and rights with the collective goals of the organization, which is what makes it such a robust and thriving model of organizational democracy.[1]

## WHAT IS THE INDIVIDUAL AND COLLECTIVE?

The Individual and the Collective are at work when the rights of both are valued and respected. This principle wisely balances an individual's rights, needs, and responsibilities with the organization's rights, needs, and responsibilities.

---

**The Individual and the Collective are at work when
the rights of both are valued and respected.**

---

This principle gets at the heart of what makes a democratic system uniquely *democratic.* If your organization is designed too heavily to value the group over the people in it, then individuals feel silenced, overlooked, undervalued, and unacknowledged. It is imperative that each person's unique individuality not be sacrificed to conform to the collective. Conversely, if your organizational design promotes too much autonomy without an awareness of team needs and how the individual is vital to achieving collective goals, then you don't have a *team*—you just have a group of individuals. While it can be tricky, to guarantee a solid, high-performing team, there has to be a *mutual* respect for an individual's rights, voice, and expression balanced with the collective's goals and needs.

Mike, the CEO of the Dillon, Montana–based bakery chain with over 230 "Freedom Franchise" retail stores across the US, explains their practice of the Individual and Collective like this: "What we did was grow as a company centered on the power of the individual over the structure of the organization." In short, individuals must feel empowered while keeping the collective goals in focus, but the collective cannot dominate over the individual.

The Individual and Collective also provide a powerful linking element within the democratic system so that people don't feel undervalued or under-recognized because leaders are constantly explaining how individual contributions help advance the growth of the organization. When individuals understand how they contribute to the whole while still feeling valued for their unique contributions, this makes them want to give even more. This is why having both individual and collective forms of recognition are vital. "We want everybody to see how their individual role fits into the larger big picture and strategy," explains Blake, the CEO of a Boulder, Colorado–based, employee-owned solar electric company. "By knowing that, they will be able to do their individual jobs better because they know how they fit in."

This is a Scale principle because if you do not consciously and intentionally balance the needs of *both* parties in your organization as you grow, your systems and processes may get off-kilter, employees may grow resentful, and the atmosphere may become toxic. In fear-based organizations, either the individual or the collective gets overemphasized, making the system shaky. With too much focus on the individual, the team becomes overly competitive and myopic, which can have unintended consequences on performance and engagement. Too much emphasis on the collective, and this can slow down decision-making, demotivate people, and leave them feeling unseen or unvalued for their unique contributions. In our research and work with hundreds of companies around the world across various industries, we've found that employees generally feel their organizations are too focused on the goals of the collective and do not give enough emphasis to their individual efforts, rights, expression, and needs. While it is critical to have team spirit, not recognizing the unique role and rights of an individual can undermine collective goals and cause employees to disengage. It can also force individuals to involuntarily conform or act like they agree with a point of view held by company leadership out of fear of losing their job. Too much emphasis on the collective can also make people afraid of being their true self at work, engender conformity, and pressure employees to self-censor, silencing valuable insights and perspectives that are vital to a healthy democratic system.

| FEAR-BASED ORGANIZATIONS WITHOUT THE INDIVIDUAL AND COLLECTIVE BELIEVE: | FREEDOM-CENTERED ORGANIZATIONS WITH THE INDIVIDUAL AND COLLECTIVE BELIEVE: |
| --- | --- |
| Cutthroat wins | Competitiveness wins |
| Individual rights don't matter | Individual rights are respected |
| A me-first attitude wins | An Ubuntu team spirit wins |
| Employees are cogs in the machine | Individuals are unique assets |
| Conformity is required | Free expression leads to better ideas |

The Individual and Collective principle is what makes an organizational system uniquely *democratic*, valuing both the individual and the team so that everyone can win. It is about a team of individuals who work in harmony toward a shared goal.

## THE PROMISE OF THE INDIVIDUAL AND THE COLLECTIVE

The principle of valuing the Individual and Collective delivers big benefits to teams and organizations in the following ways.

**The Individual and Collective lead to more genuine teamwork.** With everyone understanding how their individual performance and collective goals work together, Freedom-Centered Organizations have a spirit of teamwork, which can help a company grow faster, weather business storms without too much emotional fallout, and outperform their competitors.

**The Individual and Collective mean less waste and internal theft.** Since everyone understands how their positive or negative actions can impact achieving collective goals that could impact individual benefits, such as profit-sharing or bonuses, they make smarter decisions. This helps lower waste and internal theft in the form of time, resources, and emotional energy.

**The Individual and Collective increase innovation.** In Freedom-Centered Organizations, there is a constructive space for authentic self-expression rather than censorship, which leads to more ideas being freely explored, boosting innovation and growth.

**The Individual and Collective attract top talent.** As individuals are accepted for their unique contributions to the whole, they naturally feel more joyful at work. Happy, engaged employees stay and attract other upbeat performers as well, making a Freedom-Centered Organization a top-talent magnet.

## HOW TO SUCCESSFULLY IMPLEMENT THE INDIVIDUAL AND COLLECTIVE IN YOUR ORGANIZATION

Remember these three key things when implementing the Individual and Collective democratic principle in your organization:

1. **Keep it in balance.** Make sure you give both principles equal weight, and avoid compromising individual rights for the whole.
2. **Link the two.** Leaders must communicate how important it is for individuals to achieve their goals so that the collective can succeed. When possible, break down the specific, measurable details of how

individual successes (or failures) impact the collective performance and vice versa so everyone understands. Even in huge companies, individuals should not feel like their personal actions do not matter, and they should understand *how* they do.

3. **Communicate constantly.** Communicate through multiple channels on a regular and consistent basis about the relationship between individual and collective rights, performance, contribution, failure, and success.

# TOOLBOX

## TRANSFORMATIONAL PRACTICES IN INDIVIDUAL AND COLLECTIVE

### Intersecting Purposes and Goals | Beginner Level

In fear-based organizations, there is no connection between an individual's sense of purpose for their life and the collective goals of the organization in which they work. However, at a forward-thinking, nonprofit primary school in Haiti, staff are encouraged to use a format that helps them gain clarity about their personal sense of purpose, life goals, objectives, and values. They are then encouraged to imagine where they see the purpose of the school intersecting with their own sense of purpose and life goals, so they can see the mutual opportunities and synergies together.

For example, a number of teachers felt called to train other teachers. This outreach supported the school's goal of creating a teacher-training program, so they were able to work together to unite the individual sense of purpose with the collective goals of the organization to create a new and meaningful program.

### Shout-Outs | Beginner Level

What would the practice of Individual and Collective be without individual and collective recognition? At this Fort Collins, Colorado–based software company with five hundred employees, they make sure everyone understands their individual worth. To do this, their Freedom-Centered CEO reminds them each Friday during their all-hands meetings, during which both individuals *and* teams are recognized for their contributions through peer shout-outs and awards for hitting key milestones.

### Individual Goals, Collective Achievements | Beginner Level

In fear-based organizations, goals and objectives are often set by top managers and passed down the chain of command, with little input from the individuals responsible for achieving the goals. However, this small New Zealand company takes a different approach. It holds quarterly planning sessions where the team creates their quarterly goals together. They also craft the rewards and celebrations they will have if they meet their goals. To keep them inspired and on track, they have created posters for each team member that ask, "What have I done to contribute to the culture of our company?"

### Whole-Picture Scoreboard | Intermediate Level

Sometimes it's difficult for each team member to know where they stand if they don't clearly see how their own contributions impact the entire organization. That's why this web hosting company with 230 employees instituted a "Whole-Picture Scoreboard" that tracks the performance of customer support techs, allowing each person to measure individual daily progress, as well as the progress of small teams and the entire group, as they work toward collective goals.

The Whole-Picture Scoreboard is a visual reminder of individual and group effort, not a tool for penalizing those who fall short of reaching a goal. Seeing how they fit into the bigger picture helps team members appreciate the importance of their own role and gives them insight into where they might help others as well.

### Value Portal | Intermediate Level

This multinational IT company had a problem. They realized that thousands of their employees throughout the organization were creating incredible value for their customers, but they were not adequately documenting these individual initiatives and solutions. This meant that the company was not able to leverage these best practices as much as they would like. Additionally, leadership believed there were thousands more employees who *could* create value for customers—and wanted to do so—but had no established channel or process that enabled them to generate and contribute ideas.

They solved the problem by linking the Individual and Collective through their "Value Portal," a company-wide initiative designed to encourage, facilitate, manage, and document customer-focused innovations. They formed a group of company officers, whose members represented all vertical and horizontal business units, to guide and support the process. Everyone participated voluntarily, collaborating with each other in small teams to develop new ideas and solutions, attending periodic ideation workshops and innovation labs along the way. The officer team refined and developed promising ideas and then shared them with customers for their input and acceptance. If a customer accepted the idea, the company would implement it.

Since the group's launch, employees have generated more than five hundred ideas for the Value Portal, with millions of dollars' worth of new ideas being implemented. It has not only generated significant new opportunities for the business; it also has produced important, patentable intellectual property.

### Career Plans | Intermediate Level

Fear-based organizations don't care about their employees' life goals or how they want to advance in their career. But this company, based in Mexico, has a transformational practice called "Career Plan," where a coach supports each employee by designing a two-year plan that strikes a balance between what they wish to achieve individually and collectively at work by creating a connection between the two.

### Show and Tell | Intermediate Level

How about a fun way to show the connections between individual and collective contributions in an Agile "Show and Tell" session? That's what they do at an Ann Arbor, Michigan–based company that does software development.

Pairs of programmers map out how much time they think a task will take, so everyone knows what is coming and when. All of their tasks are broken down into small pieces and put on "story cards." These handwritten cards identify each programming pair's unique contribution toward achieving the collective goals for the week. Then, at the end of the week, team members engage in a Show and Tell session, with clients reviewing the work that has been completed. This provides collective recognition while honoring the unique contributions of each individual pair.

### Dream Balls | Advanced Level

Often, individuals feel like they have to check their dreams at the office door. But at this digital marketing agency in Brighton, England, with thirty employees, they honor individual aspirations with Dream Balls. At the start of the year, each person writes their unique dream for that year on a piece of paper and puts it inside an old-fashioned bubblegum dispenser—what they call their "dream machine."

Each month that they collectively reach their company goals, one Dream Ball is randomly selected, and the company pays to make that individual's dream come true. They've funded dreams such as skydiving, swimming with dolphins, driving the Pacific Coast Highway, and cycling across Africa. By recognizing that people have both personal and professional aspirations, and connecting them, they have been able to bring an even clearer sense of purpose to the organization and the people within it. As a result, they achieved a voluntary turnover rate of less than 5 percent, have a list of prospective clients waiting to work with them, and have doubled their revenue.

## An Organizational Constitution | Advanced Level

We normally think of countries as having some form of a constitution, so why not organizations as well? The award-winning Massachusetts-based co-op introduced earlier has several guiding documents that act like an organizational constitution, guaranteeing the rights and responsibilities of all their worker-owners, regardless of who is their top leader or on their board of directors. Guiding documents such as these, which cannot legally be changed without a worker-owner vote, even when there is a top leadership or ownership change, bring stability to their democratic design as well as peace of mind to everyone within their organization.

## It Takes a Team to Raise a Child | Advanced Level

One of the most challenging things for companies is keeping parents in the workforce when they have a baby, if they choose to stay employed. Few companies, especially small businesses, can afford to offer childcare services, which often means that parents (and usually women) leave the workforce to care for their children.

However, a sixty-person Michigan-based software company took a radically different approach. When one of their star performers told the CEO that she couldn't afford childcare and thought she would have to quit her job, his reply was, "Just bring your baby to work!" Startled but pleased, she did, and the company culture was forever changed.

"One of the first things we learned is that the team helps raise the child," explains their CEO, Rich. "At any given point you could look out across the room and see a team member holding the baby, obviously with the permission of the parent. The baby is raised by the 'village,' so when the baby does cry, the parent doesn't have to go to the child. We all help."[2]

Children can sleep in their swing, or, again with the parent's permission, they are passed around to anyone in their small, open-office environment who wants to hold them—a product of the trust generated by their Freedom-Centered Culture. If the child cries or needs their diaper changed, the parent takes care of it in a parent's room. Their CEO acknowledges that this won't work for every company or industry, but it does for them, integrating individual needs supported by the collective. Parents save on daycare costs and they don't have to suffer with separation anxiety or worry.

And what do their clients think? They've found that it makes them more "human" and even "cool."

# SUSTAIN

On-the-job democracy isn't just a lofty concept but a better, more profitable way to do things. We all demand democracy in every other aspect of our lives and culture. People are considered adults in their private lives, at the bank, at their children's schools, with family and among friends—so why are they suddenly treated like adolescents at work? Why can't workers be involved in choosing their own leaders? Why shouldn't they manage themselves? Why can't they speak up—challenge, question, share information openly?

—Ricardo Semler—

# PRINCIPLE 8

## Choice

*The greatest power that a person possesses
is the power to choose.*
–J. MARTINE KOHE–

**"W**hat if somebody comes to you and says, 'I love my job, I love the people I work with, and I'm even happy with what I'm being paid, but I
can't stand my manager'?" asked Henry, the CEO of a twenty-person,
London-based, WorldBlu certified IT training and consulting company.

Horrible bosses—we've all had them, and we know what they can do. A
bad boss or manager can devastate a company's morale, performance, organizational tone, and the well-being of its employees. Bad bosses can spike absenteeism and kill engagement. A whopping 75 percent of people voluntarily leave
their jobs because of a bad boss.[1]

Bad bosses or managers negate any investment a company makes toward
improving its performance or culture. Perks, rewards, a cushy workplace

environment, ongoing training—are all canceled out by a rotten boss. These bad managers not only harm organizational performance, but also employees' lives outside of work. How many clients have I worked with whose inept and demoralizing manager sends them home from work each day completely stressed out and exhausted? Just imagine the impact on their marriage, the way they parent their children, and their overall health and well-being. The effect fear-based managers have on a team, company, and an employee's personal life can border on immoral.

In their *Harvard Business Review* article "How Damaging Is a Bad Boss, Exactly?" Jack Zenger and Joseph Folkman studied the relationship between overall leadership effectiveness and employee satisfaction, engagement, and commitment with 2,865 leaders in a large financial services company. They found a direct-line correlation between the effectiveness of the manager or leader and how engaged the employees on their team were as a whole. Leaders in the lowest percentile for effectiveness had only 4 percent engagement, while those leaders in the ninetieth percentile had 92 percent engagement. They found that these results were consistent across the US, UK, India, the Netherlands, Spain, and the United Arab Emirates in a variety of industries ranging from 250 to 250,000 employees.[2]

So, what's to be done? Well, at Henry's company, they ask each employee an unconventional question: "Who do *you* want to be your manager?" Whoever *they* select becomes their manager—and they can change their manager at any time. They recognize that some people are not at their best managing others, so rather than promoting people to managerial roles where they won't excel, they give people the option of not being a manager at all. And if they have someone who is not picked to be a manager, no problem. They simply have them do something else. As a result, they have been able to significantly reduce—if not eliminate—absenteeism and resignations caused by poor manager–employee relationships.

Henry explains it like this: "We just celebrated our thirtieth anniversary and, for the last twenty-five years, we have based how we work on democratic principles. People work best when they are doing something they are good at and have the freedom and trust to do it to the best of their ability. We know that creating happy workplaces, based on mastery and autonomy and coupled with a clear purpose, lead to more productive and innovative environments—and to greater profitability.

"Imagine a workplace where people are energized and motivated by being in control of the work they do. Imagine they are trusted and given freedom, within clear guidelines, to decide how to achieve their results. Imagine they are able to get the life balance they want. Imagine they are valued according to the work that they do, rather than the number of hours they spend at their desk. Wouldn't you want to work there? That is the environment we seek to create.

"One crucial element is the role of the manager. We believe that their role is to coach rather than tell. We know that the manager can make a huge difference to people's well-being and to their performance, so we let people choose their own manager. That simple step has the potential to improve motivation, improve wellbeing, improve productivity, and reduce turnover."

## WHAT IS CHOICE?

Choice is at work when each individual chooses between different possibilities. Freedom-Centered Organizations recognize that when employees have the opportunity to make meaningful choices about their workplace, they feel greater empowerment, autonomy, and control, which translates to more engagement and productivity. Choice is a democratic principle, and one of the four key drivers of democracy, because without it, there is no freedom.

To make a choice, you need more than one option. And to have freedom, you must have meaningful choice. Choice is vital to self-government and free thought.

---

**Choice is at work when each individual chooses between different possibilities.**

---

Choice is in the Sustain phase of building a Freedom-Centered Team or Organization because you cannot sustain organizational democracy without consistently giving employees a choice on critical issues. Choice is also one of the four main drivers of a democratic system, so when the opportunities to make meaningful choices are increased within an organization, it enhances the level of democracy.

For example, at Henry's IT training company, rather than employees feeling forced to work on projects that don't interest them, in addition to choosing their own manager, they are free to choose the projects and tasks they actually *want* to work on. The rule is, if you don't want to work on something, you don't have to.

This is also the policy at a Copenhagen-based, WorldBlu certified Freedom-Centered training company that specializes in happiness in the workplace. There, employees are free to pick the projects they want to work on as well, with the rule that no one is allowed to assign anyone else to a project or task that they have not specifically chosen for themselves. It is these meaningful choices that give employees a greater sense of ownership, and therefore motivation, about their work.

| FEAR-BASED ORGANIZATIONS WITHOUT CHOICE BELIEVE: | FREEDOM-CENTERED ORGANIZATIONS WITH CHOICE BELIEVE: |
| --- | --- |
| Management should make the choices for employees | Employees should make the choices that impact their work |
| Employees can be controlled through an absence of choices | Employee success can be optimized through meaningful choices |
| Choice creates a paperwork nightmare | Choice leads to smarter and happier employees |
| One size fits all | Not all sizes fit everyone |
| An employee's only "power" is to do what they are told | An employee's greatest power is their power to choose |

In fear-based organizations, however, there is little meaningful choice. Such organizations may lock an employee into a never-ending relationship with a horrible boss. They give employees no choice regarding the hours they work or their schedules, what and how they're paid, what benefits may work best for them, or who they want to work with each day. This lack of choice creates a culture of fear-based dependents rather than respectful critical thinkers. Employees are afraid to question the rules, policies, systems, or processes. Without the democratic principle of Choice at work in an organization, a corrosiveness can take over, slowly dumbing employees down because they feel powerless and disengaged. They stop thinking for themselves and just do what they are told because initiative and creative thinking are viewed with skepticism and doubt. Without meaningful choices, employees are unable to self-determine and can feel infantilized, disempowered, and angry.

## THE PROMISE OF CHOICE

The democratic principle of Choice delivers several major promises to our organizations and teams.

**Choice gives us freedom.** Without meaningful choices, we are literally locked into one way of doing things, unable to consider and decide between other options and possibilities.

**Choice gives us power.** Without real choices, we aren't empowered to choose our own paths. We all know what it feels like when someone tells us what we have to do, without giving us any say in the matter. When you remove the option of choice from an individual's life, they can feel backed into a corner, without a voice. It can trigger anger, conflict, and violence. Having meaningful choices, however, helps us regain a sense of power and perspective.

**Choice cultivates self-knowledge.** If you never have to make a choice, you never have to figure out your tastes, dreams, goals, or likes and dislikes. You simply do what you are told. Giving employees meaningful choices cultivates a corporate citizenry of people who know themselves and can effectively self-govern.

When there are meaningful choices in the workplace, employees are happier, feel valued and treated fairly, and are more engaged. This translates to lower turnover, an ability to attract top talent, and greater loyalty.

## THE SUCCESSFUL IMPLEMENTATION OF CHOICE

When it comes to designing and implementing the democratic principle of Choice in your team, there are a few key things to remember.

First, reflect upon these two key questions:

1. **Is this a practice where, if meaningful choices were added, it would create more *value* for our team?** For example, most people just assume they have to be assigned a manager, but what if you let people *choose* their own manager? You've added meaningful choice to a conventional practice, which will have a profound and positive ripple effect throughout the organization. Become more aware of how you can intentionally build meaningful choices into common systems and processes, such as letting employees choose their own work schedule, projects, or teammates.

2. **Who, *really*, should be making this choice?** The decision should always be made by those most impacted by it. Again, rather than a boss assigning a manager to an employee, the employee should be given the choice.

Then, remember that the power of Choice lies in offering *meaningful* choices. Letting employees choose what they want to eat at the Friday office party is a nice idea, but not as potentially meaningful as letting them choose their own manager.

Last, the option of making choices should not just happen at the top of an organization—Choice must be democratized and decentralized throughout.

## TOOLBOX

### TRANSFORMATIONAL PRACTICES IN CHOICE

#### FlexTime | Beginner Level

One of the most helpful things for most employees is having a schedule that can flex with their personal and professional needs. A small, full-service digital marketing company in North Carolina found a way to give its employees a choice with their schedule through a practice they call "FlexTime." Employees are all free to create the schedules that fit their lifestyles, whether it's working from home one day a week, working late (if they're night owls), or coming into the office regularly, nine to five. They can also take sick days, vacations, and time off to see their children's school plays as needed. By giving their employees a choice in creating their own schedules, they eliminate the inevitable tensions that arise when balancing busy personal and professional lives.

#### Funky Fridays | Beginner Level

Every other Friday, the fifty-person product development team at this large, UK-based social intelligence company gets to choose a project they want to work on and with whom they want to work, in a transformational practice called "Funky Fridays." The goal is to use the time to come up with new ideas and innovations.

It all starts with an 8:30 AM all-hands meeting, which can best be described as an internal dating game as everyone decides with whom and what they are going to work on; then they go away and do so. Sometimes they research new areas of interest or emerging technologies, sometimes they work on a personal project, or they brainstorm how they can improve products not yet on their strategic road map.

Then, at the end of the day, everyone gets together, both locally and via video conference, and has a show-and-tell about their projects. This always includes clapping and laughter—and sometimes beer. The best ideas are voted upon and moved over to their formal product development road map. About twenty "Funky Friday" projects have made it into production in one year alone.

### Choose Your Own Job Title | Beginner Level

Have you ever had a job title that didn't fully recognize or honor the work that you did, making you feel undervalued and unnoticed? To avoid their employees feeling this way, this small digital marketing company in Asheville gives everyone the option to choose their own job title—and to amend or change it as often as they want.

### Choose Your Team | Intermediate Level

A leading web hosting and cloud services provider in California recently had to go through a reorganization, shifting from a competency structure to a product-based structure. Leaders recognized that just assigning people to new products and teams without their input could create a lot of anger and resentment. Their solution? Give employees the opportunity to choose their favorite product to work on, which meant, in a product-based structure, they also got to choose which team they wanted to join. The result was increased efficiency and performance.

### Choose What You Say | Intermediate Level

Customer service reps at this multibillion-dollar Las Vegas–based online retailer are given the rare choice of saying what they want to say and doing what they need to do for customers, without direction from a script, strict rules, or time limits. Reps may chat for hours with customers if they need to, write thank-you notes, send flowers, and even direct shoppers to a competitor if an item is out of stock. By giving their well-trained employees a choice in what they say, the company is able to connect on a more authentic and genuine level with customers, which increases customer loyalty and satisfaction. One result: during a recent tough economic climate, sales were up by double digits.

### Choose Your Own Career Path | Intermediate Level

Tired of feeling like their employees were locked into one job description that might not always fit their individual purpose or grow with them, this Mexico-based product-software development company instead gives their 250 employees a choice in their career path. New employees may receive a starting job description, but that doesn't mean they can't explore other interests and activities. The principle of Choice is put into practice through project exchanges, mentoring, work-sharing, and employee discussions, where they can learn about different roles and opportunities and then decide how they want to develop their careers. By doing all it can to help employees find their right roles, the company ensures that all individuals are happy, engaged, and working at their best.

### Choose Your Own Manager | Advanced Level

Amid increasing absenteeism and turnover due to poor relations between employees and their managers, the small IT training company in the UK that I described earlier decided to let people choose their own managers. To recap how they did it: they simply asked each employee, "Who do *you* want to be your manager?" and whoever they selected became their manager. They were also given the choice of changing their manager at any time. As a result, they have significantly reduced absenteeism and resignations caused by avoidable employee–manager strife.

### Project Incubator | Advanced Level

Modeled after the hit TV show *Shark Tank*, "Project Incubator" is an annual opportunity for teammates at this Los Angeles–based web hosting and cloud services company to propose an idea they want to develop. This could be a new product to help internal processes, or to take to market. Once a proposal is approved, teammates stop working on their regular projects for two months. Then they present their Project Incubator project to the company at their all-hands meeting. Each product or idea is taken through a critique process, and then the leadership team decides which ones to bring to life the following year.

Likewise, a Las Vegas–based online retailer created a practice where employees with product ideas (often gleaned as a result of talking with customers) can choose to prototype their idea and bring it to a group of colleagues, who then choose which to put into action. Selected ideas are given the financial and intellectual support to bring it to fruition. As a result, the company has created new ideas around adaptive footwear and clothing, among other areas, through this intrapreneurship approach.

### Challenge by Choice | Advanced Level

This private Colorado-based high school takes a democratic approach to education—including giving their students the choice of being challenged to grow. Their philosophy is that when students are *required* to do things, they are less likely to fully engage and reap the benefits of their educational experience. Instead, students are *not* required to do anything. While that might sound radical, the students understand that in order to graduate, they must accomplish their own goals and make the investment in *themselves*.

The founder of the school, Bobby, explains their reasoning for the approach like this: "Students are much more invested in their own education when they know that, rather than school being done *to* them, they have a genuine voice and choice in shaping their own experience. Students then take responsibility for their academic program and community and ensure that it is helping them be prepared for life."

## Choose Your Own Salary | Advanced Level

Many employees feel that they are not fairly compensated for the work they do. So, what if you could choose your own salary? This small UK-based social business consultancy created a group called "the Money Gang," composed of mostly elected team members (not the CEO or CFO), to assess and approve all salary decisions fairly and consistently. Employees work up their own proposals of what they think their salary should be and present it to the Money Gang. The gang then determines if the salary proposed is fair and in line with market rates as well as affordable for their organization. If it is, then it is approved.

# PRINCIPLE 9

# Fairness and Dignity

*Let not a man guard his dignity,*
*but let his dignity guard him.*
—Ralph Waldo Emerson—

My first job out of college awakened me to the need for Freedom at Work. I'd accepted a position as an advertising account executive for a local newspaper owned by a Fortune 500 company. Although I considered the job of selling ads to be far from ideal, I was still excited to be a part of a large company, where I could learn and begin making my way in the world.

However, my dreams of success were shattered when they hit reality that first day on the job. Day one was a complete culture shock. I entered the office building as a confident, bright-eyed, twenty-two-year-old college graduate who had successfully held various leadership positions throughout my school years. But by five o'clock, I left it demoralized and deflated, feeling more like a child than an empowered employee.

My first few days were spent being told what I could and could not do, how I was to behave, who was important in the organization—and who was not. I was told what my sales goals would be and how I was to accomplish those goals. Any questions I had were either shrugged off or ignored. I was assigned to a cubicle with minimal resources needed to do my job. I was not trained; instead, I was told to just "get out there and figure it out as you go." By the end of the first week I had never felt so dehumanized in all my life. I remember thinking, *If this is what I'm supposed to expect from work for the next forty years, I quit!* My passion toward service and demonstrating leadership within the company was almost extinguished.

As time went on, my attitude toward my job and the company grew worse. I witnessed the manner in which decisions were made, without input from those who did the job or would be affected by it. Experienced salespeople who knew their territories and performed well were never consulted when their sales targets were set. I quickly learned that my job was not to protest against management and its policies but to figure out how to work around them if I was to succeed. And although I was hitting all my sales goals, my work was far from meaningful.

Conversations with coworkers rarely deviated from plotting our escape strategies. I soon adopted a survive-rather-than-thrive mentality and did the minimal amount required to get the job done. I wasn't alone—it's what everyone else had learned to do as well.

Finally, I reached a point where I realized I had more self-respect than to allow myself to be treated as just another cog in the machine of corporate America. Although I had no other job prospects, I reasoned that having *no* job was better than having *this* job. Almost four months to the day, I resigned. When I handed my boss my resignation letter, he looked at me and said, "Traci, when I hired you, I knew you wouldn't last more than six months. You're too smart to let yourself be treated this way." Those were the kindest words he'd ever spoken to me.

Versions of this scenario happen around the world in millions of organizations each day. People begin working somewhere, only to quickly discover that no one is interested in hearing their ideas. They begin to feel demoralized and become disenfranchised. They don't feel treated as a human being with respect—they are simply a means to an end. No one is interested in what their purpose might be for their life and how it might be actualized within the organization. They're expected to be 100 percent committed, show up on time, and give it their all, often at the expense of their dignity and personal freedoms. Employees soon learn that they are there to serve the company—with little reward beyond a paycheck in return.

Yet at the core of democracy is the fact that each one of us matters, that each one of us has inherent worth. And in order to practice Freedom at Work, Freedom-Centered Leaders *must* believe in the inherent worth of each individual or they simply cannot uphold organizational democracy.

## WHAT ARE FAIRNESS AND DIGNITY?

Fairness and Dignity are at work when each individual is treated justly and impartially and is recognized for their inherent worth. Fairness is about understanding that we are all equal and all deserve to be treated as such in our organizations, regardless of our title or position, age, gender, race, or other attributes. Fairness does *not* mean sameness—we can't always be treated the same way, as circumstances can vary—but we *do* all deserve to be treated justly. And Dignity is when we acknowledge and treat each individual as having inherent worth. You simply cannot have a commitment to freedom if you don't believe that we all deserve to be treated with respect.

This principle acknowledges each individual's inherent worth, and therefore their inherent right to be seen and heard. When we practice Fairness and Dignity, we are building human worth into the organizational system. And real democracy is based on this fact—that we *all* have value.

---

**Fairness and Dignity are at work when each individual is treated justly and impartially and is recognized for their inherent worth.**

---

This principle is in the Sustain phase because you cannot sustain a Freedom-Centered Organization if you don't intentionally bake into its operating system practices that reinforce fairness and the worth of each individual. Without Fairness and Dignity, the entire sustainability of a democratic system is undermined.

I like to think of the democratic principle of Fairness and Dignity as the "I See You" principle. A CEO I know often signs his email to people with the phrase "I see you." It makes each individual feel special and important. They are not an anonymous cog in a machine or just another email to answer. And that's what this principle brings to building a Freedom-Centered Team: the acknowledgment that we all have value.

However, in fear-based organizations, there is little Fairness and Dignity. Fear-based leaders don't believe in their own inherent sense of worth, let alone that of their employees or colleagues. Instead, you have to earn (or prove!) your worth through your title, how much money you make, how many people you manage, or any number of things. In these organizations, you have to earn the right to be seen and respected.

Dr. Robert Fuller, former president of Oberlin College and author of numerous books on dignity, describes this phenomenon by saying that many workplaces treat people like either "somebodies" or "nobodies." In these companies, if you're a "somebody"—usually because of your positional title or how much material wealth you've accumulated—*then* you have worth. If you're a "nobody"—because you're just a minion in the machine—then you deserve to be treated with little importance or value. "Dignity means that there is a place for me, and you accept my place, and there is a place for you, and I accept your place regardless of title or position," Fuller says.[1]

In his book *Rankism: A Social Disorder*, Fuller writes about the opposite of dignity, using a term he coined called *rankism*. We've all heard of sexism, ageism, and racism, but rankism means the "abusive, discriminatory, or exploitative behavior towards people because of their rank in a particular hierarchy." Rankism is seen when a boss berates an assistant, a manager engages in one-upmanship, or a CEO pays himself hundreds of times more than the janitor. It is, as Fuller explains, "a degrading assertion of power." This kind of behavior, carried out by some fear-based leaders, is a sorry attempt at reducing multidimensional people to one-dimensional beings in order to have a feeling of power over them.

Fear-based organizations, which tend to be more hierarchical, create the conditions for an abuse of rank because of their centralized command-and-control structure. While rank or hierarchy itself is not inherently bad, it's the *abuse* of rank—rankism—that must become as embarrassing as any other form of discrimination.

Fuller says that we must stand up to the abuse of rank in our organizations. "Dignity works better in the workplace where people aren't being chronically humiliated," explains Fuller. "Organizations that respect each person's dignity make more money and are more successful."

In Freedom-Centered Organizations, systems and processes are in place to treat people fairly and to *reinforce*, rather than corrode, their sense of worth. The assumption is that each individual has inherent value, regardless of their job title, degrees, past experiences, or salary. Freedom-Centered Organizations are mindful of treating everyone like they matter, because they *do*.

| FEAR-BASED ORGANIZATIONS WITHOUT FAIRNESS AND DIGNITY BELIEVE: | FREEDOM-CENTERED ORGANIZATIONS WITH FAIRNESS AND DIGNITY BELIEVE: |
|---|---|
| Select people are somebodies | Everyone is a somebody |
| You have to earn your worth | You inherently have worth |
| Unfairness and injustice are justified | Fairness and justice are key |
| You're invisible unless you have a certain title | Everyone is seen and valued regardless of their title |
| It's OK to abuse one's power | No one is above the law |

## THE PROMISE OF FAIRNESS AND DIGNITY

The democratic principle of Fairness and Dignity, which reinforces impartiality and the worth of each individual, delivers remarkable benefits to an organization.

**Fairness and Dignity increase engagement.** In Freedom-Centered Organizations, where individuals feel seen and valued by leaders and colleagues, employees are more engaged and willing to go the distance in order to achieve a goal, together.

**Fairness and Dignity enhance leadership development.** When people know they have inherent value, it helps them let go of unhealthy and toxic behavior and become better leaders. And who wouldn't want to be part of a team in which people are daily growing and deepening their sense of worth, confidence, and interpersonal skills? All of this translates to greater trust, higher morale, and joy throughout the organization as well.

**Fairness and Dignity help eliminate drama.** When people don't feel treated fairly or with dignity, they are more likely to engage in mild to overt forms of procrastination or corporate sabotage. This creates drama, fiefdoms, and division within an organization. But when people feel seen and valued at work, there is less drama and more team spirit, less divisiveness and more community.

**Fairness and Dignity attract talent.** Organizations that treat *everyone* as a "somebody" will attract and keep top talent.

**Fairness and Dignity lower turnover and increase loyalty.** In fear-based organizations that humiliate and strip away the worth of their employees, turnover is higher—and costly. In Freedom-Centered Organizations that implement Fairness and Dignity into their systems and processes, individuals feel deeply valued and as a result, are more loyal.

## HOW TO SUCCESSFULLY IMPLEMENT FAIRNESS AND DIGNITY IN YOUR ORGANIZATION

Before you design new transformational practices to increase your company's level of Fairness and Dignity, consider these tips for success.

1. **Reflect upon your own behavior.** Is there something you as a leader are doing that is unintentionally or unknowingly (or even knowingly!) unfair or harming another's sense of worth? Become aware of your actions and take personal accountability for correcting them.

2. **Understand that sameness doesn't equal fairness.** Often organizations create one-size-fits-all policies in an attempt to be "fair" to everyone. Unfortunately, *sameness* is not the same as *fairness*. Instead, focus, when possible, on living the principle of Fairness, handling situations on an individual, case-by-case basis, rather than applying a blanket policy that only further angers people.

3. **Take a stand against rankism and for the dignity of all.** Insist on each person's worth, regardless of their title or position in your organization, and consciously and intentionally design systems and processes that build people up rather than pull them down.

## TOOLBOX ————————————————————————

# TRANSFORMATIONAL PRACTICES IN FAIRNESS AND DIGNITY

### Daily Recognition | Beginner Level

In fear-based organizations, recognition comes—if at all!—once a year in a review from your boss. But in this San Francisco–based Freedom-Centered Organization, they believe that each of their 250 employees should feel valued for their worth on a *daily* basis, whether they are in a senior role or entry-level position. Therefore, they encourage everyone to practice recognition each day, whether by thanking a colleague for help or congratulating someone on taking ownership of a project. Recognition doesn't come only from the top down, but also from bottom-up and peer-to-peer. They believe everyone should have the opportunity to give and receive praise based on performance, not position or tenure.

### Smart Services Desk | Beginner Level

Have you ever noticed that some people's feedback or ideas for how to improve things at an organization are heard—while others' just get ignored? Well, at this very large and public Freedom-Centered Organization in the IT industry, they wanted to create a just and impartial work experience for each of their employees, regardless of their rank and position.

To uphold a fair and uniform approach to employee issues, complaints, and inquiries, they implemented a Smart Services Desk: a ticket-based online system that decreases resolution times and provides more transparency across all enabling functions.

Any employee can submit a ticket electronically to any "enabling function," and only the employee who submits a ticket can close it. For instance, an employee might submit a ticket to the human resources department to request funding for higher education or to report a job-related incident. The service providers (a.k.a., enabling functions) then track service levels—resolution time, customer-satisfaction scores, and the like. Employees are guaranteed a resolution or update on the status of their request within seventy-two hours.

### Equal Pay | Intermediate Level

One of the key areas where many employees feel treated unfairly is with their compensation. Instead, at a small Virginia-based telecom company, they've decided that pay should not be automatically linked to traditional roles. For example, the president of the company is not the highest-paid employee; it's the employee who adds the most value.

And at a professional football (soccer) club based in Lewes, East Sussex, England, they decided to pay their women's team the same amount as their men's team. As the men's team's manager, Darren, put it: "We use the same pitch, the same facilities, the same ball. As football fans we all want our team to win regardless of gender. Parity means giving everyone the same opportunity and getting the same rewards."[2]

### Dignified Discipline | Intermediate Level

When there is a conflict, a lack of Fairness and Dignity can humiliate an individual in ways that could be avoided if the democratic principle had been consciously applied throughout the process. That's why this private high school in the Colorado mountains strives to practice Fairness and Dignity by employing a democratic disciplinary process with students. Students, faculty, and staff all collaborate through dialogue and listening and decide on a solution or consequence on which all agree.

When a student was dismissed recently for compromising the terms of the school's community contract, everyone in the community—including the student—agreed to the consequences. The disciplinary action was handled transparently, with input from all members of their community. The consequences then had to be agreed on by all, including the student who made the mistake, or else there would not be restorative justice. After the dismissal, the door was left open for him to return if he could demonstrate progress and if everyone in the community was willing to support his return.

The student went home and worked on the issue for six months, got the treatment he needed, made positive changes, and then appealed to return. Everyone voted in the student's favor, and he has returned very successfully. This process was unique because it was so democratic. Rather than the discipline coming from the top and resentment and confusion setting the tone in the community, they all worked together and treated the student with Fairness and Dignity. In the end, everyone shared in the successful transformation and the student grew in his sense of self-worth.

### The Blueprint of We Contract | Intermediate Level

Have you ever signed a contract and felt like it was unfair, benefiting one party over another? What if there were a more democratic way to do contracts? A Rossendale, England–based management consultancy that teaches how to build values-driven cultures takes a different approach. They use the "Blueprint of We" contract and process to make individual needs and preferences transparent and fair. The process invites individuals to write out what brought them to the company and describe what they look like on good and bad days. It also defines expectations of how best to work together and clarifies what should happen if they feel that the contract has been violated in some way. It is a radically different kind of contract, one they find honors the dignity of each individual while strengthening workplace relationships.

### Equal Benefits | Intermediate Level

Resentments are often stirred up in an organization when it appears that some leaders get extra perks simply because of where they sit in a hierarchy. But when it comes to Fairness and Dignity, this Las Vegas–based online retailer practices the principle through every program and policy, without regard for hierarchy or titles. For example, all employees, regardless of role, receive the same benefits. Compensation bonuses are given at the same percentage for all employees, and there are no "perks" provided to any group of people simply because of rank. "All for one and one for all" personifies this organization's view of everyone.

Similarly, at a Massachusetts-based co-op, when profits are distributed, all 150 worker-owners receive the same amount, regardless of rank or seniority. For example, a customer service worker with two years' tenure receives the same profit-sharing amount as the founder who's been there for twenty-five years.

### Village Fund | Intermediate Level

How often do fear-based organizations look away when one of their employees is struggling outside of work? Often, personal hardship can leave one feeling alone, overlooked, and unworthy of support. But one Denver-based healthcare company with 52,000 employees has a fund to care for their fellow teammates when times are challenging. They call their company a village, and their "Village Network" provides financial assistance to teammates during crises or difficulties. Teammates can donate from their paycheck to the Village Fund, and the company matches the amount employees put in. Over the last fifteen years, the company has provided their employees in need almost $1 million.

### Embrace Differences | Advanced Level

Individuals with disabilities are often treated unfairly and without dignity, especially in the workplace. However, this digital asset management company found a way to operationalize Fairness and Dignity while strengthening community relationships in Madison, Wisconsin, by offering employment opportunities for people with developmental disabilities.

Their CEO, Matthew, is passionate about the dignity of each individual. He explains, "We all want to go to work and have it be impactful and meaningful. But there's a group of people who have not been included in the workforce for a very long time. Some surveys have found that 81 percent of people with developmental disabilities don't have a job. And more than half of those people want a job! If our role as a business leader is to develop people to their fullest potential, create more opportunities, and include as much of the market as we can, then we need to fix this problem. We can use our entrepreneurial spirit to create a job for them, and it's easier than you think."[3]

By partnering with a local organization, they've created unique jobs such as "popcorn delivery" (passing out popcorn as a snack to those who want it) and "straightening up after lunch." This satisfies both a business need and a social integration need. They now employ six people with developmental disabilities who perform various tasks throughout the building with the assistance of their job coaches.

All employees also attend empathy training hosted by the local nonprofit Community Support Network, where they learn how to interact with workers with developmental disabilities. While the intent was to boost the employees' social and occupational wellness, the project has improved the entire organization's social and emotional wellness as well.

Kristina, one of the popcorn managers, says, "I do a little bit of everything. I feel very happy and very successful in my life now. I'm not a homebody; I like to be out and about, and I feel very comfortable working here because everyone welcomes people with a disability here very well."

## Peer Impact Bonus Award | Advanced Level

Most fear-based organizations base bonuses on rank and title, but this California-based savings and retirement company sets bonuses democratically. Each quarter, everyone gets one hundred points to distribute how they see fit to whomever they feel has made a positive impact on the company's goals and values. Each point has a dollar value assigned to it. Employees get one week to vote with their points by distributing them through an internal website. The website has everyone's picture on it with a field next to their photo to put in their points. A countdown clock lets employees know how much time is left to distribute their points.

After all of the points have been distributed, each employee can log into their own dashboard and see how many points they received and where they rank. For those who ranked higher, it's a great confirmation of their good work; ranking lower can be a great motivator. Employees cannot see anyone else's ranking—just their own.

"You might think it's a popularity contest, but it is not," shares Carrie, the Vice President of People who implemented the system. "The introverts are awarded just as much as the extroverts—even more at times. When I look at the top ten each time in the rankings, 60 percent are quiet, heads-down workers. The peers know who is working and who is not, and they reward it."

They have also tied the Peer Impact Bonus Award to other forms of evaluation. Employees can also get more than just cash for their points—they can also get more paid time off or stock. And everyone gets a certificate at the end of each year honoring how many points they have earned.

The practice has brought a much deeper sense of fairness to the bonus process and the entire organization. Individuals feel valued for the difference they make in the organization, not just for where they sit in the hierarchy. They trust that their peers will recognize and reward their hard work and contribution.

## Hire, Fire, and Promote
## Democratically | Advanced Level

In fear-based organizations, getting hired is usually up to the head of human resources, as are promotions and firings. But Freedom-Centered Organizations treat *both* the applicant and the people who will be working with them with Fairness and Dignity.

For example, at an Ann Arbor, Michigan–based software development company, they hire, fire, and promote in a very different way. Before they even look at an individual's resume, their hiring process involves between thirty and fifty people coming in at a time and pairing up with another competing candidate for several activities. Their CEO, Rich, says, "We tell them that their job is to try to get the person next to you another interview. If they struggle, help them out. We're looking for people with good kindergarten skills."

They work together for twenty minutes on a relevant activity while one of the company's team members observes them. They move through three pairs, working together for twenty minutes at a time. They are not asked a single question, just observed, but they are able to ask any questions they want.

After that process, rather than the head of HR (which they don't have!) deciding who should come back, they ask all the observers to vote on who should get a second interview, keeping the process moving quickly. The company does all work in pairs, so this process lets the observers get a feel for who's a good match.

In the second interview, the candidate comes alone and pairs up with a team member. They pay them a one-day contract and the candidate gets a feeling for what it's like to work there.

If that works out well, the candidate is invited back for a paid three-week trial. And if the trial goes well, the decision to hire the individual is not made by the CEO or HR—it's made by the *team* who will be working with them.

There are no salary negotiations because they have fifteen set pay levels. To advance, you must move through the levels. When you think you're ready for the next step, you put together a "Feedback Lunch" and invite your team to give you feedback and then vote to decide if you're ready to advance or not. If not, you get additional coaching; if yes, you advance to the next level.

And what about those rare times when someone needs to be let go? Since they have no bosses or managers, again, the team decides.

"I tell everyone that you must do it with fairness and dignity, and respect and honor the individual," explains Rich. "Then, you must ask what the best thing is to help them make a positive transition to the next stage of their life. We have to look at people as *people*, and not objects."

# PRINCIPLE 10

---

# Reflection and Evaluation

*The real man smiles in trouble, gathers strength from distress,
and grows brave by reflection.*
–THOMAS PAINE–

**A**ll the employees at a social media consultancy in Brighton, United Kingdom, are gathering in their conference room. The conference room chairs have been arranged into "pews" and a tall desk designed to look like a pulpit sits at the front of the room. One by one, all twenty-five employees are invited up to the pulpit to "confess" their failures before their colleagues. Some of them will share small blunders, like accidentally jamming the photocopier or tweeting a photo they shouldn't have. Another shares how he had completely bombed a previous pitch. Still others have epic failures and mistakes to confess.

Are you squirming yet? For many of us, reflecting on our performance and owning up to our missteps can be nothing short of torture. It's even worse when we have a leader who will take us to task for honest mistakes. And yet, here in Brighton, as individuals are called to the pulpit, the mood is far from formal or somber. Why?

It's time for the Church of Fail—a creative and even transformational experience that, as you'll see, shows just how powerful Reflection and Evaluation can be.

## WHAT ARE REFLECTION AND EVALUATION?

Reflection and Evaluation are at work when each individual and the organization are committed to continuous feedback and growth. Freedom-Centered Organizations engage in continuous improvement at both the individual and collective levels. Reflection and Evaluation are key to organizational democracy because they ensure a *learning environment* within a freedom-centered system.

------

**Reflection and Evaluation are at work when each individual and the organization are committed to continuous feedback and growth.**

------

Reflection and Evaluation represent the last Sustain principle because freedom is only sustained in an environment where there is ongoing learning and development. When we reflect, we look back upon an experience and think about the lessons we can glean from it. When we evaluate, we determine the value we can take from an experience to help us move forward and not repeat past mistakes. This helps sustain and ultimately advance the entire democratic system.

In fear-based organizations, there is little to no constructive reflection upon or evaluation of individuals, systems and processes, or the organization as a whole. Employees aren't properly trained in how to both give *and* receive feedback, instead either blowing up at each other or giving each other the silent treatment when they get upset.

This failure to self-reflect leads to the same mistakes over and over again in an endless "rinse and repeat" cycle that wastes money while dehumanizing individuals in the process. As leadership expert Margaret Wheatley puts it, "Without reflection, we go blindly on our way, creating more unintended consequences, and failing to achieve anything useful."

The Church of Fail couldn't be farther from how organizations usually treat mistakes. One of the consultancy's employees, Matt, created the practice while staying at a small cottage one weekend in Wales. "I created the Church of Fail to combat this kind of toxic environment of right and wrong," he explains. "I really think that the current system is broke, this way that we've been conditioned to think that we can't get things wrong. I genuinely believe that a new mindset is required. We need a mindset that is open, that *presumes* trust rather than expecting that it must be earned, and that creates an environment where people can feel valued and heard."

Thus, the Church of Fail was born.

After each individual "confesses," they are invited to reflect upon three questions:

1. What did I fail at?
2. How did I cope with it?
3. What would I do differently next time?

They then receive a huge round of applause and they are not allowed to leave the front of the room until that applause ends.

"The peculiar feeling that comes from standing there in the moment and receiving that round of applause coupled with the vulnerability of sharing something personal to you, whatever it may be, leaves a far longer-lasting impression on that individual and those in the audience than if you just wrote your learnings down on a piece of paper or mentally beat yourself up in the corner of the room," Matt explains.

The Church of Fail is completely scalable, no matter how many employees you have, and according to Matt, brings together three unique elements for an experience like no other:

- a theater or a church setup
- improvisation
- sound business logic, as everyone reflects both individually and collectively on how they can learn from their experiences

"There is no such thing as failure," shares Matt, "only experiences and how we respond to them."

At a time in which most leaders react to employees' mistakes by shaming or humiliating them—or worse!—the Church of Fail is a playful yet reflective way for this company to help the entire team learn from each individual's missteps, without fear of judgment.

## YOU ARE NOT YOUR MISTAKES

Another toxic practice in fear-based organizations is the failure to separate the "who" from the "what"—in other words, the failure to separate the mistake from the individual, correlating an individual's worth and value, or lack thereof, with what they *did*. When leaders lash out at an employee, or employees lash out at each other because they are triggered by fear and don't separate the action from the individual, it can erode an individual's sense of self-worth.

At the Ann Arbor software development company, they understand the value of Reflection and Evaluation and how to separate the individual's worth from the seeming mistake. The largest sign in their office reads "Make Mistakes Faster" and it hangs where all sixty employees can see it. Posting this cultural norm reminds everyone that it's not mistakes that threaten their progress, but the *fear* of making mistakes. Faster mistakes create the opportunity for quicker feedback, correction, and rapid organizational learning.

| FEAR-BASED ORGANIZATION WITHOUT REFLECTION AND EVALUATION HAVE: | FREEDOM-CENTERED ORGANIZATION WITH REFLECTION AND EVALUATION HAVE: |
| --- | --- |
| Reactionary learning | Continuous, intentional learning |
| Feedback sessions that destroy self-worth | Feedback sessions that bolster self-worth |
| A fear of self-reflection | A commitment to self-reflection |
| Failures | Learning moments |
| Once-a-year feedback | Real-time feedback |

## THE PROMISE OF REFLECTION AND EVALUATION

The Reflection and Evaluation principle brings more freedom and less fear to our teams and organizations in the following ways.

**Reflection and Evaluation help us grow, individually and collectively.** When we're afraid, we don't grow—we just hunker down and protect ourselves. But in democratically designed Freedom-Centered Organizations, leaders understand that Reflection and Evaluation bring continuous learning and promote positive growth. Fear stymies reflection and development. But if we can't reflect openly and constructively evaluate where we've been, we simply can't improve.

**Reflection and Evaluation empower each one of us to develop into our best self.** When we reflect upon lessons learned in a situation, we can accelerate our personal growth and sense of self-awareness more rapidly.

**Reflection and Evaluation promote healthy, ongoing communication.** In fear-based organizations, communciation can get bottled up because the principle of Reflection and Evaluation is not operationalized. And if we can't give feedback to each other in a healthy and positive way, then we aren't really free; we're just faking and pretending. But Freedom-Centered Organizations intentionally build systems and processes for ongoing, real-time feedback so that communication is healthy and constructive.

**Reflection and Evaluation make us less wasteful.** When we don't have the necessary feedback loop that keeps us from making the same mistakes over and over again, we waste time, money, and resources.

**Reflection and Evaluation help us make smarter decisions.** Fear gives us tunnel vision and makes us myopic so that we make dumb, shortsighted decisions. But in Freedom-Centered Teams where there is space to pause and reflect, we make smarter decisions while developing a wiser collective consciousness as well.

**Reflection and Evaluation create a positive learning environment.** In fear-based organizations, it's not a *learning* environment, it's a *punitive*, me-first environment. Reflection and Evaluation create and reinforce the conditions for a positive learning environment where everyone can express their voice respectfully while feeling listened to and heard.

The Reflection and Evaluation principle helps mitigate the fear that develops in a closed-off environment and promotes more freedom through constructive and timely feedback on an individual and collective level.

## TOOLBOX ────────────────────────────

## TRANSFORMATIONAL PRACTICES IN REFLECTION AND EVALUATION

### Gratitude Board and "Great-itude" Sessions | Beginner Level

We all know that an "attitude of gratitude" is a powerful way to transform our mindset, the way we lead, and the way we work, by creating happier and more joyful work environments where everyone feels more emotionally connected. At this small media planning and buying business in Denver, Colorado, they have a Gratitude Board on the wall by the conference room. People pin up little cards with statements of what they are thankful for, often for something someone else did for them. They have found it's amazing what this little gesture or feedback can do to make someone feel seen and appreciated.

Every last hour of the day on Friday, a company that curates the biggest online stories in Malaysia has a ritual that involves all members of the team as well as invited clients, partners, friends, and special guests. It's called the weekly "Great-itude" session. Every team member shares one thing they're grateful for that has happened in the week. This allows everyone to tune into one emotional moment from each employee, enabling them to learn more about who they are and what they value. The practice helps everyone across different teams stay connected through this weekly shared experience.

### Learning Moments | Beginner Level

Fear-based organizations equate mistakes with personal failure. At this publicly traded manufacturing company in San Diego, they don't speak of "failure," but rather of "Learning Moments" (page 150). By separating the "who" from the "what," they make it psychologically safer for everyone to admit mistakes, to be open to feedback, and to keep growing.

They believe using the language of Learning Moments prevents a punitive culture; instead they turn "failures" into opportunities to analyze what works and what does not: They emphasize taking time to pause, review progress, and look for any lessons, regardless of whether or not a mistake has been made. A key tenet of their culture is that mistakes that might hurt both the organization and an individual's reputation can be mitigated by this reflective process.

## What Have We Learned? | Beginner Level

The principle of Reflection and Evaluation creates a culture where it's safe to look back and evaluate what's been learned along the way, rather than suppressing or being afraid to talk about lessons learned. One Danish training company does this in a clear-cut way. After every meeting, presentation, speech, or workshop, they simply ask themselves, "What have we learned?" This question serves as a starting point for the discussion of what went well and what could be done better next time. They also encourage people to celebrate mistakes instead of hiding them, so everyone can learn and improve.

## Peer-to-Peer Feedback | Beginner Level

Many Freedom-Centered Leaders understand that the most transformational feedback doesn't come from the top down—it comes from peers giving each other constructive feedback. But how to do it? At the end of each month, this London-based translation services company invites each of their 150 employees to write something about their colleagues, positive or negative, if needed. The purpose of the feedback is to help people improve and to better understand their colleagues' perspectives.

### Feedback Futons | Intermediate Level

Sometimes you just need quick feedback: enter "Feedback Futons." At a New Zealand–based training company, employees can select three people they would like to get feedback from and invite them to join them on futons set up in the office. The three individuals then complete these sentences about the individual inviting the feedback:

"I really like working with you because . . ."

"I would like to thank you for . . ."

"I think you could work on improving . . ."

After each piece of feedback received, the individual is only allowed to say, "Thank you."

Further, the company asks that all feedback be tied to a specific instance to give it context. The purpose of the Feedback Futons is to practice honesty and constructive feedback.

### My Personal Growth Plan | Intermediate Level

Instead of the once-a-year performance reviews that are typically done in fear-based organizations, this publicly traded, Malaysia-based, deals and discounts business conducts their reviews on a *monthly* basis in a transformational practice called "My Personal Growth Plan."

First, every employee has a one-to-one session with their team leader to discuss their performance and achievements for the month as well as to plan their Key Performance Indicators and targets for the following month. This way, each person is clear about what is expected of them.

Next, they pair their Personal Growth Plans with Peer Feedback Reviews that are done every six months so that the individual gets a whole-picture understanding of their strengths and areas of growth. Their team leader also uses this time with each person to explore if there are any issues or assistance that the individual needs to further grow and develop themselves.

## Upward Evaluations and Open 360 Degree Feedback | Intermediate Level

In fear-based organizations, reviews are always top-down and rarely shared. But what if they could be bottom-up and shared in a transparent way? That's exactly what they do at this Nodia, India–based IT company with employees across twenty-five countries through "Upward Evaluations."

Here's how it works: All of their 120,000 employees are invited to evaluate their CEO, their boss, their boss's boss, and three other company managers they choose on eighteen questions using a 1-to-5 scale. All results are posted online for every employee to see.

Additionally, for one month each year, they have an "Open 360 Degree Feedback" portal that enables all employees to review *anyone* within the organization, including subordinates and peers, separate from performance appraisals. With a participation rate of almost 50 percent, employees greatly benefit from this feedback and feel more empowered. Employees can also voluntarily make this information public through their secure employee intranet, so others can learn and grow from the feedback shared.

## In Your Face | Intermediate Level

How do you keep controversial issues from blowing up in an unhealthy way? Consider this transformational practice called "In Your Face."

Each month, this Malaysian digital media company's teams meet at a restaurant, dining at a round table so everyone can see each other. Team leaders initiate and lead the conversation, inviting each person to reflect upon and evaluate team and individual performance by asking several questions:

1. What should we *keep*? (What is working well?)
2. What should we *start*? (What new ideas should we implement?)
3. What should we *stop*? (What can we do without? What bad habits should we put to rest?)

In Your Face sessions are designed to provide a space where team members can share their thoughts and clear the air. Open conversation helps prevent conflicts and fosters breakthrough ideas for future improvement.

### The Church of Fail | Advanced Level

Most organizations have a punitive culture when it comes to making mistakes. Not so at the UK social business consultancy I described at the beginning of this chapter. They have a unique practice called "Church of Fail," which encourages innovation rather than blame.

Gathered in a conference room, with chairs organized into makeshift "pews," participants take turns standing up to "confess" their failures.

Each individual is invited to answer three questions:

1. What did I fail at?
2. How did I cope with it?
3. What would I do differently next time?

They then are met with the cheers and applause of their colleagues. The Church of Fail helps the entire team learn from each other's mistakes, without fear of judgment.

### What Color Are Your Balls? | Advanced Level

Just how happy are your employees? Well, this web hosting and cloud services provider in Los Angeles figured out a fun (and a bit irreverent!) way to gauge the level of their employees' happiness each day with a transformational practice called "What Color Are Your Balls?"

Inspired by another WorldBlu certified company, they adapted this practice to their culture. Here's how it works for them: A container of red, yellow, and green balls sits near the exits of each office location. As they leave work, team members choose a ball to represent how their day went. When team members have a great day, they place a green ball into the voting canister. Had a bad day? A red ball goes into the can. A yellow ball means their day was neither good nor bad. At the end of each day, the number of balls in each canister is recorded. Data from all locations is tracked over time for trends, as well as the overall happiness level in each office and across the organization.

————————

You've now been introduced to the complete Freedom at Work leadership model, and, in this last section, to the 10 Principles of Organizational Democracy, which gave you the blueprint for Freedom-Centered Design. You also now have a toolkit of over one hundred proven and inspiring examples for how to practice more freedom and less fear in your team or organization.

But before we talk about how to implement Freedom at Work into your life, your team, or your organization, we need to explore one more critical element to building and sustaining something truly great: how not to mess it up.

# Seven Ways to (Accidentally) Destroy Your Successful Freedom-Centered Organization

*Eternal vigilance is the price of democracy.*
–Thomas Jefferson–

You've worked hard to build a thriving Freedom-Centered Team or Organization. Smart decisions, a checked ego, standing for each employee's worth, and countless do-overs have resulted in an organization that you and your team are genuinely proud of. You've helped better the lives of your employees and their families, your community has cheered you on for your visionary leadership, and your company is growing and prospering. What could go wrong?

Well, unfortunately, a lot. Here are seven ways we've seen leaders (accidentally) destroy the years of hard work and effort building a Freedom-Centered Culture. But forewarned is forearmed, and after reading this chapter you can stay vigilant to avoid making the same costly—and soul-crushing—mistakes.

## 1: YOU GET DISILLUSIONED ABOUT FREEDOM AT WORK WHEN THINGS GET CHALLENGING

First of all, it's easy to practice Freedom at Work when everything is humming along and everyone is happy. But what happens when, as a leader, you are challenged for being "undemocratic" or you feel like your democratic system has somehow failed you? There are times when you will get it wrong, you will feel frustrated with organizational democracy, and you will want to discredit the entire system. But let me be clear: just because you may not know how to do advanced calculus doesn't mean the math doesn't *work*. In other words, not always getting it right doesn't mean that organizational democracy doesn't work. In twenty-five years of doing this work all over the world in many different cultures and industries, I've never seen democracy fail—only our *practice* of it. What this means is that, first, you must be humble and further grow your understanding of how to practice it. Next, check in and make sure you are handling fear and practicing the skills of a Freedom-Centered Mindset and Leadership. Last, look at the issue that's creating the friction and examine if *all* ten principles are really in operation. Odds are one or two are missing, which might have made your democratic system get out of whack. So, before you kick organizational democracy to the curb, be honest with yourself and your team. How do you all need to grow?

## 2: YOU DON'T SCALE YOUR FREEDOM-CENTERED CULTURE

You've built a great company and you're growing rapidly. Now, don't forget to also scale your democratic systems and processes. So, how do you do that fast and still maintain your culture? Identify which democratic practices are working (and can scale!) and keep doing them. Some of your practices, however, may need to be upgraded, or you may need to retire some and build new entirely ones. Go back to the 10 Principles of Organizational Democracy and let them guide you as you create new practices for this stage of growth.

## 3: YOU DON'T HAVE AN ONBOARDING STRATEGY TO TRAIN YOUR NEW HIRES

You're growing and staffing up quickly, but how do you successfully onboard new hires into your Freedom-Centered Culture? I recently had a WorldBlu certified company's CEO tell me that they wanted to hire thirty new people each month, yet he had no idea how to onboard them into their thriving

Freedom-Centered culture. You can't just cross your fingers and hope your new hires will pick up your culture by osmosis; you have to teach it to them from day one and reinforce it through ongoing training, your leadership example, and democratic systems and processes. If you don't, it can easily be corrupted from within. Hire high self-worth people (see page 53) and then begin training them immediately in Freedom at Work.

## 4: YOUR BOARD OF DIRECTORS OR INVESTORS DON'T GET IT

"When are you going to grow up and run your company like an adult?" the board of directors asked the CEO of a highly successful WorldBlu certified company. Never mind that they were making billions of dollars and were completely disrupting a stagnant industry; the board wanted this CEO to be more "adult-like" with his management style (read: centralized, command-and-control leadership).

Boards and investors often don't understand the value and bottom-line benefit of a healthy democratic structure and leadership style, dismissing all its benefits. So, if you decide to have a board of directors or investors, make sure they are completely aligned with your vision of implementing Freedom at Work—or it may be a major cost to your emotional well-being, your bottom line, and your business.

## 5: YOU MERGE OR SELL THE COMPANY

It can be an entrepreneur's dream to build a thriving company and then sell it, making millions. But what happens to the successful Freedom-Centered Culture you've built? Unfortunately, we've seen many Freedom-Centered Organizations need more capital as they grow, often merging or selling the company to do so. One WorldBlu certified organization sold to a multinational firm that assured the two owners they were buying it for their Freedom-Centered Culture, which they claimed they wanted to spread to its other divisions. The cofounders believed them and sold, only to discover that the parent company had no interest in cultivating their culture elsewhere and was only paying lip service to get them to sell. The employees were devastated and mourned the loss of their once-thriving Freedom-Centered Culture. The CEO later admitted to us that he wished he'd never sold the company.

Another WorldBlu certified company had a stellar global reputation and revenues in the billions of dollars. The company's founder sold it to a Fortune

500 company to actually *save* the culture since his original investors didn't agree with what he and his team had built, despite their success. The new CEO assured the founder he could keep their democratic culture, and over the next decade, it thrived. But suddenly, the CEO went through personal challenges, so the parent company pushed him out and brought in their own guy. Shortly thereafter, the founder passed away in an accident. Rather than leave their thriving Freedom-Centered Culture as it was, the parent company offered buy-out packages for all the top employees who had built the culture, erasing their institutional memory.

Unless you make it a part of the legal structure of the sale, your Freedom-Centered Culture could easily be erased, absorbed into the ubiquitous fear-based management style found in most companies.

## 6: YOUR FOUNDER OR CEO WHO LOVES FREEDOM AT WORK IS LEAVING

It's the day everyone has been dreading: when your visionary founder or current Freedom-Centered CEO has decided to leave or retire. Now what? Will your Freedom-Centered Organization remain intact, or will a new, fear-based leader push in and destroy everything you've built?

No matter how solid your democratic systems and processes may be, and no matter how much the new CEO praises them, be on guard. Even if you're promoting from within, if that leader isn't rock solid on *why* organizational democracy is the optimal model of organizational design, things can change—fast.

I watched it happen with one of our highly evolved WorldBlu certified Freedom-Centered Organizations. They had a rock-solid Freedom-Centered Culture and were employee-owned—we thought they were bulletproof. Then their visionary CEO decided to step aside, and a replacement was hired from outside the company through what they thought was a thorough vetting process. Yet within a matter of months, the new CEO had already dismantled many of their democratic systems, putting in centralized command-and-control processes throughout and destroying morale.

So, how do you avoid the same trap? First, and especially when it comes to hiring a new CEO, you must make sure you hire someone who is a *solid ten* in self-worth.

Next, you must have some form of a (legal) organizational constitution (see page 185) guaranteeing that the current democratic rights of your employees cannot be taken away when there is a leadership change. The CEO must *not* be above these standards. Do a test run: make sure they understand what Freedom at Work is all about and are willing to uphold your democratic standards. If not, make sure you have a way to let them go before they do too much damage.

## 7: YOU STOP REINFORCING FREEDOM AT WORK

You've built a high-performing Freedom-Centered Culture, but you can't rest on your laurels. One of the biggest mistakes that leaders make is building a successful Freedom-Centered Organization and thinking that the destination is the goal, but it's not. It's the journey. So how do you stay humble, keep learning and growing, and keep reinforcing the message of Freedom at Work? One certified Freedom-Centered Organization thought they had "arrived." They earned certification and felt great about what they had built. But when things started to deteriorate because they weren't constantly reinforcing the high standard of Freedom at Work, they knew they had to do something. So, they decided to spotlight one of the 10 Principles of Organizational Democracy each month, focusing on how they were living it and what they could do to bolster their practice of it. Things quickly turned around for them as they intentionally deepened and strengthened their practice of Freedom at Work each day.

---

Building a thriving Freedom-Centered Organization is a deeply fulfilling and rewarding journey, so on your way to the summit don't give up if you hit some bumps along the way. Remember to surround yourself with investors and a board that support Freedom at Work, and hire people who get it, too! Have legal standards in place that ensure your Freedom-Centered Culture no matter *who* leads the company, and don't sell out to people who could dismantle all you've built. Freedom at Work takes discernment, trust, and eternal vigilance—and it's worth it!

---

You've now experienced why Freedom at Work is *the* winning strategy that leaders like you can use to transform the way you lead, improve your bottom line, and build a workplace culture people love. You've also discovered how to make it *last*. Freedom at Work is so urgently needed today because we're constantly up against its greatest inhibitor—fear. Fear tries to steal our light, our dreams, and our deeper connection to each other. Now that you've read this book, I hope I've further sparked something inside of you that makes you want to claim your power within, say an emphatic "no!" to fear, and seize your sacred right to shine your light, achieve your dreams, and lead fearlessly. So, what's your first step?

As we've explored, the Freedom at Work leadership model comprises three pillars: Mindset, Leadership, and Design. As an individual leader, you can practice each pillar of the Freedom at Work model with the questions and tools I've given you throughout this book. And while you may want to jump straight into Freedom-Centered Design, for example, remember that each step builds upon the last. You need to cultivate the skills of a Freedom-Centered Mindset *first* and then develop Freedom-Centered Leadership skills *before* you're ready for the more advanced work of designing, growing, and sustaining a Freedom-Centered Culture. Whether you're looking to improve yourself as a leader, or you've just started a new company, lead a team, or are the CEO of a global organization, the path to successfully practicing Freedom at Work always starts within *you*.

And if you're ready to bring these ideas more broadly into your team or organization, that process also starts with each individual cultivating a Freedom-Centered Mindset and Leadership skills. After you've worked through these two pillars of the Freedom at Work model, your team will be mentally and emotionally ready with the skill set to design a more Freedom-Centered Culture. Remember that 75 percent of your culture is determined by the design of your systems and processes. If you want to build a high-performing environment that creates the conditions for *everyone's* success, this is where you do it.

As you explored over one hundred transformational practices in the book, I invited you to highlight which practices inspired you. Now is the time to begin trying them out. Which practices do you start with? Remember, there are three phases you move through: Start, Scale, and Sustain. Begin with the practices you chose under the Start category and work your way forward, adapting the practice to fit *your* unique context, goals, and needs. Or you may be inspired to create an entirely new transformational practice inspired by one you read. In the words of Benjamin Franklin, "Without *continual growth* and progress, such words as improvement, achievement, and success have no meaning." We begin—and ultimately succeed—step by intentional step.

At this point, I hope you feel energized and ready to start practicing Freedom at Work. If you are, you may like some experienced help along the way. If that's the case, go to worldblu.com and apply for free membership with us. When you become a member, you'll get access to even more material than I could include in this book in our accompanying Freedom at Work course. The course comes with training videos, tools, tips, and our 7-Step Freedom at Work Design Map that teaches you how to create, adapt, and implement democratic transformational practices into your team or organization. And you're not just left to figure it out on your own, either. The course also includes top leadership and culture-design coaching each week.

Whether you want to take a do-it-yourself approach, or you want to join the vibrant WorldBlu global leadership community for inspiration and support, what matters *most* is that you make the commitment to freedom—not fear—transforming your life, your organization, and our world for the better.

# WHY FREEDOM AT WORK MATTERS TO FREEDOM IN OUR WORLD

*. . . the only remedy, in my judgment, for the present alarming*
*condition of affairs, is to return to this principle, decreeing*
*for all the Territories, Freedom now, Freedom forever.*
—Reuben Eaton Fenton—

The time is *now* for you, as a leader—whether you are an entrepreneur or the CEO of a Fortune 500 company, a leader of a church, sports team, school, or government—to step up and intentionally choose to lead yourself, your team, or your organization with freedom rather than fear and control. I strongly believe that leaders of all types of organizations are uniquely positioned to lead their teams using freedom and organizational democracy rather than fear and control. And, I believe they have a moral and ethical responsibility to do so. Instead of expecting our governments to be the promoters and guarantors of democracy, which often they are not, leaders committed to freedom can help build a more democratic world, team by team, organization by organization. This is a powerful (and often overlooked!) way to weave a robust web of freedom throughout every corner of our world—and transform our world for generations yet to come.

Why is Freedom at Work so urgently needed *now*? Because those with a malicious agenda to steal freedom away from each one of us are actively and silently weaving webs of fear-motivated control into every area of our lives, in ways that most of us are completely missing—and, unfortunately, they are winning. According to Freedom House, a nonpartisan organization that measures the level of freedom and democracy globally shared through their annual "Freedom in the World" report, we are in a fifteen-year global decline in the level of freedom worldwide.[1] The Index of Freedom in the World, a joint project of Canada's Fraser Institute, Germany's Liberales Institut, and the Cato Institute in the US, also reports a global decline in freedom, particularly in established democracies such as the United States and the United Kingdom.[2]

It's important to remember that democracy, while a centuries-old concept, is still generally new to our modern world. Therefore, it is under constant attack by fear-based leaders and organizations actively undermining its power and promise for humankind. The battle against oppression and for our inherent freedom has been fought for millennia. It continues today, and it is both an individual *and* collective battle that we must win together.

These tactics to subvert and undermine the growth of freedom and democracy around the world—carried out by fear-based corporations, governments, and leaders—have an immoral agenda with one singular goal: to make you more dependent on these control-based systems and leaders rather than your *own* right to self-govern and think freely and independently. And if they continue to succeed, they can and will control and manipulate you with their fear-based tactics, leading you down a path that takes you off purpose and off course. These fear-based patterns are happening aggressively all over our world today.

Throughout human history, there have been many issues that have tried to divide us. Yet when you step back and look at these core social, religious, economic, and political problems, what is underneath all of them is *fear*. Fear of what? Fear of not being accepted, fear of being left out, fear of not being good enough, fear of failure, fear of lack. But what would we do if we *weren't* afraid?

What do we lose when we submit to being controlled through fear-based systems rather than rising through Freedom-Centered Leadership? We lose the fulfillment of our fullest potential. We lose our joy. And we lose our human connection. When we put personality over principle, corruption over character, and selfishness over service, we become adrift and without an anchor. The muscles of personal discipline, which are critical to maintaining real freedom, atrophy, and we end up siding with the darkness rather than walking in the light.

So, where do we go from here? As individuals, we must *first* commit to self-government, stand for our inherent worth, and lead with freedom rather than fear in every area of our lives. Freedom and democracy are acts of love for our fellow human beings. The word *freedom* evolved from Old English and Old Norse words for *peace*—and that is its promise.[3] Freedom brings a lasting peace *within* to each one of us.

Those of you not yet leading an entire organization but leading a team or division can start there, bringing Freedom at Work to your workplace. Make everyone else in your organization wonder what it is that makes your group so unique, successful, and full of the Ubuntu spirit. You can create a positive ripple effect, beginning with your example.

CEOs and top executive leaders can use Freedom at Work to not only build highly competitive and admirable organizations that are financially sound, well run, and magnets for top talent; they can also use it to help advance freedom worldwide. Just imagine the impact of millions of small to large businesses, schools, nonprofits, and governmental institutions operating on democratic principles. What could that do to accelerate the development of a robust, mature, and engaged citizenry and its positive impact on our world?

I've shared the benefits of freedom with you in detail. Freedom at Work lifts our thought into new realms of inspiration and possibility. It gives us a proven pathway for leading with clarity, confidence, and conviction. And it provides the blueprint for building highly profitable, resilient, and ethical organizations worldwide.

My hope is that this book makes you a more discerning, awake, and passionate leader for freedom. As united freedom fighters, we must engage our heads, hearts, and hands to elevate the standard of leadership while compassionately helping those who may not yet be aware of how much fear governs them. I invite you to join our global movement of leaders committed to Freedom at Work, building our lives, families and communities, our teams and our organizations, on this proven rock. It is up to you to decide if you will rise to *this* moment, and I hope you will. Together, we *can* build a more freedom-centered world, one organization at a time. Freedom now—freedom *forever*.

# ACKNOWLEDGMENTS

This book is the culmination of over two decades of hard work, research, and experiences all over the world. Along the way, I have been supported by countless individuals who share my love of freedom and democracy. In small to big ways, you have helped broaden my view, refine my ideas and methods, and inspire me. I am so grateful for each one of you.

Specifically, I am grateful for the hundreds of WorldBlu certified Freedom-Centered Organizations and our members that I have learned from over the years, without whom there would be no book or WorldBlu. Thank you to each one of you for your model of excellence, courage, vision, and tenacity. While word count limited how many organizations I could write about, please know that I honor and recognize each one of you for the light of freedom that you shine brightly in our world.

My purpose-driven work has been supported throughout my lifetime by countless mentors, role models, spiritual teachers, cherished friends, and unwavering cheerleaders who have walked with me (and sometimes carried me!) through the battlefield of life. You know who you are. From the depths of my heart, I truly could not have done it without you, and I am profoundly grateful.

I held the dream of this book in my heart over two decades before meeting the perfect team to bring it to life. Lari Bishop, we met early on, and your developmental editorial work took all the ideas, stories, and research I had and gave me a framework for how to organize the book. Thank you for believing in me and the power of this message. Also, thank you to my wonderful literary agent, John Willig, for your integrity, humility, care, and calm—everything an agent should be.

My deepest hope was that I would meet a visionary publisher with whom I felt a philosophical alignment—and from my first call with its founder, Glenn Yeffeth, I did! Working with the world-class team at BenBella has been a joy and privilege every step of the way. A huge thank-you to my outstanding editor, Claire Schulz, for making the book into all that I hoped for and more. James Fraleigh, thank you for your exacting copyedits, Michael Fedison and Sarah Vostok for your diligent proofreading, Sarah Avinger and independent designer Rizky A. Shahrial for most of the artwork, and Jennifer Canzoneri, Tanya Wardell, and the marketing team for getting this message of freedom out to our world.

I am most grateful to my many numerous colleagues at WorldBlu over the years for your support, ideas, and encouragement. I have learned so much from each one of you. I must give special thanks to my incredible colleague, Miranda Ash, who is one of the finest human beings I've ever known. Thank you for providing a calm, joyous, and ever-supportive space for me to refine my ideas over the years. You are a world-class coach, incredibly smart, and one of my greatest teachers. You are the wind beneath my wings, dear friend, and I am so grateful for the many adventures we've had together—with many more to come!

My beautiful Australian Shepherd, Joey, has also been by my side as my steadfast companion and emotional rock for so much of this journey, faithfully fulfilling his duty as the guardian of my heart, mind, and soul.

I am so grateful for my entire family, and specifically, my incredible parents, John and Diana Fenton, who model excellence, character, and why you stand for what is right. Thank you for the rock-solid foundation you gave me, your unconditional love, for always being there for me, and for giving me the space to find and live my unique purpose in life. Last, I am so grateful to God, divine Love, for choosing me to steward these ideas forward, joining with countless other freedom fighters of the past, present, and future who believe that freedom, not fear, is our birthright. It has been my sacred honor to do this work.

# RESOURCES

## BECOME A MEMBER OF WORLDBLU

Would you like to join a global community of leaders like you committed to leading themselves, their team, or their organization with Freedom at Work? If yes, we invite you to apply for free membership in WorldBlu.

As a free member, you will get access to the Freedom at Work course which complements this book, our informative and inspiring newsletter, exclusive invitations to exciting events, and much more.

Additional paid membership levels, with access to mindset, leadership, and design courses, top coaching, and a world-class community, are also available.

Join our global community of top CEOs, leaders, and organizations committed to breakthrough success with Freedom at Work.

**Apply now for free membership at www.worldblu.com.**

## RECOMMENDED READING

### Select Books by the CEOs, Leaders, and Employees of WorldBlu certified Freedom-Centered Organizations

Barrett, Richard. *Building a Values-Driven Organization: A Whole System Approach to Cultural Transformation.*

Barrett, Richard. *The Values-Driven Organization: Cultural Health and Employee Well-Being as a Pathway to Sustainable Performance.*

Chapman, Bob, and Raj Sisodia. *Everybody Matters: The Extraordinary Power of Caring for Your People Like Family.*

Employees of Zappos.com. *The Power of WOW: How to Electrify Your Work and Your Life by Putting Service First.*

Gatenby, Nikki. *Superengaged: How to Transform Business Performance by Putting People and Purpose First.*

Hollender, Jeffrey, and Bill Breen. *The Responsibility Revolution: How the Next Generation of Businesses Will Win.*

Hsieh, Tony. *Delivering Happiness.*

Kjerulf, Alexander. *Happy Hour Is 9 to 5: How to Love Your Job, Love Your Life, and Kick Butt at Work.*

Kjerulf, Alexander. *Leading with Happiness: How the Best Leaders Put Happiness First to Create Phenomenal Business Results and a Better World.*

Lakhiani, Vishen. *The Buddha and the Badass: The Secret Spiritual Art of Succeeding at Work.*

Lakhiani, Vishen. *The Code of the Extraordinary Mind: 10 Unconventional Laws to Redefine Your Life and Succeed on Your Own Terms.*

McInnes, Will. *Culture Shock: A Handbook For 21st Century Business.*

Nayar, Vineet. *Employees First, Customers Second: Turning Conventional Management Upside Down.*

Nixon, Tom. *Work with Source: Realise Big Ideas, Organise for Emergence and Work Artfully with Money.*

Ridge, Garry. *Tribe Culture: How It Shaped WD-40 Company.*

Ridge, Garry, and Ken Blanchard. *Helping People Win at Work: A Business Philosophy Called "Don't Mark My Paper, Help Me Get an A."*

Scudamore, Brian. *WTF?! (Willing to Fail): How Failure Can Be Your Key to Success.*

Sheridan, Richard. *Chief Joy Officer: How Great Leaders Elevate Human Energy and Eliminate Fear.*

Sheridan, Richard. *Joy, Inc.: How We Built a Workplace People Love.*

Sinek, Simon. *The Infinite Game.*

Sinek, Simon. *Leaders Eat Last: Why Some Teams Pull Together and Others Don't.*

Sinek, Simon. *Start with Why: How Great Leaders Inspire Everyone to Take Action.*

Stack, Jack. *A Stake in the Outcome: Building a Culture of Ownership for the Long-Term Success of Your Business.*

Stack, Jack, and Bo Burlingham. *The Great Game of Business, Expanded and Updated: The Only Sensible Way to Run a Company.*

Stewart, Henry. *The Happy Manifesto: Make Your Organization a Great Workplace.*

Weinzweig, Ari. *Zingerman's Guide to Giving Great Service: Treating Your Customers Like Royalty.*

## Select Books About Organizational Democracy and Freedom in the Workplace

Ackoff, Russell. *The Democratic Corporation: A Radical Prescription for Recreating Corporate America and Rediscovering Success.*

Carney, Brian, and Isaac Getz. *Freedom, Inc.: Free Your Employees and Let Them Lead Your Business to Higher Productivity, Profits, and Growth.*

Cloke, Kenneth, and Joan Goldsmith. *The End of Management and the Rise of Organizational Democracy.*

Dressler, Larry. *Consensus Through Conversation: How to Achieve High-Commitment Decisions.*

Edmondson, Amy. *The Fearless Organization: Creating Psychological Safety in the Workplace for Learning, Innovation, and Growth.*

Gratton, Lynda. *The Democratic Enterprise: Liberating Your Business with Freedom, Flexibility and Commitment.*

Manville, Brook, and Josiah Ober. *A Company of Citizens: What the World's First Democracy Teaches Leaders About Creating Great Organizations.*

Semler, Ricardo. *Maverick: The Success Story Behind the World's Most Unusual Workplace.*

Semler, Ricardo. *The Seven-Day Weekend: A Better Way to Work in the 21st Century.*

## Books on Freedom and Democracy

I have read and been influenced by hundreds of books, articles, and documentaries over the years in my study of leadership and democracy. This is a small selection of readings that particularly influenced my selection of the 10 principles of democracy.

Aristotle. *The Athenian Constitution.*

Aristotle. *Politics.*

Barreiro, Jose, editor. *Indian Roots of American Democracy.*

Barton, David. *Original Intent: The Courts, the Constitution, & Religion.*

The Bible.

Blaug, Ricardo and John Schwarzmantel, editors. *Democracy: A Reader.*

Carey, Ray. *Democratic Capitalism: The Way to a World of Peace and Plenty.*

Cuomo, Mario M., and Harold Holzer, editors. *Lincoln on Democracy: His Own Words, with Essays by America's Foremost Civil War Historians.*

Dahl, Robert. *On Democracy.*

De Tocqueville, Alexis. *Democracy in America.*

The Declaration of Independence, The Bill of Rights, and The Constitution of the United States.

Dunn, John. *Democracy: A History.*

Eddy, Mary Baker. *Science and Health with Key to the Scriptures.*

Fenton, William N. *The Great Law and the Longhouse: A Political History of the Iroquois Confederacy.*

Friedman, Milton. *Capitalism and Freedom.*

Grinde, Donald A. Jr., and Bruce E. Johansen. *Exemplar of Liberty: Native America and the Evolution of Democracy* (Native American Politics Series; No. 3).

Hamilton, Alexander, James Madison, and John Jay. *The Federalist Papers.*

Hammer, Dean. *A Companion to Greek Democracy and the Roman Republic (Blackwell Companions to the Ancient World Book 116).*

Hansen, Mogens Herman. *The Athenian Democracy in the Age of Demosthenes: Structure, Principles, and Ideology.*

Havel, Václav. *Open Letters: Selected Writings, 1965–1990.*

Johansen, Bruce E. *Debating Democracy: Native American Legacy of Freedom.*

Kloppenberg, James T. *Toward Democracy: The Struggle for Self-Rule in European and American Thought.*

Landemore, Hélène. *Democratic Reason: Politics, Collective Intelligence, and the Rule of the Many.*

Locke, John. *The John Locke Collection: A Collection of His Most Important Works.*

Locke, John. *The First and Second Treatises of Government.*

McClay, Wilfred M. *Land of Hope: An Invitation to the Great American Story.*

Mill, John Stuart. *On Liberty.*

Paine, Thomas. *Common Sense.*

Plato. *Republic.*

Rahe, Paul Anthony. *Soft Despotism, Democracy's Drift: Montesquieu, Rousseau, Tocqueville, and the Modern Prospect.*

Ravitch, Diane, and Abigail M. Thernstrom. *The Democracy Reader: Classic and Modern Speeches, Essays, Poems, Declarations and Documents on Freedom and Human Rights Worldwide.*

Rousseau, Jean-Jacques. *A Discourse on Inequality.*

Rousseau, Jean-Jacques. *The Social Contract.*

Skousen, W. Cleon. *The 5000 Year Leap.*

Skousen, W. Cleon. *The Making of America: The Substance and Meaning of the Constitution.*

Slater, Philip, and Warren Bennis. "Democracy Is Inevitable." *Harvard Business Review.*

Smith, Adam. *The Wealth of Nations.*

Sorensen, Georg. *Democracy and Democratization: Processes and Prospects in a Changing World (Dilemmas in World Politics).*

Washington, George. *George Washington's Farewell Address.*

Washington, George. *Washington on Courage: George Washington's Formula for Courageous Living.*

Washington, George. *Washington's Inaugural Address of 1789.*

Watts, Edward J. *Mortal Republic: How Rome Fell into Tyranny.*

Weatherford, Jack. *Indian Givers: How the Indians of the Americas Transformed the World.*

# NOTES

## Introduction

1. Charles O'Reilly, Jeffrey Pfeffer, David Hoyt, and Davina Drabkin, *DaVita: A Community First, A Company Second* (Cambridge: Harvard Business Review, 2014).

2. Brent Tarter, "George Mason and the Conservation of Liberty," Virginia Magazine of History and Biography 99, no. 3 (July 1991): 279-304, https://www.jstor.org/stable/4249228.

3. US Congress, "All Information (Except Text) for S.Con.Res.76—A concurrent resolution to acknowledge the contribution of the Iroquois Confederacy of Nations to the Development of the United States Constitution and to reaffirm the continuing government-to-government relationship between Indian tribes and the United States established in the Constitution," accessed June 8, 2021, https://www.congress.gov/bill/100th-congress/senate-concurrent-resolution/76/all-info.

4. Noah Storer, "The Life and Times of Reuben Eaton Fenton," Fenton History Center, accessed December 10, 2020, http://fentonhistorycenter.org/the-life-and-times-of-reuben-eaton-fenton.

## Fear at Work

1. Jim Harter, "U.S. Employee Engagement Rises Following Wild 2020," Gallup, February 26, 2021, http://www.gallup.com/workplace/330017/employee-engagement-rises-following-wild-2020.aspx.

2. "Do American Workers Need a Vacation? New CareerBuilder Data Shows Majority Are Burned Out at Work, While Some Are Highly Stressed or Both," CareerBuilder, May 23, 2017, http://press.careerbuilder.com/2017-05-23-Do-American-Workers-Need-a-Vacation-New-CareerBuilder-Data-Shows-Majority-Are-Burned-Out-at-Work-While-Some-Are-Highly-Stressed-or-Both.

3. Valerie Bolden-Barrett, "Study: Disengaged Employees Can Cost Companies up to $550B a Year," HR Dive, March 8, 2017, http://www.hrdive.com/news/study-disengaged-employees-can-cost-companies-up-to-550b-a-year/437606/.

4. Elizabeth Wolfe Morrison and Frances J. Milliken, "Sounds of Silence," *Stern Business*, Spring/Summer 2004, http://w4.stern.nyu.edu/sternbusiness/spring_summer_2004/soundsofsilence.html.

5. "Zogby Poll: As Independence Day Nears, Workplace Democracy Association Survey Finds One in Four Working Americans Describe Their Employer as a 'Dictatorship,'" *Workplace Democracy Association* (blog), June 23, 2008, http://workplacedemocracy.wordpress.com/workplace-democracy-survey/.

## The Promise of Freedom at Work

1. Philip Slater and Warren Bennis, "Democracy Is Inevitable," *Harvard Business Review*, 42, 1964.

2. "2012 Release of Establishment Characteristics Data Tables, Business Dynamics Statistics," United States Census Bureau, 2014.

3. The three guiding principles of sociocracy are consent-based decision-making, distributed authority, and feedback. "Sociocracy: The Operating System of the New Economy," video, Sociocracy for All, accessed April 10, 2021, https://www.sociocracyforall.org/start-here/.

## The Power Question Practice

1. Don Joseph Geowey, "85 Percent of What We Worry About Never Happens," *Huffington Post,* updated December 6, 2017, http://huffpost.com/entry/85-of-what-we-worry-about_b_8028368; Lucas S. LaFreniere and Michelle G. Newman, "Exposing Worry's Deceit," *Behavior Therapy* 50, no. 3 (May 2020): 413–23, http://doi.org/10.1016/j.beth.2019.07.003; "(Yes—85%) of What We Worry About Never Happens," Boevink Group, February 24, 2014, http://boevinkgroup.com/2014/02/24/yes-85-of-what-we-worry-about-never-happens.
2. Geowey, "85 Percent of What We Worry About Never Happens."

## Love

1. Jennifer Robinson, "Turning Around Employee Turnover," Gallup, May 8, 2008, https://news.gallup.com/businessjournal/106912/turning-around-your-turnover-problem.aspx.

## Power

1. Matthew Gonnering, "How to Handle Brutal Online Reviews from Your Employees," *Fast Company,* October 5, 2020, http://fastcompany.com/90559764/how-to-handle-brutal-online-reviews-from-your-employees.
2. Ibid.

## Ubuntu

1. *Anything Is Possible: The Story of the 2008 Celtics,* produced by Jim Aberdale, aired May 29, 2018, on NBC Sports.
2. Ibid.
3. "Ubuntu Quotes," Global Ministries, December 30, 2014, http://globalministries.org/special_days_gm_sunday_2012_ubuntu_stories_ubuntu_quotes.

## Organizational Democracy: The Framework for Freedom

1. There is strong evidence that democracy may have started in Lycia, Turkey. Called the Lycian League, it is the "first known democratic union in history," established in 205 BC. "Lycian Turkey—Discover the Beauty of Ancient Lycia," accessed March 30, 2020, https://www.lycianturkey.com/lycian _government.htm.
2. Lisa A. W. Kensler et al., "The Ecology of Democratic Learning Communities: Faculty Trust and Continuous Learning in Public Middle SchoolsIbid," *Journal of School Leadership* 19, no. 6 (November 1, 2009): 697–734, http:// doi.org/10.1177/105268460901900604.
3. WorldBlu, LLC, *Freedom at Work™: Growth & Resilience* report, 2015.
4. Gretchen Spreitzer, "Giving Peace a Chance: Organizational Leadership, Empowerment, and Peace," *Journal of Organizational Behavior* 28 (August 23, 2007): 1077–95, http://doi.org/10.1002/job.487.

## Integrity

1. "Our Values," The WD-40 Company, accessed December 10, 2020, http:// wd40company.com/our-tribe/our-values/.
2. Stan Sewich, vice president of global organizational development at the WD-40 Company, email message to author, April 8, 2020.
3. Matthew Gonnering, CEO of Widen, email message to author, April 7, 2020.
4. Conversation with Razvan Luca, April 13, 2020.

## Dialogue and Listening

1. David Maxfield, "How a Culture of Silence Eats Away at Your Company," *Harvard Business Review*, December 7, 2016, http://hbr.org/2016/12/how -a-culture-of-silence-eats-away-at-your-company.
2. Much has been written about the Four Levels of Listening. The ideas in these paragraphs derive from the Presencing Institute, The Educare Unlearning Institute, and our own original work. Source: The Presencing Institute, "u.lab 1x: Levels of listening (part 1)," July 22, 2014, https://www.presencing.org /resource/tools/listen-desc.

3. Alex "Sandy" Pentland, "The New Science of Building Great Teams," *Harvard Business Review*, April 2012, http://hbr.org/2012/04/the-new-science-of-building-great-teams.

## Decentralization

1. Vineet Nayar, "Breakthrough for Business: End the CEO as We Know It," *Christian Science Monitor*, July 27, 2010, http://csmonitor.com/Commentary/Opinion/2010/0727/Breakthrough-for-business-End-the-CEO-as-we-know-it.
2. Ted Rau, "Consent Decision Making," Sociocracy for All, accessed December 10, 2020, http://sociocracyforall.org/consent-decision-making.
3. Charles Fishman, "Engines of Democracy," *Fast Company*, September 30, 1999, http://fastcompany.com/37815/engines-democracy.

## Individual and Collective

1. Rodney North, former vice chair of the board of directors of Equal Exchange, email message to author, March 6, 2021.
2. Laura Garnett, "Why You Should Let Your Employees Bring Their Babies to Work," *Forbes*, January 15, 2016, http://forbes.com/sites/lauragarnett/2016/01/15/why-you-should-let-your-employees-bring-their-babies-to-work.

## Choice

1. Marcel Schwantes, "Why Are Your Employees Quitting? A Study Says It Comes Down to Any of These 6 Reasons," *Inc.*, October 23, 2017, http://www.inc.com/marcel-schwantes/why-are-your-employees-quitting-a-study-says-it-comes-down-to-any-of-these-6-reasons.html.
2. Jack Zenger and Joseph Folkman, "How Damaging Is a Bad Boss, Exactly?" *Harvard Business Review*, July 16, 2012, http://hbr.org/2012/07/how-damaging-is-a-bad-boss-exa.

## Fairness and Dignity

1. Robert Fuller, "Rankism," TEDxBerkeley, filmed March 23, 2011, http://youtube.com/watch?v=djM6cZb8kak.

2. Ricard Foster, "Lewes FC: The Football Club Who Are Making Equality Pay," *Guardian,* July 16, 2019, http://theguardian.com/football/the-agony-and-the -ecstasy/2019/jul/16/lewes-fc-equal-pay-club-best-paid-player-woman.

3. Nate Holmes, "Why We Hired a Popcorn Manager," *Widen* (company blog), October 30, 2018, https://www.widen.com/blog/why-we-hired-a-popcorn -manager.

## Conclusion

1. Sarah Repucci and Amy Slipowitz, "Freedom in the World 2021: Democracy Under Siege," Freedom House, accessed June 10, 2021, https://freedomhouse .org/report/freedom-world/2021/democracy-under-siege.

2. CATO Institute, "Finding Freedom in an Unfree World," January/February 2021, https://www.cato.org/policy-report/january/february-2021/finding -freedom-unfree-world.

3. Etymology Online, "Free (adj.)," accessed June 10, 2021, https://www .etymonline.com/word/free#etymonline_v_14152.

# INDEX

## A

Abrashoff, Michael, 164
*Academy of Management Review,* 6
accomplishment, from Power Question
  Practice, 38–39
accountability
  in Freedom-Centered Leadership,
    46–47, 72
  gaining power through, 66
  from Power Question Practice,
    35–36, 39
  self-worth and, 62
Accountability (organizational
  democracy principle), xxi, 87–88,
  149–158
  defining, 151
  in fear-based vs. freedom-centered
    organizations, 152
  implementing, 153
  individual vs. collective, 153
  peer-to-peer, 153
  promise of, 152
  transformational practices, 154–158
Accountability Pledge (practice), 150,
  154–155
Accountable Tracking (practice), 154

Achievements and Objectives (practice), 154
Achievers, xxii
Ackoff, Russell, on democracy, 84–85
action, with Power Question Practice,
  37, 39
active adaptation, democracy as, 84–85
Adams, John, on principles, 83–92
Adams, Samuel, on being free, xv
adaptability, 89
adaptation, democracy as, 84–85
Aesop, 62
affirmations, for mental discipline, 59
agility, fear and, 6
Alfred P. Sloan Award for Flexibility, 10
alignment, transparency for, 139
Align with Your Clients (practice), 104
American Revolution, xix
Are We Living It? Pulse Test (practice),
  102
Auburn University, 86
authenticity, 140
awakening, with Power Question Practice, 34–35, 39
Awesomeness Report (practice), 96,
  104–105

# B

balance, of individual and collective needs, 180
Baseball Accountability (practice), 157–158
benevolent dictatorships, 22
Bennis, Warren, 12
Bill of Rights, xv, xix, 176–177
blame, 153
The BluePrint of We Contract (practice), 207
board of directors, 227
Boston Celtics, 74–77
bottom-line results, measuring, 18
Bottom-Up Accountability (practice), 157
boundaries, maintaining, 60, 71, 151
Brutal Honesty Sessions (practice), 134
bureaucracy, reducing, 99, 139
butt-kicking mantra, 59

# C

Can You Imagine? Wall (practice), 103
Career Plans (practice), 183
Case, John, 142
Cato Institute, 234
Cedar Rapids, Iowa, xviii
Center for Medicare & Medicaid Services (CMS), xxix
centralization, 163–165
CEO Dashboards (practice), 141–142
CEO Facetime (practice), 133
CEOs (chief executive officers)
    culture after departure of, 228–229
    Freedom-Centered, 163, 176
    roles of, 162–163
Challenge by Choice (practice), 197–198
change, adaptability to, 89
Change the World (practice), 103
character, Ubuntu as, 78

Choice (organizational democracy principle), xxi, 87–88, 189–198
    defining, 191
    in fear-based vs. freedom-centered organizations, 192
    implementation of, 93
    offering meaningful, 194
    promise of, 192–193
    transformational practices, 194–198
Choose What You Say (practice), 195–196
Choose Your Own Career Path (practice), 196
Choose Your Own Job Title (practice), 195
Choose Your Own Manager (practice), 196
Choose Your Own Salary (practice), 198
Choose Your Team (practice), 195
The Christian Science Monitor, xxvi
Church of Fail, 214–216
The Church of Fail (practice), 222
Circles of Change (practice), 131
clarity, accountability and, 153
Cleveland Clinic, 27
Cloke, Kenneth, on command-and-control environments, 83–84
CMS (Center for Medicare & Medicaid Services), xxix
Co-CEOs (practice), 172–173
Collective, rights of. see Individual and Collective (organizational democracy principle)
collective intelligence, 137–138
command-and-control leadership, 164–165
command-and-control work environments, 83–84

communication
about individual and collective
rights, 181
dialogue and listening to improve,
128
dysfunctional, 123
reflection and evaluation in, 217
competitiveness, 165
consensus, 167, 169–170
consent, 167, 170–171
Constitution (US), xv, xix, 176–177
control-based systems, fear in, 234
co-ops, ownership in, 173
Core Values (practice), 113
core values, establishing, 110–112
corruption, reducing, 166
Covey, Stephen, on beginning with the
end, 93
Creech, Wilbur L., on decentralization,
165
criticism, 68
culture
Freedom-Centered (*see* Freedom-Centered Culture)
organizational democracy and,
88–89
Culture Book (practice), 143

**D**

Daily Huddles (practice), 130
Daily Recognition (practice), 205
DaVita, xxii
Decentralization (organizational
democracy principle), xxi, 87–88,
159–174
centralization vs., 165
decision-making and, 166–167
defining, 161–162
in fear-based vs. freedom-centered
organizations, 164
ownership and, 167

promise of, 165–166
transformational practices,
168–174
decision-making, 5, 7
and decentralization, 166–167
in organizational democracy, 90
purpose and vision for, 99
reflection and evaluation for, 217
transparency to improve, 137–138
Decision-Making Process (practice),
168–169
Decision-Making Through Consensus
(practice), 169–170
Decision-Making Through Consent
(practice), 170–171
Decision-Making Through Majority
Vote (practice), 169
Decision Matrix (practice), 168
Declaration of Independence, xv, 174
democracy, xvii–xviii, xx. *see also* organizational democracy
as active adaptation, 84–85
building, 15–16, 90
defining, 85–86
etymology of, xvii
and freedom, xxvi–xxvii, 13
individual and collective rights in,
178–180
integrity to maintain, 113
momentum of, 12
organizational model based on, 84
resources on, 242–243
threats to, xxvi
voice element of, 122
"Democracy Is Inevitable" (Bennis and
Slater), 12
Democratic Age, 84
democratic citizens, core values of, 111
*The Democratic Corporation* (Ackoff),
84–85
democratic leadership, xx, 20, 99–100

Democratic Ownership Through
 Co-ops (practice), 173
Democratic Ownership Through
 ESOPs (practice), 173
Democratic Ownership Through
 Shared Ownership (practice),
 173–174
denials, building mental discipline
 with, 59
design. *see* Freedom-Centered Design
Design Roles to Advocate for Integrity
 (practice), 117–118
dialogue, defined, 122
Dialogue and Listening (organizational
 democracy principle), xxi, 87,
 121–134
 defining, 122–124
 in fear-based vs. freedom-centered
 organizations, 124
 four levels of listening for efficient,
 124–127
 implementing, 128–129
 the promise of, 127–128
 transformational practices of,
 129–134
Dignified Discipline (practice),
 206–207
Dignity. *see* Fairness and Dignity (organizational democracy principle)
Directions Retreat (practice), 104
Discover Your Purpose and Vision
 (practice), 101–102
disengagement, 6, 109
disillusionment, about culture, 226
drama, reducing, 204
Dream Balls (practice), 184
dysfunctional communication, 123

E

Eddy, Mary Baker, on conscious self-
 worth, 58

Edmondson, Amy, 33
Educare Unlearning Institute, 126
efficiency, improving, 99, 166
Einstein, Albert, on freedom, 11
Embrace Differences (practice),
 208–209
Emerson, Ralph Waldo
 on becoming what you think, 59
 on dignity, 199
 on principles and methods, 91
empathetic listening, 125, 126
empathy, 69
employee satisfaction, 18, 74, 190
employee stock ownership programs
 (ESOPs), 173
*The End of Management and Rise of
 Organizational Democracy* (Cloke
 and Goldsmith), 83–84
engagement, increasing, 6, 89, 203
Enron, 109
*Entrepreneur Magazine,* xxvi
Equal Benefits (practice), 207–208
Equal Pay (practice), 206
ESOPs (employee stock ownership
 programs), 173
Evaluation. *see* Reflection and Evaluation (organizational democracy
 principle)

F

factual listening, 124–126
failure, learning moments from, 150
Fairfax, Thomas, xix
fairness, sameness vs., 204
Fairness and Dignity (organizational
 democracy principle), xxi, 87,
 199–211
 defining, 201–203
 in fear-based vs. freedom-centered
 organizations, 203
 implementing, 204

promise of, 203
transformational practices, 205–211
*Fast Company,* xxv
fear, 33–41
  in control-based systems, 234
  dialogue and listening to reduce, 128
  purpose and vision statements to reduce, 98
  reflection and evaluation to reduce, 217
  shifting mindset from, 27–31
  transparency to reduce, 138
  utilizing integrity to reduce, 109
  at work, 3–10
fear-based leadership, xvi–xvii, 7–8
  accountability in, 152
  facetime with CEO in, 133
  fear-and-control tactics in, 46
  integrity in, 109
fear-based organizations, 22
  centralization in, 163
  choice in, 192
  decentralization in, 164
  dialogue and listening in, 123–124
  employee life goals and, 183
  fairness and dignity in, 202–203
  feeling heard in, 132
  individual and collective rights, 179
  integrity in, 110
  recognition in, 205
  reflection and evaluation in, 214, 216
  transparency in, 136–137
fear-based power, 66–67
Fear Gap, 36
fearlessness, 40, 69
*The Fearless Organization* (Edmondson), 33
Fear Purge, 35–36
feedback, 61, 214, 219, 221

Feedback Futons (practice), 220
Fenton, Reuben Eaton, xix, 233
*The Financial Times,* xxvi
Fireside Chats (practice), 141
firing, 210–211
Fleming, Renée, 161
Flextime (practice), 194
Folkman, Joseph, 190
*Forbes,* xxv
forgiveness, 59
*Fortune,* xxv, xxix, 18
Fortune 500 companies, 45
Forward-Thinking Models, 22
founder, culture after departure of, 228–229
Frank, Open, and Honest Conversations (practice), 129–130
Fraser Institute, 234
freedom, xvii–xviii, 233–235
  choice and, 193
  and democracy, xxvi–xxvii
  in Freedom-Centered Leadership, 46–47
  leading from a spirit of, xxiii
  mental, 27
  momentum of, 12
  organizational democracy and, 85
  peace in, 235
  resources on, 242–243
  threats to, xxvi
  without fear, 38
Freedom at Work, xxii–xxiv
  defined, 13–14
  fear at work vs., 3–10, 14
  Freedom-Centered Culture to reinforce, 229
  promise of, 11–23
  resources on, 241
Freedom at Work course, 231
Freedom at Work Leadership Model, xxiii–xxiv, 13

Freedom at Work Scorecard, xxv–xxvi, 18

Freedom-Centered CEOs
  decentralization for, 163
  fear of change and, 176
  resources from, 239–241

Freedom-Centered Culture, 225–231
  after founder/CEO departure, 228–229
  after merger/sale of company, 227–228
  board of directors and investors in, 227
  disillusionment about, 226
  integrity to develop, 110
  reinforcing Freedom at Work with, 229
  scaling your, 226
  training new hires in, 226–227

Freedom-Centered Design, xxiv, 15, 22

Freedom-Centered Leadership, xxiv, 15
  accountability in, 46–47, 72, 151–152
  constructive feedback in, 219
  core values for, 112
  decentralization in, 165–166
  defined, 47
  fearlessness as, 69
  freedom in, 46–47
  inherent worth of individuals in, 201
  maintaining boundaries in, 71
  morality in, 68
  order of, in Freedom at Work model, 21
  power and self-worth as, 71
  purpose and vision statements for, 69, 98–99
  recognizing humanity in, 77
  self-government as, 72
  self-worth in, 49–50, 54–55, 60–61
  three attributes of, 45–47
  transparency for, 137–138
  truth in, 68
  Ubuntu for, 75

Freedom-Centered Mindset, xxiv
  for high performance, 15
  order of, in Freedom at Work model, 21
  shifting from fear to, 27–31

Freedom-Centered Organizations, 16–17, 22. see also WorldBlu Freedom-Centered Organizations
  accountability in, 152
  avoiding accidentally destroying (see Freedom-Centered Culture)
  choice in, 91, 191–192
  core values for, 110–111
  decentralization in, 162, 164–167
  decision-making in, 166–167
  democratic rights in, 177
  dialogue and listening in, 122–124, 129
  fairness and dignity in, 201–203
  fostering democratic citizens in, 111
  individual and collective rights in, 178–179
  integrity in, 110, 113
  purpose and vision for, 97–100
  reflection and evaluation in, 216
  self-worth in, 52–55
  teamwork in, 180
  transparency in, 136, 137, 139–140
  Ubuntu and, 73

Freedom-Centered Power, 65–72
  accountability as, 72
  compassion as, 69
  fear-based vs., 66–67
  fearlessness of, 69
  knowing truth as, 68

maintaining boundaries, 71
morality as, 68
purposefulness of, 69
for self-government, 72
self-worth as, 71
Freedom-Centered Teams. *see* Freedom-Centered Organizations
Freedom Franchises (practice), 172
Freedom House, 234
"Freedom in the World" (Freedom House), 234
free thought, choice as, 191
Fuller, Robert, on dignity, 202
Funky Fridays (practice), 194–195

**G**

Gallup Organization, 6, 54
Gandhi, Mahatma, on truth, 135
GE Aviation Durham, xxii
generative listening, 125, 126
Get "Stoked" and Earning Values/ Medallions (practice), 116–117
Get Upgraded Plan (practice), 156
goals
bottom-line, 89
linking individual and collective, 180–181
long-term, 112
Goldsmith, Joan, on command-and-control work environments, 83–84
Governance Matrix (practice), 168
Governed by Same Standards (practice), 114–115
gratitude, 60
Gratitude Board (practice), 218
Great Depression, 20
Great-itude Sessions (practice), 218
Great Law of Peace, xix
Great Recession (2008), 3–4, 8–12, 16–21

gremlins, as negative self-talk, 39, 58–59
"Grow" framework, 156
growth
bottom-line, 5–6
reflection and evaluation for, 214, 217

**H**

*Harvard Business Review,* 5, 12, 123, 190
Harvard University, xxii, 161
Hay System, 145
HCL Technologies, xxii
Henry, Patrick, on fear, 7
Hewitt Associates, 18
Hiawatha, xix, 49
Hire, Fire, and Promote Democratically (practice), 210–211
hiring, 63–64, 138, 226–227
Hoops for Hope, 75
horrible bosses, effects of, 189–190
"How Damaging Is a Bad Boss, Exactly?" (Zenger and Folkman), 190
"How would I feel without the fear?" (question), 38
Hulu, xxii
Human Dynamics Laboratory, 127
humanity
honoring, 77
organizational democracy and, 88–90
humanness, Ubuntu as, 74
humility, 28, 69
Hussein, Saddam, 85
hypocrisy, accountability and, 153

**I**

identity, 58
*Inc.* (magazine), xxvi, 10, 142

Index of Freedom in the World, 234
Individual and Collective (organizational democracy principle), xxi, 87, 175–186
  defining, 178–180
  in fear-based vs. freedom-centered organizations, 179
  implementing, 180–181
  promise of, 180
  transformational practices, 181–186
Individual Goals, Collective Achievements (practice), 182
Industrial Age, 8, 84
information, sharing, 140
innovation, 6, 99, 180
Integrity (organizational democracy principle), xxi, 87, 107–120
  defining, 108–112
  in fear-based organizations, 109, 110
  Freedom-Centered Organizations use of, 110
  promise of, 112–113
  transformational practices of, 113–120
Integrity at the Board Level (practice), 115
interconnectedness, Ubuntu as, 76–77
Intersecting Purposes and Goals (practice), 181
intuition, 40
investors, 227
In Your Face (practice), 221–222
Iroquois Confederacy, xix
*It's Your Ship* (Abrashoff), 164
It Takes a Team to Raise a Child (practice), 185–186

**J**
Jefferson, Thomas
  on eternal vigilance, 225
  on mental attitude, 27

John, King, xv, xx
Jones, Roger, 5
judgmental, being, 40

**K**
Kensler, Lisa, 86
King, Martin Luther King, Jr., on humanity, 175
Kohe, J. Martine, on power of choice, 189
Korn Ferry, 145

**L**
leadership. *see also* fear-based leadership; Freedom-Centered Leadership
  bad, 54
  command-and-control, 164–165
  courses for, 60
  decentralization to develop, 166
  democracy as framework for, 86
  democratic, xx, 20, 99–100
  dialogue and listening to improve, 128
  effectiveness of, 190
  modeling accountability in, 153
  reflecting upon your, 204
  WorldBlu's model of, 13
leadership development, 7, 203
Leadership in Energy and Environmental Design (LEED), xxix
learning environments, 129, 214, 217
learning moment, "failure" as, 150
Learning Moments (practice), 218–219
LEED (Leadership in Energy and Environmental Design), xxix
Level 4 Meetings (practice), 133–134
Lewis, C. S., on integrity, 108
Liberales Institut, 234
Lincoln, Abraham, xix

Link to Strategic Anchors (practice), 105
listening
    and dialogue (*see* Dialogue and Lis-
        tening [organizational democ-
        racy principle])
    four levels of, 124–127
Localized Leadership (practice), 171
love, 49–64. *see also* self-worth
loyalty, encouraging, 04
Lunch + Learns (practice), 141

## M

Ma, Yo-Yo, 161
Madison, James, on people and power,
    159
Magna Carta, xv, xx
majority rule, 167, 169
Mandela, Nelson, on Ubuntu, 74
Marquette University, 75
Mason, George, xix
Massachusetts Institute of Technology
    (MIT), 127
Matheny, Dale, 18
Matungulu, Kita, 75
meaning, 90, 140
Menlo Innovations, xxii
mental discipline, 59, 206–207
"mental door," shutting your, 59
mental freedom, 27
mental health, 6
mergers, 227–228
*Merriam-Webster Dictionary,* 108
micromanaging, 52, 150
military organizational model, 84
Milliken, Frances J., 6
mindset
    Freedom-Centered (*see* Free-
        dom-Centered Mindset)
    shifting your, 22, 57–58
Mindvalley, xxii
mission statements, 97

mistakes, reflection on and evaluation
    of, 216
MIT (Massachusetts Institute of Tech-
    nology), 127
MIT Media Lab Entrepreneurship
    Program, 127
Mitsubishi, 161
Model It at the Top (practice), 155
money, using integrity to save, 112
Montaigne, Michel de, on misfortune,
    36
moral compass, 68–69
morale, 6, 139
morality, 68, 78
Morrison, Elizabeth Wolf, 6

## N

Nasdaq Stock Market Educational
    Foundation, 28
National Bureau of Economic
    Research, 20
National Science Foundation, 27–28
National Wellness Institute, 119
NBA Championship (2008), 75
net worth, self-worth vs., 56
"The New Science of Building Great
    Teams" (Pentland), 127–128

## O

Oberlin College, 202
Objectives and Key Results (practice),
    156
One on Ones (practice), 132
Open Board Meetings (practice), 144
Open Book Management (practice),
    142
Open Office (practice), 140–141
Open Salary Ranges (practice),
    144–145
Open 360 Degree Feedback (practice),
    221

Open to Competitors (practice), 144

Open Town Halls (practice), 142–143

Organizational Constitution (practice), 185

organizational democracy, xxiv–xxv, 17–18, 83–92

building Freedom-Centered Organizations with, 91–92

democratic rights and, 177

freedom as goal in, 85

humanity and, 88–89

principles of, xxi–xxii, 86–89

principle- vs. practice-based approaches to, 15

reasons for adopting, 89–90

resources on, 241

self-worth and, 55

organizational design, 22

ownership

accountability to cultivate, 152

decentralization and, 167

organizational democracy to inspire, 89

transparency to foster, 138

**P**

Paine, Thomas

on accountability, 151

on reflection, 213

Pandora, xxii

parity, 206

peace, freedom and, 235

Peace, Great Law of, xix

Peer Impact Bonus Award (practice), 209–210

Peer-to-Peer Feedback (practice), 219

Penney, James Cash, on growth, 147

Pentland, Alex "Sandy," 127–128

performance, improving, 56, 153

Personal Growth Plan (practice), 220

physical health, 6

Podio, xxii

Positive Pairing (practice), 157

power, 47. *See also* Freedom-Centered Power

definition of, 66

fear based, 66–67

from having choices, 193

transparency to decentralize, 138

Power Answers, 38, 41

Power Question concept, 29–31

Power Question Practice, 31, 33–41, 60

Power to the Edge (practice), 172

practicing being a ten, 60

"Practising Ubuntu and Leadership for Good Governance" (Nzimakwe), 74

praise, 61

The Presencing Institute, 26

Principia College, 18

principles, defined, 88

productivity, fear and, 6

profitability, 89

Project Incubator (practice), 197

Promise Pledge (practice), 113–114

promotion, 210–211

Purpose and Vision (organizational democracy principle), xxi, 87

defined, 97–98

at every level, 98–99

finding your organization's, 99–100

knowing, as self-knowledge, 75–76

promise of, 99

transformational practices, 101–105

Purpose and Vision statements

examples of, 100

for Freedom-Centered Leadership, 69

for Freedom-Centered Organizations, 97–100

implementing your, 100
mission vs., 97
refreshing your, 100
Put It on the Card (practice), 115–116

**R**
Rankism, 202, 204
*Rankism: A Social Disorder* (Fuller),
    202
The Recall Game (practice), 101
Reciprocal Accountability (practice),
    155–156
Reflection and Evaluation (organiza-
    tional democracy principle), xxi,
    87, 213–223
    defining, 214–216
    in fear-based vs. freedom-centered
        organizations, 216
    on mistakes, 216
    promise of, 216–217
    transformational practices, 218–223
Republican Party, xix
resilience, 20–21
responsibility, 76, 151, 233
"results zone," 40
RevAsia, xxii
revenue growth, 19–20, 85
"Rich Dad or Mom" organizations, 22
Rights and Responsibilities (practice),
    143
Rivers, Glenn Anton "Doc," 74–75
Roosevelt, Franklin Delano, on free-
    dom, xv–xvi

**S**
Safe Place for Whistleblowers (prac-
    tice), 116
sale of company, 227–228
sameness, fairness vs., 204
scaling Freedom-Centered Culture,
    226

self-awareness, 38, 39, 217
self-confidence, 51
self-government, xx, 47
    choice as, 191
    in Freedom-Centered Leadership,
        72
    integrity to improve, 112–113
self-knowledge, 47, 75–76, 193
self-talk, negative, 59
self-worth, 47, 49–64
    accountability to develop, 153
    characteristics of, low vs. high, 53
    conscious, 58
    defined, 50–51
    fairness and dignity to recognize,
        201
    as Freedom-Centered Leadership, 71
    improving your, 57–60
    inherent value of, 56
    knowing your, 55–57
    leadership and, 51–53, 60–63
    WorldBlu on, 52, 55
Semco, xxvi
Semler, Ricardo, on on-the-job democ-
    racy, 187
shared ownership, 173–174
*Shark Tank* (TV show), 197
Shout-Outs (practice), 181–182
Show and Tell (practice), 184
Slater, Philip, 12
Smart Services Desk (practice), 205–206
Solon, xix, 65
South by Southwest, xxii
S&P 500 companies, 18–20
Spiritual Wellness Groups (practice),
    118–120
stability, organizational, 90, 166
Stanford University, 161
Stern Business, 6
stress, 6
Summitt, Pat, on accountability, 149

**T**

Team Charter (practice), 129–130

teamwork, 76–77, 127, 180

"ten-ness," self-worth and, 62

10-Word Rule (practice), 130

theft, reducing, 180

3 Most Important Questions (practice), 102

Town Hall Meetings (practice), 131–132

Tracy, Brian, xviii, 95

training, in Freedom-Centered Culture, 226–227

transactional listening, 124, 126

transformational practices

    Accountability Pledge, 154–155

    Accountable Tracking, 154

    Achievements and Objectives, 154

    Align with Your Clients, 104

    Are We Living It? Pulse Test, 102

    Awesomeness Report, 96, 104–105

    Baseball Accountability, 157–158

    The BluePrint of We Contract, 207

    Bottom-Up Accountability, 157

    Brutal Honesty Sessions, 134

    Can You Imagine? Wall, 103

    Career Plans, 183

    CEO Dashboards, 141–142

    CEO Facetime, 133

    Challenge by Choice, 197–198

    Change the World, 103

    Choose What You Say, 195–196

    Choose Your Own Career Path, 196

    Choose Your Own Job Title, 195

    Choose Your Own Manager, 196

    Choose Your Own Salary, 198

    Choose Your Team, 195

    The Church of Fail, 222

    Circles of Change, 131

    Co-CEOs, 172–173

    Core Values, 113

    Culture Book, 143

    Daily Huddles, 130

    Daily Recognition, 205

    Decision-Making Process, 168–169

    Decision-Making Through Consensus, 169–170

    Decision-Making Through Consent, 170–171

    Decision-Making Through Majority Vote, 169

    Decision Matrix, 168

    Democratic Ownership Through Co-ops, 173

    Democratic Ownership Through ESOPs, 173

    Democratic Ownership Through Shared Ownership, 173–174

    Design Roles to Advocate for Integrity, 117–118

    Dignified Discipline, 206–207

    Directions Retreat, 104

    Discover Your Purpose and Vision, 101–102

    Dream Balls, 184

    Embrace Differences, 208–209

    Equal Benefits, 207–208

    Equal Pay, 206

    Feedback Futons, 220

    Fireside Chats, 141

    Flextime, 194

    Frank, Open, and Honest Conversations, 129–130

    Freedom Franchises, 172

    Funky Fridays, 194–195

    Get "Stoked" and Earning Values/Medallions, 116–117

    Get Upgraded Plan, 156

    Governance Matrix, 168

    Governed by Same Standards, 114–115

    Gratitude Board, 218

Great-itude Sessions, 218
Hire, Fire, and Promote Democratically, 210–211
In Your Face, 221–222
Individual Goals, Collective Achievements, 182
Integrity at the Board Level, 115
Intersecting Purposes and Goals, 181
It Takes a Team to Raise a Child, 185–186
Learning Moments, 218–219
Level 4 Meetings, 133–134
Link to Strategic Anchors, 105
Localized Leadership, 171
Lunch + Learns, 141
Model It at the Top, 155
Objectives and Key Results, 156
One on Ones, 132
Open Board Meetings, 144
Open Book Management, 142
Open Office, 140–141
Open Salary Ranges, 144–145
Open 360 Degree Feedback, 221
Open to Competitors, 144
Open Town Halls, 142–143
Organizational Constitution, 185
Peer Impact Bonus Award, 209–210
Peer-to-Peer Feedback, 219
Personal Growth Plan, 220
Positive Pairing, 157
Power to the Edge, 172
Project Incubator, 197
Promise Pledge, 113–114
Put It on the Card, 115–116
The Recall Game, 101
Reciprocal Accountability, 155–156
Rights and Responsibilities, 143
Safe Place for Whistleblowers, 116
Shout-Outs, 181–182
Show and Tell, 184

Smart Services Desk, 205–206
Spiritual Wellness Groups, 118–120
Team Charter, 129–130
10-Word Rule, 130
3 Most Important Questions, 102
Town Hall Meetings, 131–132
Upward Evaluations, 221
Value Portal, 183
The Values Crew, 118
Village Fund, 208
Vote-o-Rama, 171
What Color Are Your Balls?, 222–223
What Have We Learned, 219
Whole-Picture Scoreboard, 182
World Cafés, 132–133
Transparency (organizational democracy principle), xxi, 87–88, 135–145
defining, 136
in fear-based vs. freedom-centered organizations, 137
implementing, 139–140
promise of, 137–138
transformational practices of, 140–145
trust, 122, 138
truth
and fear, 6
in identity, 58–59
knowing, 68
transparency as, 136
Tutu, Desmond, on Ubuntu, 77
Tyco, 109

U
Ubuntu, 47, 73–79
defined, 73–74
dialogue and listening to develop, 128
honoring your humanity as, 77

Ubuntu (*continued*)
  interconnectedness and teamwork
    as, 76–77
  moral character as, 78
  self-knowledge as, 75–76
understanding, listening for, 122
University of KwaZulu-Natal, 74
University of Pennsylvania, 84
University of Southern California, xxii
Upward Evaluations (practice), 221
US Air Force Tactical Air Command,
  165
US Environmental Protection Agency,
  xxix
US Naval Academy, xxii, 163–165
*US News and World Report,* xxvi
USS *Benfold,* 164
US Securities and Exchange Commis-
  sion, xvi, 135

**V**

value, using choice to create, 193
Value Portal (practice), 183
values
  core, 110–113
  defined, 88
The Values Crew (practice), 118
value zone, 16
Vaughan, Bill, on freedom, 73
Village Fund (practice), 208
Virginia Declaration of Rights, xix
vision. *see* Purpose and Vision
VitalSmarts, 123
voice, building your, 122, 128
Vote-o-Rama (practice), 171
voting, 85

**W**

*Wall Street Journal,* xxvi, 10
Washington, George, xix, 107

waste, reducing, 89, 180, 217
The WD-40 Company, xxii
well-being, fear and, 6–7
Wharton School, 84
"What am I afraid of?" (Power Ques-
  tion Practice), 34–35
"What CEOs Are Afraid Of" (Jones),
  5
What Color Are Your Balls? (practice),
  222–223
What Have We Learned (practice),
  219
"What would I do if I weren't afraid?"
  (Power Question Practice), 37
Wheatley, Margaret, on reflection,
  214–215
Whole-Picture Scoreboard practice,
  182
"Why am I afraid?" (Power Question
  Practice), 35–36
"Why is it okay to let the fear go?"
  (Power Question Practice),
  38–39
Workplace Democracy poll, 7
workplace environments
  command-and-control, 83–84
  learning, 129, 214, 217
  self-worth in, 51–52
  transparency in, 138–139
WorldBlu
  core values of, 111
  four levels of listening at, 124
  leadership courses at, 60
  leadership model of, 13
  measuring bottom-line results at, 18
  membership in, 239
  on self-worth, 52, 55
  principles of organizational democ-
    racy for, xxi–xxii, 87
  Ubuntu and, 76–77

WorldBlu Freedom at Work Scorecard,
    xxv–xxvi, 18
WorldBlu Freedom-Centered Organi-
    zations, 18–20, 30–31
    accountability in, 150–151
    certification for, xxv–xxvi, xxix, 4, 10
    culture in, 88–89
    fear and change in, 175–176
    during Great Recession, 98
    organizational democracy in, 91
    purpose and vision statements for,
        100
    resiliency of, 20–21

    resources from, 239–241
World Cafés (practice), 132–133
WorldCom, 109
World Movement for Democracy, 73

**Y**
Yale University, xxii

**Z**
Zappos, xxii
Zenger, Jack, 190
Ziglar, Zig, xviii, 33
Zogby International, 7

# ABOUT THE AUTHOR

**T**raci Fenton is the founder and CEO of WorldBlu, a global leadership education company teaching top leaders and their organizations how to lead with the proven Freedom at Work™ leadership model. Traci is also a globally recognized keynote speaker, author, and transformational coach to CEOs and top leaders worldwide.

Traci is a "Thinkers50 Radar" award winner, received the Game Changer award for "Outstanding Results in Shaping the World," was named a "World-Changing Woman in Conscious Business," has been recognized in *Inc.* magazine as a "Top 50 Leadership Thinker," and as a Marshall Goldsmith "Top 100 Coach."

Traci founded WorldBlu in 1997 and has helped spark and lead the global conversation around leading and reinventing workplaces using freedom and organizational democracy rather than fear and control. Traci and her team have transformed hundreds of top companies and leaders at world-class organizations such as The WD-40 Company, DaVita, HCL Technologies, Mindvalley, Pandora, Podio, RevAsia, GE Aviation, Zappos, and more in over 100 countries worldwide.

Traci developed the groundbreaking Freedom at Work™ leadership model based in part on the WorldBlu 10 Principles of Organizational Democracy as well as numerous mindset, leadership, and organizational design courses, all of which are delivered on BluSpark™, the cutting-edge gamification learning technology she developed.

Traci frequently speaks worldwide to top leaders and their teams. She has spoken at numerous organizations such as Harvard, Yale, Yahoo!, and the US Naval Academy, and at events such as South by Southwest and TEDx. Her work has been featured in *Fortune, Forbes, Fast Company*, the *Wall Street Journal*, the *Christian Science Monitor*, the *New York Times, Inc.* magazine, *BusinessWeek*, NPR, the BBC, and dozens of other media outlets around the world as well as in over three dozen books. She is the author of the book *Freedom at Work: The Leadership Strategy for Transforming Your Life, Your Organization, and Our World.*

Traci holds a BA in Global Studies and Entrepreneurship from Principia College and an MA in International Development from American University in Washington, DC.

# ABOUT WORLDBLU

**W**orldBlu, founded in 1997, is a global leadership education company teaching CEOs and top leaders how to build, scale, and lead their organizations using the proven Freedom at Work™ leadership model. WorldBlu's founder, Traci Fenton, developed the Freedom at Work model, which is used by thousands of leaders of for-profit and nonprofit organizations worldwide.

Members of WorldBlu get access to exciting events, top thinkers and training, and world-class courses based on the three pillars of the Freedom at Work model: how to cultivate a fearless mindset, how to lead yourself and others with freedom rather than fear and control, and how to design your culture based on WorldBlu's 10 Principles of Organizational Democracy.

WorldBlu has worked with thousands of top leaders and companies such as Zappos, The WD-40 Company, DaVita, HCL Technologies, Mindvalley, Pandora, Hulu, Great Harvest Bread, Zappos, GE Aviation, and more worldwide. WorldBlu also recognizes and certifies the most Freedom-Centered Organizations™ each year using their rigorous Freedom at Work Scorecard.

WorldBlu has been featured in the *Wall Street Journal,* the *Christian Science Monitor,* the *New York Times, Fast Company, Inc.* magazine, *BusinessWeek, US News & World Report, Fortune, Forbes*, NPR, the BBC, and dozens of other media outlets around the world as well as in over three dozen books. WorldBlu's purpose is to transform the way leaders lead with Freedom at Work. WorldBlu's vision is to see a world where everyone can live, lead, and work in freedom.

**Learn more and become a free member at www.worldblu.com.**